Internet Resources for Leisure and

Internet Resources for Leisure and Tourism

William Theobald and H. E. Dunsmore

OXFORD BOSTON JOHANNESBURG MELBOURNE NEW DELHI SINGAPORE

Butterworth-Heinemann
Linacre House, Jordan Hill, Oxford OX2 8DP
225 Wildwood Avenue, Woburn, MA 01801-2041
A division of Reed Educational and Professional Publishing Ltd

A member of the Reed Elsevier plc group

First published 2000

British Library Cataloguing in Publication Data
Theobald, William F.
   Internet resources for leisure and tourism
   1. Leisure industry – Data processing   2. Tourist trade – Data
   processing   3. Internet (Computer network)
   I. Title   II. Dunsmore, H. E.
   338.4'791'02854678

Library of Congress Cataloguing in Publication Data
A catalogue record for this book is available from the Library of Congress

ISBN 0 7506 4644 6

Composition by Genesis Typesetting, Rochester, Kent
Printed and bound in Great Britain by Biddles Ltd, Guildford and King's Lynn

Contents

Preface

Welcome to *Internet Resources for Leisure and Tourism*, a comprehensive introduction to the Internet and World Wide Web as well as an expansive guide to hundreds of tourism and leisure sites that may be found there.

Communication methods have dramatically changed over the past twenty years. Prior to the 1970s, communication with others was either by post, by telephone or in person. In the decade of the 1980s, communication methods underwent marked change with the introduction of cellular telephones, fax machines, personal computers, electronic mail and other new telecommunication technologies.

During the time that this book was under development, the authors have seen evolutionary, and sometimes revolutionary, changes in computer technology. At the beginning stages of the Internet, pages on the World Wide Web were rather drab combinations of grey backgrounds, large black text, blue links, and often large photographs that loaded extremely slowly. Within a few years, graphic designers and artists have exerted their influence. Now, web page design and programming often incorporate fill-in forms and clickable links and image maps.

When we first started working on this book, we were worried that there would not be enough sites to fill the pages. Instead, we found more than we could mention. And every day, we were happily surprised by at least one new discovery that may or may not have had anything to do with the subjects of this book – tourism and leisure. The planning, imagination and intelligence that make for the best sites on the Web simply boggle the mind. We are looking forward to seeing even more advances.

Introduction

Internet Resources for Leisure and Tourism is designed for those in the leisure and tourism businesses, academics, students and all others who want one central Internet resource. The Internet's hundreds of sites can help you locate the latest economic statistics and demographics, get information about government agencies and their programmes, learn about universities from which you may wish to access their web sites or which you might want to enrol in a distance learning course, and much, much more.

This book can benefit practitioners in the tourism and leisure industries as they learn of the many and varied opportunities the World Wide Web offers in providing important information on professional developments within their career fields. In addition, the Web provides up-to-the-minute statistics on international as well as domestic visitor arrivals and departures, information on upcoming meetings and conferences, tables of contents for current periodicals, as well as a host of other related pertinent information.

Although this book assumes that you have some knowledge of the World Wide Web and other Internet features, you can always refer to the glossary in Appendix A for basic definitions and information.

It should be understood that although there are vast amounts of information to be found on the Web, not all of that information is current, accurate or correct. For example, a number of websites provide data that may be relatively old or out-of-date. Also, some of that data may be incorrect since errors do indeed occur when individuals post information on a particular site. Such errors may be by omission or commission, so it is always prudent to check both the sources and the data itself.

Finally, readers should recognize the fact that there are significant differences between information that can be accessed at no cost, and that where a fee or fees are charged to users. Everything on the World Wide Web is <u>not</u> free. For example, some information providers such as the World Tourism Organization provide a free organization web page that allows users to view without cost their press releases, official speeches, list of members, publications, etc. However, if individuals wish to access their statistical service, a password is required and a charge is made for each search. Likewise, the National Employee Services Recreation Association website allows users to access their buyers guide, press releases, bookstore, conferences, and the like. However, another part of the website is for members only, and also requires a password to enter. In order to get a password individuals must first be fee-paying members of the association.

The contents of this book

This book is an introduction to the Internet and the World Wide Web, and contains information on hundreds of Internet tourism and leisure sites. You will also find a number of special features such as:

- a wide variety of Internet topics – from how to find a provider to how to compress and decompress files that you download
- interesting sites highlights that are not to be ignored – for content, design and/or specific information
- notes emphasizing important information about a site
- short cuts and easy-to-use methods for performing functions.

Text conventions used in this book

In this book, italicized text represents variables (for example, a filename or a value to be typed) and new terms, and as usual any publications and foreign-language words/phrases. This font **http://www.yahoo.com** indicates uniform resource locators (URLs) that you type to go to a particular site.

How to use this book

Each entry in *Internet Resources for Leisure and Tourism* is a snapshot of a site <u>at the time</u> that the authors wrote about it, when a technical editor checked it, and possibly when one of the authors changed it. One thing that we have learned is that the Web is constantly changing: students graduate, professors move on to other interests, webmasters change folder and file naming conventions, and businesses switch to new providers or obtain a new domain name. During this project, we have seen URLs change from one day to the next, and sites that we thought would be permanent simply disappeared. Some sites provide forwarding information; others do not.

Therefore, while a great deal of care has been taken to provide both accurate and current information, nevertheless, owing to the nature of the Internet, there will be some errors and omissions in particular regarding websites.

However, there are a number of ways that you can search for a site that has moved from one part of the Internet to another without leaving a 'forwarding' link. Most of the time, one of these methods results in success.

Finding a site: part 1

If you are willing to try a short cut, think of a logical name for a site. For example, if we could not find the World Trade Organization at **http://web.fie.org/web/wld/wto**, we successfully tried **http://www.wto.org**/. Starting with **http://** is obvious, following with **www.** is a good bet, using an abbreviation such as **wto** is an excellent first (and probably only) initial try, and **.org** represents the organization domain. However, there are exceptions to every rule. Not every address includes **www.** Some addresses simply start with the company or agency name, and others start with **web** or some other identifier. To confuse things more, not all organizations use the **.org** domain; the agency may be a government organization (**.gov**) or even a private–public commercial (**.com**) site. If you try this with Gopher sites, the best bet for the first part of the URL is **gopher://gopher**.

Finding a site: part 2

One way to find a missing site is to take apart its URL piece by piece. Let us say that you are looking for an outdoor recreation research site and the address for which you are looking is **http://www.vt.edu:10021/Y/yfleung/recres.html**. You can either remove all the address after the main domain name (leaving **http://www.vt.edu**/) or remove the address in stages from one slash to the next (for example, **http://www.vt.edu/1021/Y/yfleung**/ to **http://www.vt.edu/1021/Y**/, and so on) until you see a link that looks as though it might work. Sometimes you find yourself looking at the folders that form the under-structure of a site, but sometimes you hit pay dirt. This works for both Web and Gopher sites.

Finding a site: part 3

If guessing a URL or taking it apart and putting it back together again does not work, use a search engine (for the best of them, see Chapter 6). In the text box, type the title of the site, the name of the author, or a keyword you think will clearly identify the site. Then, click on the button to start the search. On the page of results, look for the link that most closely resembles the site for which you are looking. Then, click and hope for the best. If the first results do not pan out, try a new search using a different keyword.

Abbreviations and acronyms

ACED-I	Association of Conference and Events Directors – International
ADSL	Asymmetrical digital subscriber line
AFTA	Australian Federation of Travel Agents
AH&MA	American Hotel and Motel Association
AHT	Articles in Hospitality and Tourism
ANTOR	Association of National Tourist Offices
AOL	America Online
ARPANET	Advanced Research Projects Administration Network
ASAE	American Society of Association Executives
ATLAS	European Association for Tourism and Leisure Education
ATTT	Association of Tourism Teachers and Trainers
Bcc	Blind courtesy copy
Bit	Binary digit
Bitnet	Because It's Time Network
Blaise	British Library's Automated Information Service
CARL	Colorado Alliance of Research Libraries
CASO	Cape software
Cc	Courtesy copy
CD	Compact disc
CD-ROM	Compact disc – read only memory
CENL	Conference of European National Librarians
CERN	Conseil European pour la Recherche Nucleaire
CGI	Common Gateway Interface
CIA	Central Intelligence Agency
CPRA	Canadian Parks and Recreation Association

CREN	Computer Research and Education Network
CSNET	Computer Science Network
CWIS	Campus-wide information systems
DARPANET	Defense Advanced Research Projects Administration Network
DNS	Domain Name System
DOD	Department of Defense
DSL	Digital subscriber line
DVD	Digital video disc
EIU	Economic Intelligence Unit
Email	Electronic mail
ENTER	International Conference on Information and Communications Technologies in Tourism
ESD	Ecologically sustainable development
FAQ	Frequently asked question
FTP	File Transfer Protocol
GNN	Global Network Navigator
HCIMA	Hotel and Catering International Management Association
HTML	HyperText Markup Language
HTTP	HyperText Transfer Protocol
IACC	International Association of Conference Centers
IACVB	International Association of Convention and Visitor Bureaus
IAEM	International Association for Exposition Management
IAFE	International Association of Fairs and Expositions
IAHC	International Ad Hoc Committee
IAMI	International Association Managers, Inc.
IATA	International Air Transport Association
ICHA	International College of Hospitality Administration
ICOMOS	International Scientific Committee on Cultural Tourism
ID	Identity
IFITT	International Federation for Information Technology and Tourism
IGU	International Geographical Union
IJCHM	International Journal of Contemporary Hospitality Management
IMPS	Internet Meeting Planners Site
Internet	Interconnected network of networks
IP	Internet protocol
IPng	Internet protocol: the next generation
ISO	International Standards Organization

ISP	Internet service provider
ITA	International Trade Administration
JPG/JPEG	Joint Photographic Experts Group
LAN	Local area network
LC System	Library of Congress Classification System
LC	Library of Congress
LIN	Leisure Information Network
LOCIS	Library of Congress Information System
LOUIS	Louisiana Online University Information System
LRU	Least recently used
MIME	Multipurpose Internet Mail Extensions
Modem	Modulator/demodulator
MPI	Meeting Professionals International
MRI	Magnetic resonance imaging
NCSA	National Center for Supercomputing Applications
NIC	Network Information Centre
NIRRPS	Natural Resources Research Information Pages
NISO	National Information Standards Organization
NISS	National Information Services and Systems
NREN	National Research and Education Network
NRPA	National Recreation and Park Association
NSF	National Science Foundation
NTU	Nanyang Technological University
OAS	Organization of American States
OPAC	Online Public Access Catalogue
OSI	Open Systems Interconnection
PC	Personal computer
PCMCIA	Personal Computer Memory Card International Association
PGP	Pretty good privacy
Pim	Personal information manager
PIRT	Partners in Responsible Tourism
PRIT	Pacific Rim Institute of Tourism
SHI	Swiss Hospitality Institute
SMTP	Simple Mail Transfer Protocol
SR	Search and Retrieval
TCP/IP	Transmission Control Protocol/Internet Protocol
THOR	The Online Resource
TR	Therapeutic recreation
TRDC	Tourism Reference and Documentation Centre
TTI	Travel and Tourism Intelligence
TTRA	Travel and Tourism Research Association

UCLA   University of California at Los Angeles
VCR   Videocassette recorder
WAN   Wide area network
WLRA   World Leisure and Recreation Association
WTO   World Tourism Organization
WTTC   World Travel and Tourism Council
WWW   World Wide Web

1

What in the world is the Internet?

The Internet: a wide world of information
How the Internet works
Internet protocols
Internet node names and numbers
Internet domains
Internet protocol: the next generation

The Internet: a wide world of information

Imagine that you had volunteered for a deep space mission in the year 1980. You were placed on board a space vehicle and rocketed into outer space. You have been travelling now for nearly twenty years and are eagerly anticipating your return to good old planet Earth. One of the negatives of your journey has been that (due to travel on the other side of the Sun) you have been cut off from communications with Earth. You know nothing about what has been going on since 1980. You anticipate that you have much to catch up on. Many world leaders have likely changed. The nature of political boundaries has almost certainly changed. Some nations have risen in prominence, while others have fallen. There have likely been many new inventions and many new developments that you will want to find out all about.

You are approaching Earth and make your first radio contact in nearly twenty years. The first conversation, after it gets past the 'Hi, hello, how have you been?' stage proceeds to you telling the prime communicator, 'Please tell me the most striking development on planet Earth since I have left'. She ponders this question a bit – considers the array of world leaders that have come and gone in the last twenty years; the fall of communism and rise of democracy; the linking of international commerce; the many incredible inventions such as large-screen televisions; cellular phones; open MRI (magnetic resonance imaging) machines – but, finally, she blurts out, 'I would have to say the Internet!'

'The what?'

'The Internet may be the most important development of the past twenty years! This is a computer network linking many of the world's computers and allowing the transfer of electronic mail, software, private data files, and web pages.'

Many of these words mean very little to you. What is a computer network? What is electronic mail? And what in the world (on Earth) are 'web pages'?

Let us come back down to Earth! You have not been on such a journey. So, you are not totally in a communications blackout concerning the Internet. But, you may not know as much about the Internet and the World Wide Web as you think everyone else does. The interesting thing is that many people do not know as much about the Internet and the World Wide Web as they think everyone else does. These phenomena have developed so rapidly and have spilled out of such a specialized research area that many people are scrambling to figure out what these things are and how they impact or may impact on their own lives.

You are aware that the Internet is a computer network, although the term 'network' may be a bit fuzzy. You know what a television network is, but that analogy does not seem to help much in working out what a computer network is. But, whatever this Internet computer network is, you know that there is purportedly a tremendous amount of information available to those who seem to have the magic key to unlock its secrets.

The Internet has information about research centres and research projects, detailed admissions and course information from most universities, and vast amounts of news and information from various governmental organizations. It is possible to access information about:

- the books and holdings in many libraries
- airline schedules and ticket prices
- rooms available in hotels
- festivals and special events all over the world
- how to join a biking club and what trips they are planning for the coming season
- sports scores and schedules
- records and statistics for your favourite sports team
- the current weather where you are as well as on the other side of the globe
- local and international news.

The fact that the Internet is growing in usefulness and importance is confounding. What started as a research project has rapidly become an important information resource for many people in both their professional and private lives. Some people now use the Internet many times each day in their work and then go home and continue to use it for private communication and pleasure purposes. The same Internet that can give you travel information for your next big business trip to London can also yield information useful for planning your upcoming holiday in Cancun, Mexico.

The Internet is replacing many other entities in the way it is used. People now turn to the Internet in the way they used to turn to libraries, encyclopaedias, newspapers, magazines, catalogues, brochures, travel agents, ticketing agents, weather maps, governmental pamphlets or even physicians, for advice.

An anecdote may serve to exemplify the way the Internet is beginning to permeate what many people do and how many people think to use the Internet in place of resources that they might have used before. Recently a young man was exploring under water with his father, but found it difficult for them to communicate with each other. Talking under water is, of course, impossible, and hand signals were not terribly useful. The young man wanted to invent a device to allow two people to talk under water. So, he went to the Internet, specifically the World Wide Web (the Web) on the Internet, to do some research. There he learned from several people and in various parts of the world how sound travels in water and what devices had previously been tried. He went to the Internet and the Web for this information, rather than to his encyclopaedia, school library or local library, because he knew that there

3

would likely be a wealth of information about this (or any) topic and that the information would be more current than any he could find in an encyclopaedia or any book. (We will talk more about the joys and dangers of finding things on the Internet in Chapter 6.)

By the way, the young man described above used the information he got from the Internet to invent a device that can be held up to the mouth and spoken into under water. The sound waves travel through water and can actually be heard by someone close to the speaker. The young man received a contract from a toy manufacturer to manufacture and market his invention.

Before we move further into discussing the Internet and the Web, let us first make it clear that there are two terms we will not use in this book:

1 'Information Super-Highway' – This childish term cropped up in the mid-1990s to serve politicians and members of the news media who wanted to talk about a science fiction entity that they felt only they could envision. The so-called Information Super-Highway was a way that anyone could access information anywhere in a matter of seconds. This information would be in any format – text, pictures, sounds, video, etc. The problem with the term is that while its users were employing it to represent something that they thought was decades away from fruition, researchers were already using the Internet in a manner very similar to that which the politicians and media were predicting would be available only in the distant future.

2 'Surfing the Net' – If 'Information Super-Highway' is childish and frivolous, then 'Surfing the Net' trivializes the access of information on the Internet even more. When the World Wide Web first came into use there were (and still are) many users who were infatuated with the hours that could be spent (wasted?) just travelling from one entry on the Web to another – reading about movies in India, cookie recipes from Belgium, magic clubs in Indonesia, farmers' associations in Kansas, etc. The mindless term 'Surfing the Net' came to be equated with using the Internet and the Web for purely trivial pursuits. This hid the fact that many scientists, students, physicians, chemists, etc. were using the Internet and World Wide Web every day in very serious pursuits of information related to their work. Instead of 'Surfing the Net', we will use the more precise (and more stately) term 'Browsing the Web'.

Since this is a book about travel, leisure and tourism, let us do some time travelling to learn where the Internet has come from and where it is going. In the next section of this chapter we are going to go back in time to see where the Internet came from. But first, let us travel forward in time and consider a typical day in the life of a typical person five years from now.

Let us call our typical person 'Fred Owens'. Fred's day begins when the alarm goes off. But, Fred's alarm is not a clanging clock or gently singing clock radio. It is a personal computer. Now, remember that it is five years from now and the term 'personal' computer has taken on a new meaning. The old computers sitting on desks that stay in the same location all the time (even if they are quite small and take up very little of the desk's surface) are now referred to as 'desktop computers'. They typically have large screens, lots of storage space, and have sophisticated colour graphics printers attached to them.

But, these are not portable computers. The computer of choice five years from now is what were called 'laptop' or 'notebook' computers when they were first introduced and are now (five years hence) referred to as 'personal' computers. The new breed of personal computer is light (about 1 kg or 2 lb) with a large colour screen, possesses an incredible amount of built-in storage, and runs extremely fast with the Pentium 2000 chip. Perhaps the most important feature of the 'personal' computer is its access to the Internet. Each personal computer has an antenna through which it communicates with mobile networks (exactly the same way that cellular phones work) so that the personal computer may access the Internet from any place in your home or office – even in the car or on board a ship or an aeroplane.

These personal computers are now the primary way of accessing the Internet. But, desktop computers play an important role, too. They contain 'docking stations' where the smaller, more portable personal computers can be 'docked' to transfer information between the desktop and the smaller machines and to enable the personal computers access to computer networking capabilities even faster than that available via the mobile network.

Five years from now, carrying a personal computer around and accessing the Internet with it has become standard fare. Back to our story of Fred Owens. Fred's bedside alarm is his personal computer. This morning the audio that awakens him is a listing of his schedule for the day, 'spoken' in a voice that mimics exactly how it would sound if read by his daughter, and presented in a gradually increasing volume until Fred awakens and clicks the mouse on the appropriate icon to stop it.

After showering and shaving, Fred goes down to the kitchen and begins to prepare breakfast for his wife Carolyn, their two children David and Lisa, and himself. By the time Carolyn joins him for her first cup of coffee of the day, Fred is sitting at the breakfast table engrossed in reading the local newspaper. But, reading the local paper is much different than it was five years ago. Fred reads it on his personal computer. Some of the stories report events that have occurred only minutes ago. A fire in a broom closet in city hall happened only ten minutes ago and appears in the paper. Throughout the day stories are updated so that at lunchtime he is able to check to see if they have any idea then what started the fire. Carolyn is reading the newspaper on her personal computer, too. But, she is a little 'old-fashioned', and is sending two of the stories to the colour graphics printer in the den to make 'hard copies' of them so that she can keep the paper versions in a folder.

Fred chuckles to himself that it may be difficult when he has grandchildren to explain to them why it is called a 'newspaper', as it is not on paper. Fred will explain that back in the old days it was printed on something called newsprint, transported by truck to areas in the city, transported by bicycle by a kid from the neighbourhood, and finally thrown on to Grandpa's porch. Then, Grandpa would come out, look for the paper, take it inside and read it. 'They'll never believe this,' Fred chuckles to himself.

When Fred arrives at the office, he docks his personal computer in the docking station of the desktop computer at work. Any files that he modified at home last night are transferred to the desktop and any company files that Fred needs that were changed since he left work are transferred to his personal computer.

Fred begins the working day and his personal computer is an intimate part of everything he does. Of course, a lot of communication in his company is by electronic mail. Fred devotes an hour or so at the beginning of the day to responding to electronic mail from colleagues that have arrived since yesterday. Also, there are a number of electronic mail messages that arrived during the night from the other side of the world.

Fred sends an electronic mail message to a professor at a small local college. They are planning a meeting in the next few weeks, and Fred has thought of two more issues he would like to explore when they get together.

Fred will use electronic mail all day long to communicate with colleagues and several people outside the company. Fred cannot imagine how he got along years ago when his communication was limited to the postal service, telephone calls, faxes and personal visits. Electronic mail is so much more convenient than many of those media, but Fred still believes that there are times when there is no substitute for a phone call or personal visit. In fact, these are even more important now than they used to be because they are used so sparingly in a world in which electronic mail has become the predominant communication medium.

At lunchtime, Fred walks down to the company cafeteria – carrying his personal computer under his arm. After a lively chat over bagels and cheese with several of his colleagues, Fred moves outside to a small picnic table overlooking the beautiful lake just beside the company grounds. As a gentle wind whispers through the trees and carries a hint of lilac bushes to his nostrils, Fred opens his personal computer and turns his attention to some personal electronic mail.

Of course, Fred would never consider reading personal electronic mail during regular working hours; this would violate most companies' policies. But, with some of his lunchtime left, this is a perfect time to catch up on some personal items. First, he finds a message from his eternally optimistic brother, telling Fred about another hare-brained moneymaking scheme in which he wants Fred to invest. The last time it was some sort of South American bean that could be used for medicinal purposes. This time it is a travel club in which the customers can make airline reservations, but their destination city is determined randomly. Fred decided to respond to that one later.

Fred also found an electronic mail message from his mother. Fred felt guilty that he had not called or written lately. So, he quickly put together a reply to her – including the picture of his son David that he had taken last week with the new digital camera – and promised to send an electronic mail message with the video from daughter Lisa's dance recital on Sunday night.

Finishing his personal correspondence with a few minutes still left before he had to leave the picnic table and return to the office, Fred decided to try to catch up on the latest national and international news through his *Time* magazine subscription. A few keystrokes and mouse clicks later and Fred was reading the day's latest news on his personal computer. This is so much better, he thought, than back in the old days. Then, by the time the magazine was printed on paper and delivered to his mailbox, much of the information in it was out of date. The new *Time* magazine also allows Fred to delve in tremendous detail into stories of interest to him. He is able to reread all previous *Time* magazine articles on a subject as well as a lot of material gathered by the author that could not have been included in the old days when a story had to 'fit' the space set aside for it. Fred found a story on new developments in architectural steel that he was sure Carolyn would want to read. He sent that story to the colour graphics printer at home so that Carolyn could read it in bed tonight. She does not like to balance the personal computer on her lap while reading.

Back to the office and the day winds down. Fred begins the long commute in bumper-to-bumper traffic as always, although today a little later than usual because of a meeting that ran late – in fact, too late today to listen to his favourite news programme on public radio. 'No problem,' thought Fred as he clicked to the public radio site on the Internet and began listening to a recording of the same news programme that was transmitted to his personal computer.

While driving home Fred began to notice a slowdown in the traffic ahead of him on the turnpike. He really needed to avoid this in order not to be late for supper. On his personal computer he brought up a traffic map showing all major roads in the area – with those flowing smoothly marked in green, those slowing down marked in yellow, and those that were stopped (or nearly so) marked in red. The turnpike Fred was on had just turned yellow on the map. But, the parkway that runs parallel to the turnpike was nice and green. Fred left the turnpike at the next exit, slipped over to the parkway, and drove home without further incident.

So goes a day five years from now. Notice the tremendous use of computers and computer networks in that day. The interesting thing is that much of what Fred did can already be done right now using the Internet and World Wide Web. Perhaps the only science fiction aspect of Fred's story is the continual access to the Internet from a portable computer through mobile networking. But, this capability is coming quickly and will likely be available for us to use in the next five years.

How the Internet works

Now that we have travelled forward in time, let us turn our attention in the other direction. For many of you there may have been several terms in the last section that you do not fully understand yet. For example, 'computer network', 'Internet', 'electronic mail', 'World Wide Web' and 'web pages', to name just a few. Most people have some idea what these things are but many of us would not feel comfortable if we were asked to explain to others exactly what they are. Let us remedy this by going back in time, to the Prehistoric Era of the Internet – way back to 1975! We will work our way forward from there, being sure that all concepts and terminology are well defined and understandable.

The first computers (even the first personal computers) were *stand-alone machines*. This meant that a computer could operate only using the software and information stored on that computer. There was no way to communicate with another computer.

With stand-alone computers, the only way to transfer information from one computer to another is to do it physically. Historically, one of the first media for doing this (and certainly the workhorse of information transfer from the early years of computing) was the punched card. Each card was about 7.5 cm (3 inches) by 18 cm (7 inches) and was divided into eighty columns of information. Each column could represent any letter, number or punctuation by the presence of one or more rectangular holes punched in the column. Typically, one of the early large stand-alone computers would have a device attached to it called a card punch. Several blank cards could be run through this device. Afterwards, the punched cards could be transported across the room or across the world to another computer with a card reader. This information – output from one computer – could then serve as input to the other computer.

For larger quantities of information it was common to use a magnetic tape or magnetic disk. Both take advantage of the fact that information in the memory of an electronic digital computer (the kind we all use) is stored by translating it into the binary number system. Every letter, number, and special character can be represented by a binary code. Thus, the lower case letter 'g' is represented by the binary code 1100111, while the character '$' is represented by the binary code 0100100.

Information is recorded on the surface of the magnetic tape or magnetic disk as a series of binary digits. The short name for 'binary digits' is *bits* – obtained by taking the first two letters of 'binary' and the last two letters of 'digits'. During the recording process ('writing' the information) the recorder rearranges the binary digits that are already there to represent the desired information. During the 'reading' process the machine interprets the binary digits that are stored on the surface of the tape or disk. The main difference in these two media are how each is written and read. A magnetic tape must be accessed in sequential order from beginning to end. A magnetic disk may be accessed in a random manner writing and reading binary digits from various places on the surface as desired. Thus, a magnetic disk is much faster in retrieving arbitrary information that might be anywhere on the disk. But, magnetic disks and their associated reading and writing equipment are generally more expensive and can usually store far less information than a magnetic tape.

9

More modern information transfer devices include the diskette — a small, easily transportable version of its bigger cousin the disk – and the CD-ROM (compact disk – read only memory) – a round, flat piece of plastic coated with a magnetizable material containing a highly dense set of binary digits. This allows a tremendous amount of information to appear on a very small CD-ROM surface. Diskettes are rapidly giving way to CD-ROMs because of the tremendous difference in amount of information that can be stored on the latter. But, diskettes may be re-recorded as needed, while writable CD-ROMs are still not yet very common.

Back in the Prehistoric Era of the Internet (around 1975) a small group of computer scientists began to speculate that there must be a better way to share information among computers than transporting it via cards, tapes, disks, diskettes, etc. They envisioned the use of a connection between any two computers in much the same manner that two children might connect a string between two tin cans, pull the string tight, and then talk to each other by speaking into and listening to the tin cans. (Try it if you have never done it. It really works!)

The computer equivalent of a string connection is a wire running from one computer to another. One computer can transmit a series of bits to the other. Actually, most wire connections begin by translating the bits into analogue waves that are translated back into bits at the other end. For more about how this works see the section titled 'Connections to the Internet' about modems in Chapter 2.

The wire connection between two or more computers creates a primitive form of what we now call a local area network (LAN). A LAN is any group of two or more computers with communication access to each other so that they may share information. This all sounds terribly easy – connect a wire from computer A to computer B and then begin immediately transmitting information from computer A to computer B – but, this is not at all the case.

You are probably well aware what happens when you give a computer a command that it does not understand or when you respond to a request from a computer with information that it cannot handle. The computer's reply is frequently a rude error message like 'Unknown command' or 'File not found' or 'Go away and find out how to do what you want'. Imagine what would happen if you approached a computer and suddenly gave it hundreds of lines of information that it did not anticipate and that it had no idea what to do with. That was exactly the problem facing computer network researchers in the Prehistoric Era. How could information be packaged at computer A in a way that it could be sent to computer B? Then, how could computer B know what to do with the information when it arrived?

Much of the early computer network research was to develop a set of standards, procedures and protocols for transmitting and receiving information sent from computer to computer. You may think you know nothing about communication standards, procedures and protocols, but you really do. For example, suppose that the phone rings in Mary McNairy's apartment. Mary picks up the phone and says, 'Hello'. The caller says, 'Hello, this is Jill Armstrong. May I speak to Mary McNairy?' Mary replies, 'This is Mary McNairy. How are you today, Jill?' Jill replies, 'Just fine, Mary. The reason why I called is . . .'

We all know the protocol for making phone calls. After the initial 'handshaking' – establishing who we are – we proceed to the purpose for the call. There are, of course, minor variations of this ritual that some people use. But, by and large we all obey the same set of 'phone call protocols'. Imagine what would happen if the call had gone like this: The phone rings in Mary McNairy's apartment. Mary picks up the phone and says in a deep, booming voice, 'Whadda you want?' Jill would likely be frightened and hang up. If Jill did stay on the line, it would take a good deal longer to establish the communication connection and valuable talking time would be lost. So Mary and Jill, like millions of us, use the standard 'phone call protocols'.

That is exactly what had to be developed for computer networks – the protocols for sending information from one computer to another so that the sending computer could identify itself and could tell the receiving computer what should be done with the packet of information.

You might think that, although this presents an interesting problem to computer scientists, what good is a computer network? Why spend so much time and effort to allow such communication to take place from one computer to another? What do computers have to say to each other? Why do we want to do this?

There were three major motivations for establishing LANs: information transfer, software sharing and device sharing.

1 'Information transfer' is what typically comes to mind when we talk about the benefits of a computer network. Reports, newsletters, technical papers and a wealth of other information can be sent from one computer to another if the person at the second computer needs any of this information.
2 'Software-sharing' enables a person at one computer to use a word-processing program, a simulation package or a graphics tool that actually

'lives' on the disk of another computer. The software can be sent over the LAN to the computer that needs it (subject to any legal restrictions on sharing software among computers, of course).

3 'Device-sharing' is a group of computers on a network that can all have access to an expensive laser printer, to image scanning hardware or to a large database file server as long as any one of the computers on the LAN has access to such a device.

Local area networks typically use technology such as wires or fibre optic cables that work well when the distances between machines are small. So most LANs consist of computers in the same room, on the same floor or in the same building. When distances become larger, the LAN model no longer works. But do not worry, we have an effective way to handle that, as discussed below.

Many people believe that computer networks were developed so that electronic mail could be sent from one person to another. This is not the case. In fact, electronic mail was an unexpected result of computer networks. The following anecdote illustrates how electronic mail (usually shortened to the term *email*) actually came into popular use.

An early LAN in a Computer Science department in a major university in the USA connected computers used by two professors and three graduate students. Late one evening Professor Bob was about to depart for home. But, first, he sent a file of experimental results from that night's work to his colleague, Professor Sally. Then, he sat down at his desk to write her a note. It began, 'Sally, the file I just sent you contains results from 100 trials. The first column is trial number, second column is time, third column is number of errors . . .'. Professor Bob stopped. 'Why am I bothering to write this in longhand on a piece of paper that I am going to put into Professor Sally's mailbox in the main office? I could type this same information into a computer file and send it to Professor Sally over the computer network.' Tossing aside the piece of paper, Professor Bob opened a computer file and began typing, 'Sally, the file I just sent you contains results from 100 trials . . .'. Thus what would have been a piece of paper in her mailbox became an item of electronic mail that Professor Sally read the next morning on her computer. Electronic mail was born!

Although many scientists recognized immediately the usefulness of electronic mail, a lot of people were much more sceptical. In fact, an early research proposal sent to a major funding agency in the USA contained a section on electronic mail. It talked about what electronic mail was, how it could be used, and what work needed to be done to make it feasible on computer networks. That proposal was rejected by the funding agency with a note to remove the section on electronic mail. 'We do not fund research concerning computer games!' What some people thought initially was simply a frivolous way for two people to send notes back and forth using a computer network has become one of the most important aspects of today's Internet. Millions of people every day communicate critical information using email. Chapter 3 contains more information about what email is today and how it is used.

The early development of what is now the Internet demonstrates again, as if we need to be reminded, that whatever new and better capability you give people to use, they will want something even better. Early LANs were pretty much self-contained. Organizations might have five or six LANs, but no way for someone on one LAN to send email to or to share software with someone on another LAN. That situation simply was unacceptable to people whose appetite for connectivity had been whetted by the first LANs. Fortunately, many of the standards, procedures and protocols that had been developed for connecting individual computers on a network could be used for connecting networks to each other. Usually one computer on the network was selected to be the 'gateway' (sometimes called 'bridge') computer to another network. For example, an email message from LAN A would travel to computer 4, which would send it to computer 37, from which it could travel to any other computer on LAN C. Thus, computers 4 and 37 are gateways between LANs A and C. This enabled the creation of a 'network of networks'.

Now, we may loosely think of everyone on LANs A–C as being on the same network (although really there are three separate networks which are themselves connected as a network). Now, suppose that LANs A–C completely connect everyone in Department I and LANs D–H connect everyone in Department II. Then, a computer in either of these departments may be used as the gateway between them. Now we have a 'network of networks of networks' connecting everyone in Departments I and II. Continuing this process through multiple levels of networking has allowed what we now call the Internet to connect a tremendous number of computers to each other. Notice how simple the process is – computers on the Internet communicate by sending information along the gateways that connect, perhaps through tens or even hundreds of networks, one LAN with another.

As information moves from one LAN to another, often the distances start to require different transmission technology than wire or fibre optic cable. Networks of networks often require microwave or satellite transmission. Information can move on the Internet from Belgium to Kansas in seconds.

This is made possible because of the high-speed satellite connections that the Internet employs between Belgium and Kansas.

What we now call the Internet began as a set of research projects largely funded by the US National Science Foundation (NSF) in the late 1970s and early 1980s, and conducted by researchers in several American universities and at a few research organizations in the USA. The work was fast and furious. Researchers seemed to be filling in pieces that other researchers needed to make a new development just in time for that new development to take place in a timely manner. The Internet was being born, but no one truly comprehended how it would change the world in another ten years. Most of the researchers involved realized that this new tool would be a tremendous boon for computer scientists, physicists, engineers, etc.; but none of them envisioned a lady in her living room in Dubuque, Iowa, communicating with her grandson in his apartment in Copenhagen, Denmark, via the Internet. No one envisioned someone in Tokyo checking airline schedules between London and Paris via the Internet.

One aspect of what we now call the Internet that made it particularly attractive to the US Department of Defense was the multiple paths that information can travel to get from one computer to another. For example, an email message travelling from New York City to Los Angeles might go from New York to Buffalo, to Detroit, to Seattle, to San Francisco, to Los Angeles. Or, depending upon the traffic in various directions on the Internet at the time, it might travel from New York to Atlanta, to St Louis, to Phoenix, to San Diego, to Los Angeles. The sender of the email would not have to care about the path the message was going to take, nor would the recipient be concerned with the path the email message followed in arriving. Furthermore, any particular connection being unavailable would not significantly delay the message, For example, if the St Louis to Phoenix connection were unavailable because of a computer failure in Phoenix, then the email could simply travel from St Louis to Denver and continue its journey from there.

This aspect of computer networking – that a computer network can withstand failures of some connections and still continue to operate – really interested the US Department of Defense. They were concerned about the perceived threat that nuclear missiles might wipe out connections from one military base to another. If there were multiple (almost infinite) ways to transmit information from one base to another, then the loss of any one location would not be significant (militarily speaking, of course). Thus, the Department of Defense joined the NSF in funding the research and development projects that led to what we now call the Internet.

So, to summarize, the Internet is the result of a number of research and development projects in the 1970s, 1980s and 1990s sponsored by the NSF and Department of Defense (DOD). The research was conducted principally in several universities and research organizations. Some early networks that resulted from this work include Advanced Research Projects Administration Network (ARPANET), Defense Advanced Research Projects Administration Network (DARPANET), and Computer Science Network (CSNET). Finally, all of this work coalesced into what we now call the Internet.

A word about what the term 'Internet' really means. Some think it is a shortened form of 'International network'. This sounds very plausible, because the Internet has become international – particularly in this era of the World Wide Web. But, the term is actually a shortened form of 'Inter-connected network of networks'. Thus, technically speaking it would be possible to call it the 'Internet' even if it were still limited to use in the USA. But, of course, the Internet has become a truly international phenomenon. So, the confusion over the term is to be understood. Furthermore, some people have begun to shorten the term simply to 'The Net', but this is considered bad form by true Internet *aficionados* and a sure sign of an 'Internet rookie'. The negative connotations of 'Internet rookie' – a new and somewhat clueless user of the Internet – will be explored further in Chapter 3's discussions of Internet rookies and email.

The Internet has now become a massive worldwide network of computers. It is gaining roughly 2–3 million new users per month. These new users join an existing group of Internet users now exceeding 250 million. How do we know these statistics are accurate? From where do they come? Is there a main Internet headquarters in Washington, DC, London, Paris, Berlin or Tokyo? Is there an organization somewhere that controls all access to the Internet and can tell us accurately how many people are using the Internet and for what purposes? Quite simply, the answer to these questions is 'No'. By its very nature of being a network of networks of networks of networks of . . . , the control of the Internet is diffused throughout the world literally in the hands of individual network administrators. Each of them decides who will be on a network and such people are notoriously difficult to pin down in terms of number of users, etc. There is no central authority figure deciding who gets to use the Internet.

So, estimates of Internet usage are likely to be wrong, but the best information we have available at the time of publication of this book suggests that the 250 million Internet user figure is probably fairly accurate (even conservative), that at least 2–3 million new users begin to use the Internet

Table 1.1   Numbers of Internet users

Year	Users (millions)
1985	0.015
1989	0.245
1991	0.900
1993	3.000
1994	7.000
1995	16.000
1996	31.000
1997	63.000
1998	125.000
1999	250.000
2000	500.000

each month and that there are at least 20 million US households using the Internet. Furthermore it seems realistic, based on current numbers and projections, that by the year 2000 approximately 500 million people will use the Internet.

The growth of the Internet from its earliest origins was gradual at first, but lately has become extremely rapid. The figures in Table 1.1 are all estimates (certainly the ones for years that have not yet arrived!), but are likely to be conservative ones. Notice seven to ten years after the 'Prehistoric Era' (i.e., in 1985), there were only about 15 000 of us using the Internet. Four years later (in 1989) this number had multiplied by a factor of sixteen to 245 000 Internet users. The growth rate has been nothing short of phenomenal in the last several years. We believe that there are now easily more than 250 million Internet users with the potential for 500 million or more by the year 2000.

Is there any limit to this growth? The obvious answer is that the entire population of the Earth is about 6 billion people. When there are 6 billion Internet users, then the growth will stop. Or will it? This assumes that every Internet user is a person, which is approximately correct right now. But, what if your videocassette recorder (VCR) has an Internet connection so that it can peruse the television guide on the Web in order to tape exactly those television programmes that you request? Then, your VCR will likely be an Internet user. Perhaps this would also apply to your car, your heating and air-conditioning system, your watch and your refrigerator. It is possible that in a world of 6 billion people, there could 25 billion Internet users – or more!

Internet protocols

What is it that makes the Internet the Internet? The critical element is the Internet 'protocols' – standardized methods for communication among Internet computers. The most important of these protocols is what is known as the Transmission Control Protocol/Internet Protocol (TCP/IP). This is the software that every Internet computer must have, that sends and receives Internet messages.

In the early days of computer network research it became obvious that sending a message from one computer to another one character at a time was extremely slow and inefficient. It made much more sense to break a message up into packets of characters (in the order of about 4000 characters each) and send each packet separately. This is very similar to what happens when you move your office from one location to another. Suppose that you have a large filing cabinet. The contents of each file drawer are removed and placed in order in a cardboard box. Each box is labelled '1 of 4', '2 of 4', '3 of 4' and '4 of 4'. The boxes can then be placed in the removal van in any order. They can even be moved on different removal vans. They can even be moved at different times. But, when they arrive at the new office, the four boxes (assuming these all show up!) can be lined up in numerical order, opened and the contents placed in order into the new filing cabinet.

This is exactly what happens with Internet messages (such as email messages and Web pages). Transmission Control Protocol/Internet Protocol software divides each message into packets of characters that are sent along the Internet. These packets can travel the same path or different paths. But, when they arrive at the recipient computer, the TCP/IP software there 'opens' the packets and reassembles the original message. Any computer with a connection to the Internet and running TCP/IP is referred to as an *Internet node*. Thus, TCP/IP is the underlying protocol – the primary way that information travels from one computer to another. However it is not the only protocol, as we will see later when we talk about email and Web protocols.

Internet node names and numbers

With millions of Internet node computers (and even hundreds more since you started reading this chapter) there must be some addressing protocol to refer to each. If not, this would be the same as a large city with thousands (or millions) of houses with no street names and no house numbers. This obviously would not work. Every Internet node has an IP (Internet protocol) node number (sometimes called an IP host number). The following numbers are a few actual IP node numbers:

128.10.2.28
199.3.65.1
40.33.1.1
128.231.128.7
129.92.1.2
128.91.1.141

Thus, someone using computer 40.33.1.1 can send a 'message' to computer 128.10.2.28 by simply routing a message to that IP node number. Each number actually may be thought of as a quartet of numbers separated by periods (or dots):

xxx.xxx.xxx.xxx

Each of the numbers must be from 0 to 255; an 8-bit field is used to store each number and an 8-bit binary number ranges from 0 to 255. These numbers are assigned to new Internet nodes by a local network administrator who has been given a range of such numbers that can be used at her or his site.

But, these numbers are unwieldy for us humans. For some reason 128.10.2.28 is not easy to remember and, since most Internet users send and receive messages from hundreds of Internet nodes, imagine trying to remember hundreds of such forbidding numbers. For that reason, most Internet nodes – in addition to their IP node number – also have an Internet node name. For example, the set of IP node numbers above is equivalent to the following list of IP node names:

ocean.cs.purdue.edu
indynet.indy.net
inet.d48.lilly.com
alw.nih.gov
blackbird.afit.af.mil
philadelphia.libertynet.org

Internet protocol node names are read from right to left. For example, ocean.cs.purdue.edu is from the education (edu) domain of the Internet. Within that domain it is part of the Purdue University (purdue) – located in West Lafayette, Indiana sub-domain. Within that sub-domain it is a computer in the Computer Science (cs) department. And, finally, it has been given the name 'ocean'. There is only one computer in the world with the IP node name ocean.cs.purdue.edu – and it is located on one of the authors' desk. There are many other computers whose names end in .edu, or .purdue.edu, or even .cs.purdue.edu. There are other computers whose names begin with ocean, for example, ocean.ic.net. But, there is only one computer in the world that is ocean.cs.purdue.edu. Thus, an email message or web page sent to ocean.cs.purdue.edu will find its way to this computer.

(*Note*: It is not absolutely necessary for every IP node to have a name. Some do not. They go only by their Internet node number.)

Internet domains

In the last section it was mentioned that ocean.cs.purdue.edu is from the education (edu) domain of the Internet. In the early days of the Internet, the decision was made to divide IP node names into six principal divisions or *domains*. For Internet node names in the USA the last three characters specify the domain in which the Internet node may be found.

Education

The oldest domain is the education (edu) domain of the Internet. For a long while it was the only domain with many computers. Most of the Internet traffic in the 1980s was from one .edu computer to another. This domain is used for universities, colleges and some research organizations.

Government

As the Internet began to catch on, it was used by governmental officials and employees in the Federal, state and even local governments. All those computers are in the government (.gov) domain.

Military

The US military – including the Department of Defense, Army, Navy, Air Force and Marines – have computers in the military (.mil) domain.

Commercial

The fastest growing domain on the Internet is the commercial (.com) domain. From a start in the 1980s of almost no .com computers at all, this is a rapidly expanding collection of networks in most of the businesses in the USA. At first slow to embrace the Internet because of the fear of security problems and not being able to see any clear reason to join this national and international network, industry has begun to connect to the Internet at a rate far exceeding the speed with which educational and governmental institutions joined the Internet. A typical scenario has been that a company cautiously considers whether it wants to use the Internet for electronic mail and to present information on the World Wide Web. After a short test period they wonder how it ever took them so long to take advantage of all the Internet benefits.

Internet

The Internet (.net) domain is a relatively small one, consisting primarily of Internet service providers and Internet administrative-type organizations.

Non-profit organizations

The .org domain is in a way the miscellaneous domain. This is also quite small compared to the others and includes primarily institutions that cannot be categorized easily into any of the other domains. For example, libertynet.org is the sub-domain of .org for LibertyNet – a non-profit corporation formed in 1993 'to provide resources and direction to help the [Philadelphia, Pennsylvania] region's non-profit organizations use the Internet'.

How are these domains used? In various ways, but one important use is in routing Internet messages. An email message or web page being sent to www.cancun.com starts at the .com domain. A computer routing the message does not need to know anything about where computers are in the .edu or .gov or any other domain. It can simply follow tables from the .com domain to determine the best way to route the message to www.cancun.com.

For many years this set of domains has been sufficient. But, the incredible increase in use of the Internet and the Web in recent years is stretching the domain system and causing it to 'bulge and crack'. There are two principal problems with the existing domains. The first is what we call 'domain collision' – more than one company or organization wanting the same domain name. For example, imagine that you have just started a travel bureau named Wilson Travel. You would like wilson.com for your domain, but this has already been given to the Wilson Electric Company in Scottsdale, Arizona. How about travel.com? Sorry, this belongs to Travel Online, Lake St Louis, Missouri. Most of the most attractive domains are already taken. Requests for domain names frequently are met with the response that these are already being used by someone else. By the way, it turns out that, as this book is being written (but probably not today), wilson-travel.com is available.

This problem has led to the second problem – what we call 'domain speculation'. Until recently it was fairly easy to obtain a domain name even if there did not seem to be any reason for you to have it. That is, you did not have to be named 'Ford' or even have a company with 'Ford' in the name to ask for the ford.com domain. Many domain speculators grabbed a number of attractive domain names and have waited to sell or rent them for lucrative amounts of money. While we do not mind people making money using the Internet, this is not at all what was intended.

There has been some suggestion that far more than the original six domains are needed. As you might suspect, ford.com belongs to the Ford Motor Company of Dearborn, Michigan. How about extending the set of domains to include the following:

ford.model – Ford Modelling Agency
ford.gum   – Ford Bubble Gum Company
ford.clean – Betty Ford Center for the treatment of alcohol and drug
              dependence

On 4 February 1997, the International Ad Hoc Committee (IAHC) of the Internet Society proposed seven new generic top-level domains (Table 1.2).

However, at the time of the writing, these have still not been fully approved and are not yet in use. There are those who are philosophically (almost theologically) opposed to adding new top-level domains. The politics of this still needs to be worked out. One thing is clear. The system as it is cannot serve the growing needs of the Internet into the next century.

Notice that all the current top-level domains are three letters (.edu, .com, .gov, etc.) long. But what about the Internet node name mitsubishi.co.jp? What

Table 1.2 Proposed new generic top-level domains

.firm	for businesses, or firms
.store	for businesses offering goods to purchase
.web	for entities emphasizing activities related to the Web
.arts	for entities emphasizing cultural and entertainment activities
.rec	for entities emphasizing recreation/entertainment activities
.info	for entities providing information services
.nom	for those wishing individual or personal nomenclature

domain is that in? A two-letter suffix at the end of an Internet node name is what we call a country code. For example, mitsubishi.co.jp is in Japan (jp) in their commercial (co) sub-domain. The computer toronto.cbc.ca is in Canada (ca). The computer club.eng.cam.ac.uk is in the United Kingdom (uk); in fact, it is a computer in the Department of Engineering at the University of Cambridge. In general the two-letter suffixes are not used for computers in the USA, but there are some exceptions, such as lsc.k12.in.us – a computer in the Lafayette, Indiana, School Corporation.

Internet protocol: the next generation

Early researchers establishing what is now the Internet had no idea how much its use was going to increase. There were almost no clues early on to suggest how quickly and on what a scale the Internet would be embraced by the industrial sector, and how much commerce would be done via the Internet.

The ongoing changes in the use of the Internet are placing incredible strains on it. The current Internet protocol (IPv4) is running out of network addresses. The address 'space' for the Internet was made sufficiently large to handle the anticipated growth. It was suggested that most computer scientists, perhaps even most scientists in the world, might eventually use the Internet. The existing address space is more than adequate to handle these kinds of numbers.

No one ever imagined that a grandmother in Dubuque, Iowa, would want to have an Internet node to exchange email with her grandson in Copenhagen, Denmark. So, would address space for the 6 billion people on Earth be good enough? No, based on the argument that each of us one day may have several 'appliances' (VCR, car, watch, refrigerator, etc.) all of which need to be an Internet node.

The *Internet protocol: the next generation* (Ipng; i.e., IPv6) is the proposed new Internet protocol to replace IPv4. The IPng address size will increase from 32 bits to 128 bits. This raises the potential Internet address space from 4.3 billion (4.3 $\times$ 10 to the 9th power) to 3.4 $\times$ 10 to the 38th power. That should be enough for a while.

The IPng also was designed with security in mind and will provide more capabilities for authentication and confidentiality than the current Internet protocol.

2

How to use the Internet

Connections to the Internet

The way that most of us get access to the Internet at home is through a telephone connection. This is the means of Internet connection for some people at work, as well. A telephone connection is achieved through a MOdulator/DEModulator device (whose jaw-breaking title is thankfully shortened to *modem*). A modem works by converting (that is, modulating) digital computer information into an analogue signal which can then travel as a very strange, high-pitched, whining sound along telephone lines. Upon reaching its destination, the analogue whine is converted back (that is, demodulated) into digital computer information and delivered to the computer to which the modem is attached.

As a side note, telephone systems are going to change from their analogue signals to purely digital operation in the future. That is, your phone call to Aunt Sally will be digitized – much as if you had gone into a recording studio and made a CD for Aunt Sally. One side effect of this will be that digital computer information will be able to travel along phone lines with no modulation/demodulation required. Modems, if they exist (and if we continue to call them 'modems'), will simply collect and distribute digital information with no conversion required.

Back to the present: Modem speeds are measured in what is called 'baud rate' or *bauds*. To keep you from sounding like one of those dreaded Internet rookies, the term 'baud' is not pronounced 'bode'. It is pronounced 'bawd'. This has nothing to do with some bawdy information available on the World Wide Web – more about that later. The term 'baud' is in honour of J. M. E. Baudot, who invented the Baudot telegraph code.

One baud corresponds roughly to one bit per second. So, a baud rate of 56 000 baud is roughly 56 000 bits per second. Due to the way information is encoded for transmission, it takes about 10 bits to represent one letter, character, or number. So, 56 000 baud is roughly 5600 letters, characters or numbers per second.

As baud rates get larger we start to use the capital letter K to stand for 1000. Actually, computer scientists have long used K to stand for 1024, which is 2 to the 10th power. But, we often use K for 1000 as well – which is much easier. Thus, a baud rate of 56 000 will usually be reported as '56K baud'. It should not surprise you that 28 800 baud is 28.8K baud and 38 400 baud is 38.4K.

Images sent along the Internet can range wildly in size, but a small image might be 60 000 bits while a larger one might be 200 000 bits. At 56K baud the smaller one will take a little more than a second to transport, while the larger one will take between three and four seconds. An enormous image file of 5 000 000 bits (yes, some can be that large or larger!) will take about ninety seconds to arrive – even at the very fast 56K baud rate.

When you go into a store to purchase a modem, the burning issue usually is, 'What speed modem should I buy?' 'Should I buy the 56K modem, or the 38.4K (which will be a little cheaper), or the 28.8K modem (even cheaper)?' One consideration is that, no matter how fast your modem is, information transmission speed is restricted by the speed of the slower modem. That is, if you have a 56K modem and your Internet service provider (ISP) has modems that are limited to 38.4K, then the transmission speed can be no greater than 38.4K.

So, in that situation should you buy the slower modem? There is a simple, but effective, rule of thumb for modem purchase: 'Always buy the fastest modem in the store!' You can rest assured that ISPs are always upgrading their modems, so that they will be able to handle your speed before long. Even following this rule, be prepared for the comment in about two years' time from your brother-in-law, 'Are you still using that old 56K modem? Gee, I didn't think there were any of those slow things still around!'

What do you buy when you buy a modem? Well, in the old days (translation 'a year or so ago') this meant buying an 'external' modem – a small piece of hardware that looked like a small telephone answering machine. You connected the phone wire from the wall to the modem and then strung another phone wire from the modem to your telephone.

But, most external modems are rapidly giving way to internal Personal Computer Memory Card International Association (PCMCIA) cards (often called 'PC' cards). These are about the size of a (thick) credit card. They are simply plugged into an appropriate slot in the computer. The PCMCIA was chartered in 1989 to establish and maintain a set of hardware and software standards for such cards. The age of the 'external' modem is rapidly coming to an end.

Commercial Internet gateways

Some of us are lucky enough to have on our desk at work a computer that is directly connected to the Internet. We do not have to do anything special to reach the Internet. There is simply a wire into the wall that somehow magically connects the computer to a LAN and from there to the Internet. However, many of us are not so fortunate. And few of us have a computer at home that is directly connected to the Internet. In all those cases, we must usually have a modem and a telephone connection to access the Internet.

But, how does this work? Suppose that I have a computer, a modem and a telephone connection. What phone number do I dial? What kind of connection do I need to make to access the Internet?

Internet service providers

There is a rapidly growing industry of small, local companies known as ISPs that provide Internet access. Typically you visit their office, fill out an application form, give them some money, and head home with a diskette or CD-ROM of software to install on your computer. After installation you have a new icon available on your desktop computer. Clicking on that icon causes your modem to call a modem that belongs to the ISP. This is almost always a local phone call so it costs you nothing except for the normal monthly amount you pay for your phone service.

After a certain amount of chirping, clicking and clacking, you will be informed that you have an Internet connection. What does this mean? You have access to the Internet through a computer belonging to the local ISP. Anything you send on the Internet goes first to that computer from where it is routed anywhere in the world. And, anything coming to you is routed to that computer at your ISP, and then on to you. It is your link (while you maintain that phone connection) with the rest of the Internet. That computer at the ISP is most likely always connected to the Internet so that it can provide service for you any time of the day or night (as long as you can get through to the ISP without encountering a busy signal).

Many of today's computers have email software, web-browsing software, and other Internet tools available on them with no effort required on your part. Also, sometimes that diskette or CD-ROM provided by your local ISP will contain some email software (like Pegasus or Eudora) or a web browser (like Netscape) that gets installed on your computer as well. If not, it is not too difficult to 'download' software from the Internet to your computer. Much email and web-browsing software (in addition to a lot of other software) is free, so the only cost for downloading it is your time and the amount of your computer disk space that it occupies.

In most cases the only charge (since the use of the telephone is effectively free) is the monthly charge you pay to the local ISP. Standard at this time is approximately $20.00 or $25.00 per month (in the USA) for unlimited access. Some service providers charge a little less for people who do not plan to use the Internet very much – like $1.00 per hour. This sounds good until the monthly bill arrives and you realize that you spent 127 hours on the Internet last month. Then, the $20–$25 unlimited access charge looks much more attractive.

Most of these ISPs are small businesses who used their entrepreneurial instincts, saw an opportunity and seized on the chance. Lately there has been some consolidation in this industry with larger ISPs buying smaller ones to form conglomerates of co-operating local ISPs.

Competition from telephone and cable television companies is also facing the ISPs. Telephone companies can offer 'global' Internet access – that is, toll-free phone numbers that can be called from almost anywhere to gain Internet access without incurring long-distance charges. (In some instances, phone companies provide local phone numbers that can be used in other cities rather than toll-free numbers, but the effect is the same.)

Telephone companies can also offer digital subscriber line (DSL) technology with two very striking features. The first is that it does not interfere with the standard voice phone service. You can make and receive phone calls while your computer is connected to the Internet. In the DSL technology the digital information travels on its own bandwidth – making it possible to be 'logged on' to the Internet for long periods of time (always!) without disrupting family or office phone use. The second striking feature is the speed of information flow with DSL. The speeds are roughly ten times the speed of a typical telephone modem – making information reception (especially web pages) a much faster proposition.

By the way, DSL technology comes in many flavours. So, usually this will be called 'something DSL' as in 'asymmetrical digital subscriber line (ADSL)'. The word 'asymmetrical' simply refers to the fact that information comes into the computer at a very high speed but goes out at a much lower speed. This is usually not a cause of serious concern. Most of us do not care how long it takes things to go from our computer to somewhere else. But, we care very deeply how quickly we can receive email messages and web pages at our own computer!

All is not completely perfect with today's ISPs. Some are terribly overloaded with customers. This makes it difficult to make a connection with one of the ISP's modems and can lead to many frustrating busy signals when you want to use the Internet. With many customers, sometimes their systems run slowly as a result, dragging down the speed with which you can receive Internet material. Some ISPs have too few employees and take forever to fix problems and answer questions. For example, if something goes wrong with the ISP's email system it may take hours, or even days, before the badly overloaded technical staff can fix the problem. Furthermore, some ISPs have almost no previous business experience, are badly under-capitalized, and do not stay in business very long. It is best to get a recommendation from trusted friends before signing up with an ISP.

We offer a few rules of thumb for choosing a good ISP:

■ Choose an ISP that is physically close in case you have to visit their office. Sometimes nothing succeeds in drawing the ISP's attention to a problem like showing up on their doorstep and demanding some help.

- If you have a Macintosh, choose one that is 'Mac-friendly'. Most ISPs deal predominantly with people who have PCs. Ask specifically if a candidate ISP has Mac customers and even talk to some of them.
- Choose an ISP that makes it very easy for you to load Internet software (like Netscape, Pegasus, Eudora, telnet, ftp) on to your machine. Downloading software from the Internet seems remarkably easy to a lot of people, but quite forbidding to others. Especially if you fall into the latter category, choose an ISP that provides 'local copies' of software – perhaps even on a disk or CD-ROM.
- Choose an ISP that makes it very easy to establish a dial-up connection (with very few busy signals during times you want to use it). Ask to try their service for a few days at the typical times that you will want to use it. Be sceptical of claims like, 'We're usually not nearly this busy. Usually you can get through at 7:00 p.m. with no busy signal at all'.
- Sign up for no more than a month (maybe a free trial month) and see if you like the service. If a company requires a full-year contract, negotiate with them for a trial month or two before signing that contract. Unfortunately, some people have signed up for a year (or more!) with an ISP only later to regret their long-term financial commitment to a service that does not really meet their needs.

Major commercial Internet service providers

As the Internet era moved into the 1980s, a company named CompuServe appeared in the USA to provide Internet-like services to people who had no access to the Internet. CompuServe was the original such 'online' service and was owned by a company more famous for tax preparation – H&R Block. CompuServe provided their customers diskettes with easy-to-install and easy-to-use software. By typing a simple command or clicking a distinctive icon, the customer's computer dialled a local phone number which connected it to CompuServe's LAN in Columbus, Ohio. The CompuServe user had access to a large amount of 'online' information such as news, weather, sports, home shopping and even email.

Later, a competitor named Prodigy appeared. Begun as a joint venture between famous retailer Sears and major computing power IBM, Prodigy was based in White Plains, New York. Still later, America Online (AOL) (based in Vienna, Virginia) entered the commercial provider market. Prodigy and AOL were very similar to CompuServe in terms of method of access and kinds of services provided.

But, in their early days CompuServe, Prodigy and AOL were all distinct from the Internet. Each was a separate LAN with no connection to each other or to the rapidly expanding Internet. This might have continued, had it not been for the emerging popularity of email in the middle to late 1980s.

CompuServe, Prodigy and AOL customers became unhappy because they could not exchange email with family members and friends on the Internet. In fact, they could only exchange email with people who were customers of the same service. A great clamour among subscribers arose for email access to the Internet. This led each company to make its LAN effectively an Internet node. This, of course, allowed email to begin flowing from CompuServe to the Internet, from the Internet to Prodigy, from AOL to CompuServe, and all such combinations. The genie was out of the bottle. CompuServe, Prodigy and AOL were now part of the Internet family.

Even the great computing software giant Microsoft decided to enter the commercial service provider market. When Microsoft released its Windows 95 operating system in August 1995, it simultaneously announced the Microsoft Network (which it called msn). The Microsoft Network followed the same model as CompuServe, Prodigy and AOL. It was a dial-up service with Internet connectivity. Even AT&T decided to venture into this market – beginning its WorldNet Service in March 1996. (There are other commercial ISPs, but those mentioned above are the major ones.)

It is now possible, of course, to send e-mail among AOL (@aol.com), CompuServe (@compuserve.com), the Microsoft Network (@msn.com), Prodigy (@prodigy.com), AT&T WorldNet (@worldnet.att.net) and the Internet. An email message coming from a customer of any of these commercial Internet service providers is identified by the suffixes above.

The pioneering commercial ISPs will always be remembered for bringing the promise of computer networks to the public when it was difficult to experience this thrill any other way. America Online now boasts approximately 11 million subscribers and is the most prosperous. By contrast, CompuServe now has only about 2.6 million subscribers. In a complex financial deal in September 1997, CompuServe was taken over by AOL. The Microsoft Network (msn) has grown to 2.5 million subscribers, but has not experienced the outrageous success of almost everything else that Microsoft founder Bill Gates has touched. Prodigy now has only about 1.3 million subscribers and was sold in May 1996 to an investor group including members of its management team. AT&T WorldNet Service has less than a million subscribers.

What does the future hold for these companies? The services give mixed signals about what they intend to do, but the best guess is that all will likely become ISPs for home and office use with little or no proprietary content of their own. That is, the era of logging on to AOL to see what information it has available will likely give way to logging on through America Online to take a look at information anywhere on the Internet.

Internet security

The Internet was not designed with security in mind. The predominant goal of the earliest computer networks was to share information, not prevent some people from being able to get at some information. So, not surprisingly, the Internet has not been (and continues not to be) the most secure vehicle for storing and transmitting information. Newer versions of Internet protocols are more security conscious. In time the Internet may become quite secure as it becomes more of a vehicle for commerce and for transmitting sensitive industrial and governmental (not to mention military) information.

Information available via the Internet and World Wide Web falls into several categories:

1 Some information is meant for 'public access'. In this category are items that are to be made available freely to anyone with an interest in them such as advertising, product information, service information, phone numbers, certain company information, etc. But, the term 'public access' refers only to seeing the information. Even public access information has severe restrictions on who can create and modify it.
2 The next category is 'restricted access' information – restricted to customers, potential customers, suppliers, company personnel, etc. Such information is not available to the general public. Access to such information may be controlled by special passwords or similar means of shutting out those for whom the information is not intended.
3 The final category is 'no access' information – private company information about sales, employees, expenses, profits, etc. that is not intended to be viewed by anyone outside the organization – and perhaps by only a few individuals inside the organization.

It is debatable whether any information in this last category should even be stored on a computer that is an Internet node. If it is, it should be carefully placed behind a *firewall*. What is a 'firewall'? Architecturally, of course, we all know that a firewall is a wall built between two rooms that is so secure that in time of emergency (like a fire) the contents of one room can be sealed completely away from the other. You will not be surprised to find that this is approximately what 'firewall' means in computer network jargon. A firewall is any device that keeps information safe from external access.

One example of a firewall, although not a very realistic one, would be a LAN with no access to the Internet. That would certainly protect the network's contents from outside access, but at the expense of being able to reach the Internet (with all the many benefits thereof) from the network. More realistic (and generally what is meant by a 'firewall') is a LAN with very restricted Internet access.

With a typical firewall all Internet access is really done by 'proxy programs'. So, what in the world is a 'proxy program'? Think of it this way. Suppose that you have a 'proxy' person to drive you around in your car. This person (perhaps a robot!) acts very much like you, drives much like you, even drives the car to the places you want to go. But the proxy person never exceeds the speed limit, never drives fast when the roads are icy, never makes a dangerous turn in traffic – in short is much more safety and security conscious than you are. This is exactly what a proxy program does. It does the same thing as an email tool or web-browsing tool, but is careful that no information flows out of the firewall that should not. It is also careful that no dangerous programs are let inside the firewall that might destroy or modify local information.

Many organizations have computing security policies and practices to which there must be strict adherence. The firewall can become the embodiment of this corporate policy with proxy programs that enforce each element of it. Frequently, the hardest part of beginning to use the Internet, is not justifying the expense or effort, but convincing management of an organization that it is safe to do so. The firewall can provide real security and often plays an important role as a security blanket for management.

The firewall can also act as a corporate 'ambassador' to the Internet. Proxy programs, while being careful not to let out sensitive information or to let in potentially dangerous programs, can provide the public with information about corporate products and services, program and data files that can be obtained, and bug fixes. Someone from outside attempting to access non-public information (perhaps 'accidentally') can be gently nudged by a proxy program with a response of, 'Gee, we're sorry. That information is not available to you. But take a look at the following information that is available.'

Generally, firewalls are configured to protect against unauthenticated logins from the 'outside' world. That is, the only people who should be able to access a system for the purpose of creating new information, modifying existing information or running software should be those who are allowed to login to the system.

There is a strange irony in all this concern about people outside an organization accessing, modifying and destroying valuable information. To date nearly 80 per cent of such security breaches are internal, that is, the problem is caused by a disgruntled (or stupid) employee or, even, a former employee who still has access codes that were not changed when he or she left. This latter point might sound ridiculous, but it is not uncommon for an employee to leave an organization, go to a competitor and then find out months (or even years) later that the security codes they used at their old organization were never changed and they still can access some very sensitive information.

Encrypting messages to make them secure

Another line of defence against unwanted access to information is to 'encrypt' that information. Remember when, as a child, you had a secret decoder ring that allowed you to do letter shift of a message that you wanted to send to a friend. Perhaps the decoder ring told you to change all letter As to Rs, Bs to Ds, Cs to Qs, etc. If your friend had an identical decoder ring, he or she could 'decrypt' the message upon receipt.

Encrypting is any process of transforming information so that, even if accessed by someone undesirable, it is unintelligible to him or her. Decrypting is the process of translating the encrypted information back into its original form. Notice that encrypting can be done before sending information along the Internet (in case it is intercepted in transit) or can be done to a data file that may never be sent on the Internet (to protect it in case of system break-in).

Sadly, the time-honoured decoder ring encryption process is far from secure. For example, in English the letter 'e' is used most often. So, if a message has many letter 'gs', that is probably the encrypted letter 'e'. A simple computer program can break a decoder-ring encryption in seconds.

The state-of-the-art encryption and decryption procedure now in use with the Internet is what is known as a public–private key procedure. In such a process, encryption and decryption require two keys (or sometimes even four) to be used in a very specific manner.

A two-key security system works like a padlock that has two keys. One is inserted into the keyhole to lock the lock, but that key cannot unlock the lock. The second key is necessary to unlock the lock.

A very popular two-key procedure is known as 'pretty good privacy' (PGP). This was developed by Philip Zimmermann and uses the concept of public and private keys. For example, PGP can be used so that one person can lock (encrypt) an email message and send it to another person who can unlock (decrypt) it – assuring that only the receiver of the email message can read it. Anyone else intercepting it has only gibberish.

To explain how this works, first we need to establish some terminology. 'Plaintext' is what we call the actual message, text, data, program, image file, etc. Plaintext can be read, run or viewed by anyone. 'Ciphertext' is what plaintext becomes after it is encrypted. Ciphertext is unreadable, unrunnable, unviewable except by a person with a key to decrypt it. So, encryption is simply the process of taking plaintext and turning it into ciphertext. Decryption is the process of taking ciphertext and turning it back into plaintext.

In PGP, everyone has both a public key and a private key. By the way, a 'key' in PGP is not a metal thing that you stick into a keyhole. It is a seemingly meaningless string of letters, digits and characters. It could be something like mQCNAi3YBBkAAA+ZLoJ7ov/yBS, although real PGP keys are much longer.

How are these public and private keys used? Let us look at a very typical scenario. Ann wants people to be able to send her email messages that are encrypted, so that anyone intercepting them gets only gibberish, and so that she, Ann, is the only one who can read them. What does Ann do? She makes her public key available to all her friends. Heck, she may even make it available to all her enemies. In fact, she makes it available to anyone who might ever want to send her an email message. How does she do this? Well, she can email her public key to people or (even more modern and cool), she can post her public key on her website for anyone to copy.

Now suppose that Ann's friend Bob wants to send Ann an encrypted email message. He writes the email message in plaintext. Then, he runs the plaintext message through PGP encrypting software – giving the software both the email message and Ann's public key. The PGP encrypting software produces a ciphertext version of the message which Bob mails to Ann.

When Ann receives the message, she runs it through PGP decrypting software – giving the software both the ciphertext email message and Ann's private key. The PGP decrypting software returns the original plaintext message. Notice that anybody (including Bob) can have a copy of Ann's public key in order to encrypt a message for her, but Ann is the only person in the world with her private key. Again this 'key' is another of these seemingly meaningless string of letters, digits and characters. Ann keeps her private key in a very secret, private, secure location to be sure that no one else can decrypt a message meant for Ann.

This all seems wonderful. Ann can be sure that messages sent to her are secure. Notice that she can reply to Bob's message by encrypting her reply with Bob's public key. He can then decrypt her reply with his private key.

There is a potential problem with the Bob and Ann scenario above. What if nasty old Charlie wanted to throw a monkey wrench into Bob and Ann's budding relationship. If he were clever enough, he could write an email message to Ann, encrypt it with Ann's public key, and then send it to her under the disguise of coming from Bob. How can Ann really tell that an email message to her comes from the person that appeared to send it? This is the problem of authentication. 'Authentication' means to determine that the source of a message is who it appears to be.

Pretty good privacy's keys can be used to solve the authentication problem. Here is the way it works. As before, Bob encrypts his message to Ann with Ann's public key (which he and everyone else have). But, before sending the message to her he puts the ciphertext through another encrypting step, this time with his own private key (which only Bob has). When Ann receives the message, she puts it through a two-step process as well. First, she decrypts it using Bob's public key (which she and everyone else have) to 'unlock' the effect of 'locking' it with Bob's private key. Then, she decrypts it with her private key to 'unlock' the effect of 'locking' it with her public key. *Voila*! The message is no longer gibberish, and Ann can be certain that no one else has read it and that it really did come from dreamy Bob.

But, is there really a serious problem that requires that messages and files be encrypted and decrypted as a matter of course in using the Internet? No, not really. With millions of email messages, information files and web pages flying across the Internet every day, what are the odds that someone would intercept one of these files and actually know what they have? Not very high. In fact, web browsers now routinely encrypt personal identification numbers, credit card numbers and bank account numbers before transporting them along the Internet. I am much more concerned about the waiter in a restaurant who takes my credit card and is gone for five or ten minutes, than I am having that number fly along the Internet. The waiter is aware of what he has and could make several charge slips before returning the card to me.

Internet security measures

The use of the Internet is growing rapidly in many organizations. Most computer systems are becoming increasingly dependent on the Internet. That, of course, means that they are also becoming more vulnerable to attack via the Internet, that is, outside intruders no longer need physically to break into an organization to read, alter or even destroy important information. They can enter fairly unobtrusively through a computer network. No doors are broken down. No windows are smashed. Seldom is a telltale clue left.

It is becoming increasingly important to test computer networks for such vulnerability. One way to do this is to hire outsiders to try all possible forms of illegal access to break into the organization's computer system and files. It is important to determine if some forms of legal access can also be used as a loophole to illegal access. For example, is it possible for someone visiting an organization's website to guess the name of a private information file and actually retrieve it?

Some software tools have been developed to help systems administrators determine how secure their computer network really is. These tools recognize several common network-related security problems. Even better, the tools report the problems without exploiting them. The report explains each problem, what its impact could be and what can be done about the problem.

Some sample problems that such software might identify include entire 'private' file systems that are actually accessible to knowledgeable outsiders, password files accessible to outsiders, and email software with security gaps that allow snooping or destructive programs to be delivered to and run by computers inside the organization.

Passwords

A very effective way of restricting access to computers, networks and files is by assigning an identity (ID) and password to allow access to such things. For example, suppose that the fictional organization International Travel, Incorporated, allows individual resort operators to update information about costs, packages, availability dates, etc. for their resort. Club Cote d'Azur could be given the ID 'azur' and the password 'Lv2501$a'. Whenever the operators of the Club Cote d'Azur want to make a change in their information as stored at International Travel, they access the ID 'azur' and must give the password 'Lv2501$a' before being allowed to edit Club Cote d'Azur information. Someone might guess the ID 'azur', but the password 'Lv2501$a' is bizarre and has nothing to do with the Club Cote d'Azur. Someone could guess for days, months, or years and never try that combination of letters, numbers and special characters.

That is what makes a good password. It should use letters, numbers and special characters. It should be fairly long. Some systems have restrictions that passwords cannot exceed, for example, eight characters. But, it should certainly be more that two or three. Suppose that a password is only three characters built from the twenty-six lower case letters, twenty-six upper case letters, ten digits, and perhaps twenty-five special characters (like commas and dollar signs). There are only 658 503 combinations to try to guess the password – more than you and I want to try by hand, but at 100 guesses per second the password could be guessed by computer software in a little under two hours.

Yet another way of 'guessing' a password involves trying obvious words. For example, a smart interloper trying to break into the 'azur' account would try 'azur', 'cote', 'club', 'French', 'Riviera', 'Nice', 'Mediterranean', etc. You would be surprised how often people use passwords such as these for easy recollection later, that greatly aid break-ins. It is a good rule of thumb not to use any word that appears in any dictionary, as well. Smart break-in software usually tries all the words in a dictionary. But certainly it is unlikely to find 'Lv2501$a' there.

The final bastion of defence is to change the password occasionally. It is amazing how many organizations have a really good password – so good, in fact, that they have kept it for two or three years. During that time several employees have left the organization and, perhaps, gone to work for competitors. You would never think of letting a former employee keep his or her keys to the office. That is exactly what you are doing if passwords are not changed when employees leave the organization.

The future of the Internet

It is obvious that interest in the Internet is growing. There are so many potential benefits of using it. The Internet (especially the World Wide Web) can be an excellent means of marketing, advertising and encouraging sales. It is a very effective way for communicating with potential clients and customers on their own terms and at their own pace.

Many organizations are using the Internet for internal communication via email, secure private files, and even a restricted access local network (called an *intranet*). The Internet can be used as a tool for communicating technical information with employees, suppliers, distributors and even some customers. 'Help' information can be made available for distributors, clients and customers. Some organizations have found that they can scale back drastically their expensive-to-operate toll-free helplines by putting a set of frequently asked questions (FAQs) on a website.

One of the major benefits of the Internet is its feature of 24-hour worldwide access. While the staff of a Lazer Tag equipment distributor is home in bed in Ohio, people in China, Hong Kong and Russia can be perusing company information on the World Wide Web. The Web also allows the use not only of text, but also of high-quality colour images, sounds and video.

Using the Internet (especially the Web) to display product and service information can be far superior to the more traditional techniques such as a printed catalogue. A printed catalogue by its very nature is probably out of date by the time it is shipped to employees, distributors and customers. With the Internet, a change to a single document, changing a price or description, immediately updates that document for all employees, distributors and customers. If the price of Lazer Gun 2000Z is changed at 9.00 this morning to $19.00, anyone looking at the website at 9.01 will get the updated information.

That is all well and good, but in what direction is the Internet going? What changes do we expect to see in the Internet and World Wide Web over the next few years that will make it better? Here are a few suggestions.

True mobile computing

Right now the standard computer is connected to the Internet via a wire into the wall or a phone connection. These will begin to give way to transmitters mounted on the side of a computer screen sending and receiving information to and from a reception station which will be the ISP. Such a system will work essentially like cellular telephones work now. This will allow computers to be repositioned as necessary within an office or entire building with no need for re-cabling. This will also allow Internet access while strolling along carrying a personal computer, or even while driving. We can envision a world in which the aphorism 'Don't drink and drive' is joined by 'Don't compute while driving'.

Better Internet accessibility for everyone

Research work is proceeding at a rapid pace to make sure that the Internet and World Wide Web are truly accessible – in the sense that buildings must be accessible – to the visually impaired, hearing impaired or individuals with other impairments (such as using the keyboard or using a mouse). Computer software and hardware hold great promise for solving such problems.

Long-distance calls

The Internet is becoming a truly global communications medium and as many computers are now equipped with audio and video playing and recording devices, it is entirely possible that the long-distance calls of the future will happen over the Internet. In fact, some have boldly predicted that the entire phone system as we know it (including local calls) may some day be viewed as simply one of the features of the Internet.

A merging of the Internet and television

As the World Wide Web begins to look a lot like television with animated images and streaming audio and video, why not simply combine the two? Why not allow me to access my favorite television programmes by selecting them via computer? This will allow me to watch television programmes either 'live' or at any time more convenient to me. Many people use video recorders to time shift television. But, there is no reason for each of us to do this if television programmes can be accessed at any time from the Internet.

Replacing CD-ROMs with the Web

A CD-ROM device stores a tremendous amount of information and makes it available quickly to a computer. But, the CD-ROM suffers from the same problem as any collection of information; it becomes out of date. And in today's world things seem to become out of date more quickly than ever. By the way, the CD-ROM is already giving way to the digital video disk (DVD) with seven to ten times the capacity of a CD-ROM. But, even DVDs will suffer from the out-of-date problem. We might simply think of CD-ROMs and DVDs as a stopgap measure until bandwidths and computer speeds get so good that anything now on a CD-ROM can be accessed just as quickly over the Web.

Using the Web as a book supplement

Nothing will ever replace the satisfaction of sitting down to touch, hold and ultimately read a good book. But, of course books suffer from the out-of-date problem as well. One possibility (actually being used by the authors of this book) is to have a supplementary website for a book with information constantly updated so that the combination of the book and the website are as current as possible. As a side note, this will also allow detailed information that an author might think is not worth putting into the book, because only a few people might find it interesting, to be included on a website. This opens a whole new world of personalized publishing. The website can be customized by each individual reader to make the supplementary material be exactly what he or she wants.

The postal service goes almost completely to email

Why bother to carry a piece of paper from Canton, Ohio, to Paris, France, at great expense if only the words on that paper are what the recipient in Paris really needs to see? Why, indeed? A large portion of what is now sent as mail (words and images printed on paper) will be able to be delivered just as well, more cheaply and much more quickly via email. Magazine publishers are already exploring this option.

Distance learning

Our concept of teaching and learning may get turned upside down by the Internet. The Internet (especially the Web) permits all course material – including readings, assignments, supplementary materials and exams (see Chapter 8) – to be available on a computer network. Great advances are being made in digitizing audio and video, so that lectures, discussions and even laboratories could be made available on the Internet. It is possible to imagine a student in rural Iowa 'attending' Yale University via the Internet. There are incredible challenges in getting such a scenario to work. The quality of education is terribly important and should not be allowed to suffer at the expense of technology use, but if all the problems can be solved, distance learning could become the prevalent paradigm of the twenty-first century.

3

Computers and electronic mail

PC or not PC – that is the question

Most of the world's computer users now use what we call a personal computer (PC; also called an 'IBM PC' or even an 'IBM PC clone'). Such a computer is usually a desktop machine with keyboard, screen, mouse, modem and printer. Typical PCs these days are very fast, have an enormous amount of disk storage space and memory space, and usually have audio and video-playing and recording devices. Such a machine has become the main workhorse of the computing arena. It is increasingly common that these once stand-alone machines have access to the Internet – either through a direct (wire) connection or via a modem.

But, such PCs are not the only means to access the Internet. 'Laptop' and 'notebook' computers are very popular as well. These are lightweight, portable PCs with keyboard, screen, mouse and modem generally all built in to the notebook-like container. These computers are attractive because of their mobility and small amount of space they take on a desk surface, plus the ease with which they may be put away when not in use.

Another major competitor to the PC is the Apple computer. Actually, the Apple is simply a brand of PC but, due to incompatibilities between the two, Apples are often spoken of as if they are completely distinct from PCs. The Apple computer most in use these days is the Apple Macintosh. The 'Mac', its usual appellation, is very popular in schools because of the ease of use that its point-and-click mouse-driven interface provides.

In addition to PCs (desktop, laptop and notebook) and Macs, there are various other popular computers that Internet users have available to them. Many of these, for example the very popular Sun workstation, use a command-based operating system called Unix and some combine point-and-click and windowed interfaces with the Unix operating system.

Much of the early work on what is now the Internet was done by computer scientists using the Unix operating system. But, one of the beauties of the Internet is the way it provides an interface among people – independent of the kind of computer they are using. The computer and operating system you are using is sometimes referred to as your *platform*, as in 'I've been reading my email from a Sun workstation Unix platform' and 'I like the way the new Netscape Web browser runs on my Windows 98 PC platform'. In general there are similar Internet tools available regardless of the platform in use.

For the remainder of this book we will make the assumption that our reader is using a PC with a Microsoft Windows (Windows 95 or Windows 98) operating system. But, because of the nature of the Internet, nearly all of what we say from here on will still be applicable even for those of you using a Macintosh or a Sun workstation or virtually any other platform.

Using PCs

The most popular computer operating system in use today is the point-and-click, Windows-based operating system from Microsoft. What is a window? It is simply a rectangular area on the computer screen in which you may view what a running computer program is doing. Windows can be very small so that several of them can be seen simultaneously. Windows can be arbitrarily large so that they may cover all the other windows and appear to be the only program running at the time. We will talk below about how to change the size of windows for programs that are running.

Most modern computer operating systems and programs use *icons*. What is an icon? This is a little picture that conveys the meaning of the thing that the operating system or program will do if you click on it. These are generally small, cartoon-like images. The philosophy employed with icons is that 'a picture is worth a thousand words', that is, rather than having a wordy command to do something, click on the icon that represents that something. For example, a picture of a letter with a stamp on it or a mailbox makes a fine icon for starting up an email tool. A picture of a garbage can is an excellent icon for representing where data files go when you do not need them anymore. On the other hand, icons can be just as bad as commands if they do not visually convey their meaning very well. What if you run across an icon that shows a snake eating a rat? Could that be the icon you click on to delete a file or is the icon to shut down the computer so that you can go to lunch?

Windows 95 (which was introduced in August 1995) is giving way to its newer version Windows 98 (first available in June 1998). Without dwelling on the specifics of either one (which are well documented by online help information from Microsoft) let us talk a little about how most modern computer operating systems work, the kinds of things you can do with them and how they can be used to access the Internet. In order to avoid confusion and because Windows 95 and Windows 98 are so similar for the kind of discussion we are having, we will simply refer to both as Windows 95/98 in the remainder of this book.

First, Windows 95/98 is an *operating system*. But, we really have not defined that term. Suppose that you are going on a trip to Turkey, where you have never been. It is a good idea to have a tour guide in Turkey to help you get to where you want to go and to make life generally easier for you during your visit. That is exactly what an operating system does. When you turn on a computer, what you see on the screen is usually what the operating system presents upon 'startup'. With the Windows 95/98 operating system the startup screen contains icons that you can click on (using the mouse, of course) to run programs, view the World Wide Web, send email, etc.

There was a good deal of hype when Windows 95 was introduced. Some declared that 'Windows 95 is the most important development in the history of computing', which was wrong. Windows 95 was just an operating system, a good one, but in many ways simply a better version of the old Windows 3.1 that people had been using for years. On the other hand, some naysayers chimed in that, 'Windows 95 is not really a significant advance in operating systems', which was also wrong. Several things were done much better by Windows 95 than many existing operating systems could boast, not the least of which was to make it much easier for a computer to be able to access the Internet. The hype was scaled down a bit with the introduction of Windows 98, because most observers realized that Windows 98 is primarily just a better quality version of Windows 95.

The desktop

The desktop computer is the starting point for all Windows 95/98 computing. The choice of the word 'desktop' is a good one. Think of the screen of the computer like the surface of a desk. You can do a lot of work by accessing things on the desktop and moving them around. The individual things you can do are called *applications* and are such things as using a web browser or using email software. If you envision these applications like something in a folder stored just under the desk surface, then it makes a lot of sense to talk about 'opening' an application (to start it running), 'closing' an application (to stop it running) and even 'hiding' an application (so that it continues running but does not appear on the desktop). At the bottom of the desktop, there is a start button (which is nothing more than a little rectangular icon with the Microsoft logo on it) for opening application programs and the taskbar for managing all of the application programs that are running or hiding. The location of the start button, taskbar and system tray trio (all discussed below) is by default at the bottom of the desktop. But, you can configure your Windows 95/98 desktop so that this trio is at the top or either side of the desktop.

The start button

A single left-click on this button pops up a menu. As you move your cursor up and down this menu, the various menu items are highlighted as the cursor passes over them. Some menu items (for example, the Eudora email tool) are applications on which you can simply left-click to get them started. Lingering the cursor over other menu items (for example, 'web browsers') will bring up a sub-menu of applications (for example, a set of web browsers) along with possibly other sub-menu starters. There is no limit to the number of sub-menus that may spread out from the start button, but pretty soon the screen can get very cluttered, so most Windows 95/98 menu sets do not go more than three or four sub-menus deep.

The taskbar

The Windows 95/98 taskbar extends to the right next to the start button. When you click on an application program, in addition to starting running, most programs place a button (another little rectangular icon) on the taskbar when they are opened. A quick glance at the taskbar shows all the applications running and/or hiding. Any program that is hiding can be brought back out on to the desktop by clicking on its button in the taskbar. Also, if several programs are running, but the window in which one is running is covering one or more of the others, a covered window can be brought to the front of the computer screen by clicking on its button in the taskbar.

The system tray

The Windows 95/98 system tray is located to the far right of the start button and taskbar, making a start button, taskbar, system tray trio across the bottom or top (or down the side) of the screen. The system tray contains smaller icons than the ones in the taskbar. These are icons for operating system programs that get started for you automatically – such things as battery meters and modem connectivity displays – just to show you that they are running. You can also click on these little icons to learn more about what that particular program is doing (or not doing). The system tray may also contain a clock.

Application programs

Windows 95/98 application programs are usually displayed on the screen in a window. Each program runs in its own private window. Windows 95/98 programs generally use a standardized set of controls as described below.

The title bar

Every Windows program has a title bar at the top of its window. It usually contains the name of the program being run – sometimes with other information, like the name of a file being edited by an editor program or the title of a website being visited by a web-browser program. The title bar can be used to reposition (move) a window. By clicking and holding down the left mouse button on the title bar, you can drag the window anywhere you want on the computer screen via a process known (not surprisingly) as 'click and drag'.

There are three little special icons to the extreme right of the title bar. A left-click on the 'flat line' icon minimizes or 'hides' the window. The program is still running. The application is still available. It just does not appear on the screen when hidden. To make it reappear, click on the window's button in the taskbar. If the middle of the three little icons is one box, then this means that the window is currently occupying only a portion of the screen. Left-clicking on the box makes the window grow to fill the entire computer screen. If the middle of the three little icons shows two boxes, then this means that the window is currently occupying the entire computer screen. Left-clicking on the two-box icon makes the window shrink back to occupying that same portion of the screen it did just before you last clicked on the middle icon. The third of these three little special icons (to the far right) is a letter 'X'. Think of this as a reminder of the word 'eXit' because left-clicking on this icon will cause the program in the window to stop running and the window to disappear. Also, think of this as the 'X' that sometimes appears on road signs to indicate a warning, because you should think carefully before eXiting a program in this way. Have you done all you have wanted to do? Have you saved all the changes you have made, etc.? By the way, virtually all Windows 95/98 programs can be exited by clicking on an option in the 'File' menu of the program itself. This is usually easier and safer, so think of that 'X' as an icon usually to stay away from.

Whenever a window is not currently occupying the entire screen (that is, the little middle icon shows two boxes), you can generally change its size. By clicking and holding down the left mouse button on the lower right-hand corner of the window, you can move the mouse in any direction making the window wider, narrower, longer or shorter. Some windows cannot be resized. This is due to the way their application programs have been written; they only run in windows of a specific size. In that case left-clicking on the lower right-hand corner of the window and moving the mouse around has no effect on the window's size.

Desktop icons

In addition to the start button, taskbar, and system tray trio visible on the desktop, there are sure to be several little icons sitting around on the desktop, like familiar file folders that you are likely to use often. These can be 'short cuts' to application programs. By left-clicking rapidly twice (known as 'double-clicking') on one of these icons, the program it represents starts running exactly as if you had found it on the main menu or one of the sub-menus of the start button. There are several other standard icons usually found on the desktop. The most common are:

1 My computer – an icon showing a single computer with the words 'My computer' below it. Double-clicking on this icon shows all the disk drives, printers and similar things to which this computer has access.

2 Network neighbourhood – an icon showing two computers side by side. Double-clicking on this icon shows the networks and other computers (if any) to which this computer has access.

3 Recycle bin – an icon showing a trash can with papers in it. Double-clicking on this icon shows you all the things currently in your recycle bin. But, how do things get there in the first place? Usually any time you delete a data file, it does not go away completely. It goes first to the recycle bin. This can be extremely useful for those times of 'brain fade' when you delete something and then immediately wish you had it back (like closing the locked car door and seeing the car keys sitting on the seat just as the door latch clicks). To recover a file in the recycle bin, left-click on it and then select the word 'Restore' from the File menu. Obviously you cannot keep everything you ever delete in the recycle bin. In time it (which occupies space on your computer's disk just like every other folder) will become so full that you will have no available disk space. Periodically go to the recycle bin, click on items, and select the word 'Delete' from the File menu. This is like emptying some of the contents of a trash can next to your desk into the dumpster out in the alley. But be warned, files deleted from the recycle bin really are gone.

Email

In the 1980s it was very common for scientists and academics to communicate with some of their colleagues, family and friends using email. This seemed a very pervasive activity to those of us who were doing it, but in reality less than 1 per cent of the Earth's citizens were participating. With the increasing popularity of the Internet and especially the World Wide Web, access to electronic mail is growing. It has been estimated that in the late 1990s somewhere between 25 per cent and 50 per cent of the population of the USA and between 2 per cent and 5 per cent of the total world population are regularly using email.

From its humble beginning as a side effect of transmitting files from one computer to another on a computer network, email's popularity rose in the early 1990s – making it the predominant activity (in terms of bytes moved across the Internet). It is only in 1998/9 that the World Wide Web has surpassed (which we think is the case) email in moving bytes. But, the popularity of email stays strong and may get a boost from the oncoming promise of easy multimedia email – discussed below.

First some basics. With electronic mail, people have mailboxes – data files into which Internet software can write incoming electronic mail – even if that person is not currently 'logged on'. So, even if you are not using your computer, someone can send you an email message. The next time you turn on the computer and check for email, anything that has been sent to you recently will appear.

Note that most people have only one email mailbox. They have only one email address to give people, saying for example, 'Send me email at wilson@travelcenter.com'. But, some of us have several email addresses on several computers and some email addresses are read by several people. For example, cruises@travelcenter.com might be an email address whose incoming messages could be read by any of several agents at the Travel Center who work on setting up cruises for customers.

The speed of email is astounding. An email message can be sent to the person in the office next door and to a colleague on the opposite side of the world and both can arrive at approximately the same time. Since most 'opposite side of the world' messages travel by satellite at the speed of light, this should not seem amazing, but still seems so.

However, email sent to a building two miles away might not arrive for several hours or several days. What is the problem here? Not an inherent problem with email, but this is usually due to problems with procedures, network connections and/or computers.

Some organizations 'batch' email messages and send them out on to the Internet as a group. So, the earliest email message in the group might have to wait several hours for a large enough batch to build up. Some organizations only connect to the outside world email servers every few hours, pick up all incoming messages, and deliver them to individual mailboxes as a 'batch'. Both of these 'batching' techniques were prevalent when email was not so important and connections to the Internet were more difficult. But, with many organizations now dependent upon immediate receipt and delivery of email, 'batching' is losing popularity.

If one of the authors of this book sends an email message from West Lafayette, Indiana, to a colleague in San Diego, California, it might travel first to Chicago, then to Minneapolis, then to Denver, then to Spokane, then to San Francisco and, finally, to San Diego. (By the way, each stop along the way is referred to in Internet parlance as a 'hop'.) But, if the Internet connection between Minneapolis and Denver is experiencing a lot of traffic or one of the sending/receiving computers is briefly unavailable, then that message might go from Chicago to Kansas City, to Phoenix, to Los Angeles, to San Diego.

If critical nodes are unavailable (like the one that sends email to the Internet for me or the one that delivers email to my colleague in Los Angeles) then an email message may be delayed. Otherwise it can be rerouted as shown above.

Email addressing

Delivering email is similar to delivering standard mail. The sender must know your address. A full email address consists of user-id@IP-Host-Name, that is, first is the 'user-id' of the recipient. This is usually a name like 'wilson' or 'davis' or 'bobwilson' or 'betty.davis' or 'floyd-wilson'. Next comes the @ symbol followed by the IP node name (see Chapter 1) of the computer on which 'user-id' has his or her mailbox. So, 'fkjohnson@zeus.personnel.lilly.com' is the full email address of 'fkjohnson' (Frances K. Johnson) and her mailbox is on the Internet computer 'zeus.personnel.lilly.com'. This is the computer named 'zeus' in the Personnel Department at the Eli Lilly company.

But, a full email address is not always necessary. For example, you may be able to send email to Frances K. Johnson by sending it to fkjohnson@personnel.lilly.com. Why do you not need the 'zeus'? Because, 'personnel.lilly.com' is the IP node name of a computer in Eli Lilly that knows that Frances's mailbox is on zeus.personnel.lilly.com. You might even be told just to send email to her at fkjohnson@lilly.com. This works if 'lilly.com' is the IP node name of a computer that knows that Frances's mailbox is on zeus.personnel.lilly.com.

Within the company, email addresses get even simpler. Most of her Eli Lilly colleagues can probably send email to her at fkjohnson@personnel. The internal email system will affix 'lilly.com' to any partial email addresses making it easier to send email to colleagues without using such long addresses. Even better, one of Frances's colleagues in the Personnel Department can probably send email to her by simply using the address 'fkjohnson'. From within the Personnel Department, the email system will likely affix '@personnel.lilly.com' to any email addresses that do not have an '@' symbol.

Using some typical email systems

Most people are now fortunate enough to have at their disposal some simple Windows-based visual email tools like Eudora, Pegasus or Netscape Mail. These tools are characterized by having nice visual icons – like buttons and letters and mailboxes and pens – and are generally very easy to use even without much instruction. We will not attempt to make you an expert user of these tools, but let us give you some basics to try.

Eudora was named in honour of Eudora Welty's short story 'Why I live at the post office'. Eudora is a very popular email tool that is available for several computer and operating system platforms. It comes in several versions (of increasing capabilities). But, the simplest version is usually fine for most beginner emailers.

Pegasus was named for the winged horse of classical mythology. Netscape Mail (also known now as Netscape Messenger) is the email tool that comes bundled with the Netscape web browser. Both are similar, in terms of features, to Eudora.

So, the following refers to Eudora, Pegasus, Netscape Mail and several other similar email tools. Each offers the following capabilities:

1 Create a message – click on a New Message button or icon of a letter to bring up a window with a text editor in which you may compose your message.
2 Send the message to one or more people – enter the email address of one or more primary recipients into a line labelled 'To:'.
3 Send 'courtesy copies' (cc) to one or more people – enter the email address of one or more secondary recipients into a line labelled 'Cc:'. By the way, 'cc' used to stand for 'carbon copies' back when people actually typed letters on typewriters (remember typewriters?) and made copies using carbon paper (remember carbon paper?). Also, on the Internet any address that appears in the 'Cc:' line is really just there for courtesy. The person(s) who must know and perhaps must act upon and reply to the message are listed in the 'To:' line. Those in the 'Cc:' line are not expected to reply to or act upon the information.
4 Send 'blind courtesy copies' (bcc) to one or more people – enter the email address of one or more recipients into a line labelled 'Bcc:'. These people will all get the email message, but no one else (including each other) will know that they got it. Bcc is rarely used, except perhaps by spy organizations. Its prime use in email is to send yourself a bcc. In this way you can see exactly what your primary and secondary recipients have received (always a good idea) without the strange look of having a message sent from Bob Wilson to (among others) Bob Wilson.
5 Get messages – ask your email system to deliver to you any new email messages that have arrived since the last time you 'got messages'.

6 <u>Save a message</u> – most email tools allow you to establish a set of mail 'folders' in which to put messages you want to keep after reading them. A few such folders are usually provided by the email tool itself, such as the 'Inbox' folder where new messages arrive, the 'Sent' folder for keeping a copy of recent messages you have sent, and the 'Trash' folder which functions exactly like Windows 95/98's recycle bin (in this case a recycle bin for no-longer-wanted email messages). You can create and name any folders you want to use as well, such as the 'Cruise' folder for email concerning your upcoming nautical vacation or the 'Afghanistan' folder for email concerning your next business trip. By the way, most novice emailers err in favour of filing messages in folders that they really need not keep. The bad news is that folders can become overrun with email messages that were only meaningful months ago. The good news is that email messages can be sent or filed to the 'Trash' folder from the 'Inbox' or any other folder, as well.

7 <u>Forward a message to someone else</u> – sometimes you receive an email message, look over its list of primary (To:) and secondary (Cc:) recipients and realize that someone else really should see this message. By clicking on the 'Forward' button or icon, you can painlessly send a copy to the new person and even include a little greeting of your own, 'Barbara, I really thought you would like to know about the cholera epidemic in Tunisia . . .'. This leads to a very important rule about email on the Internet. Assume that anything bad you say about anyone in an email message will eventually be seen by that person. Email sometimes has a funny life span, which may include several incidents of courtesy copies, blind courtesy copies and forwarding – perhaps eventually getting to the person you were griping about.

8 <u>Reply to a message</u> – click on the 'Reply' button or icon. Most email tools will bring up a window with a text editor in which you may compose your reply. Already in that window will be the email message sent to you – each line of which is preceded by a > (greater than sign). This is an established convention on the Internet that conveys that 'All the lines that you sent to me are preceded by >. All the other lines are what I am sending back to you.'

9 <u>Create aliases for often-used email addresses</u> – most email tools let you make an 'address book' of the email addresses you use most often. Suppose that I want to make an entry in my address book for my friend Frances K. Johnson. I would likely enter into the address book:

First Name:	Frances
Last Name:	Johnson
Email address:	fkjohnson@personnel.lilly.com
Nickname:	Fran

Then, any time I want to include Frances Johnson in either the To: or Cc: lines of an email message I am creating, I simply type 'Fran' which is immediately converted by the tool into fkjohnson@personnel.lilly.com – saving me much typing time and, given my tendency to mis-type, several incorrect email addresses like fjkohnson@personnel.lilly.com. You can even make aliases for several people, so for example, the alias 'officers' could be a list of the email addresses for all four officers of an organization.

Minding your online manners: netiquette

The Internet represents a new and emerging culture. Cultures are characterized by having standard ways that they do things. In Japan there are some places that you simply do not enter with your shoes on. In most places in the world it is absolutely forbidden to burp or belch following a meal, while in other cultures such behaviour is considered a supreme compliment to the cook!

No other activity on the Internet has as many cultural standards as electronic mail. Long-time Internet users have developed a set of informal rules, regulations and expectations about email use. Violators of these rules are generally dismissed as 'Internet novices' – a horribly pejorative term that none of us want to have attached to us. Serious violators find that no one will correspond with them or, even worse, find their email privileges denied by the organization that issued them an email account.

So, to keep you from the dreaded ranks of 'Internet novices' in your conduct of emailing, the following points are offered as a public service:

1 Make the subject line useful – try to encapsulate in the subject of your email message what it is about. Subjects like 'Hi' or 'Message from me to you' provide no help at all concerning the subject of the message. Many busy people who receive hundreds of email messages each day pay attention to the subject. If the subject looks important, they may read it right away. Otherwise the message might be filed for later reading (see 'Managing a lot of email' below) or simply deleted as unimportant and not worth their time. So, subjects should be things like 'Meeting about the trip to Italy' and 'Warnings about travel in the southern African climate'.

2 Check your spelling and your grammar – it is amazing how many very intelligent people come across as total dunces when you read their email messages. Lines like 'I am go to check with the State Depratment before proseading' can make the most competent writer sound rather stupid. Keep in mind that in oral conversation (for example, on the phone or in person)

51

a number of other impressions can be created due to your physical appearance, way of speaking, tone of voice, etc. But, in an email, that text is all you have. Check your spelling and grammar in order to convey your conscientiousness and intelligence.

3 Use (but do not overuse) *asterisks* or CAPITAL LETTERS for emphasis – part of the Internet culture is using asterisks around words or phrases or putting those words or phrases in capital letters to emphasize what is there. This is equivalent in speaking to simply raising your voice. For example, the phrase 'I had no idea that you would steal the car' takes on different meaning depending upon whether 'you' or 'car' is emphasized, as in 'I had no idea that YOU would steal the car' and 'I had no idea that you would STEAL the car'. Use asterisks or capital letters any time that you would raise your voice for emphasis. But, do not overdo it, as in 'I had NO IDEA that YOU WOULD STEAL the CAR'. As in life, shouting loses its effectiveness if done too much.

4 Include relevant original material in your reply – when replying to someone else's email message most email tools make life easy for you by putting the original email message in the text editor with each line preceded by a > (greater than sign). You may then simply type your reply to the entire message below the previous one. Or, you can go back and intersperse your reply among the original message lines making more of a conversation, as shown:

> Do you think we should have the meeting at 2:00 today
> or would it be better to have it tomorrow?

I would prefer tomorrow.

> Should we talk about both trips or just the upcoming
> trip to Venezuela?

Let's try to discuss both if we have time.

It is very important to include the original message lines so that the reply lines are in context. How would you like to receive an email message that simply said:

I would prefer tomorrow.
Let's try to discuss both if we have time.

or even worse:

No.

5 <u>No flaming</u> – sadly, one of the negative factors of email is that some people seem much more inclined to be rude and nasty in this type of conversation than they would ever be face to face or even over the phone. This has become so much a phenomenon that there is even a name for it – *flaming*. 'I could not believe all the things she wanted me to do, so I sent her a flame.' 'I really got flamed by the guys at the travel bureau over the missing passports.' Often the flamer has second thoughts later and wishes that he or she had not sent the nasty and crude email message. We have a very simple rule to end flaming: never say anything via email that you would not say face to face in front of your mother. Always think of having to read each email message you write in person to the recipient with your dear, sweet mother listening. If you would be willing to say the things you are considering saying in an email message under those circumstances, then go ahead and send the message.

6 <u>Keep line lengths to seventy characters or less</u> – many email tools have trouble with long lines in email messages. Either the ends of the lines seem to disappear or else you have to use a scroll bar to slide back and forth to read the email message – very annoying! Usually this line length issue is something you do not even have to think about. The text editor provided by your email tool should 'wrap' lines (end one line and begin another) after about seventy characters. However, if your email tool does not do this, you should either adjust the tool or end lines at about seventy characters yourself. Why seventy characters when most screens can display up to eighty characters? Because seventy characters fit nicely on the screen – even if preceded by a > (greater than) symbol to indicate text from another message.

7 <u>Keep signatures to six lines or less</u> – many people like to end their email messages with a *signature*, that is, a set of lines that identify them and provide additional contact information. For example, the following is the 'signature' for one of the authors of this book:

Dr H. E. Dunsmore	765-494-1996
Department of Computer Science	dunsmore@cs.purdue.edu
Purdue University	http://www.cs.purdue.edu/people/bxd
West Lafayette, IN 47907-1398	765-494-0739 (fax)

Something this lengthy is generally inserted automatically by prior arrangement with the email tool and may come from a little data file that contains this 'signature'. But, the signature above is about as long as you should use – six lines or less. More lengthy signatures (the authors have received email messages with signatures of twenty-five to thirty lines!) take valuable Internet transmission time, often convey little useful information and may even make it difficult to find the email message.

8 Use *emoticons* to convey what you really mean – you have probably seen in an email message the little smiley face consisting of a colon, dash, and right parenthesis, i.e. :–). This is only one of a legion of 'emotional icons' or 'emoticons':

> :–) happy (smiley emoticon)
> :–(sad (frowney emoticon)
> :–o shocked

When speaking in person or by phone you can use your voice and facial expression to convey additional information beyond what the words seem to say. Consider the phrase, 'I'm really disappointed'. When spoken slowly with a tone that stays flat and a serious look in your eyes, this conveys real disappointment. But, when spoken with a rising voice and a grin, this conveys exactly the opposite. In email we would make the latter say 'I'm really disappointed :–)'. We might even represent the former by 'I'm really disappointed :–('. The smiley and frowney are by far the most standard of these emoticons. Do not use some of the more exotic ones (like :–& to mean 'I am tongue-tied by your last statement') unless you are sure the recipient of the email knows what it means.

Managing a lot of email

When you first begin to send and receive email, each new arrival is treated with the same joy as the first birds that arrive each spring or the first buds to poke their heads through the late winter snow, 'Oh joy, I have received an email message!' After some time, however, your joy at new email arrivals begins to subside. When you reach the point, as have the authors of this book, at which you receive hundreds of email messages each day, you start looking for a rifle to shoot the birds and weed killer to use on the buds. The point is that handling incoming email can become a problem for some people – eating up large portions of their day.

We suggest that you counter this problem with what we call 'email triage' – modelled after the hospital emergency room procedure of sorting incoming patients (particularly when several arrive at the emergency room simultaneously) into three categories:

1 Those patients who require immediate attention.
2 Those patients who need medical attention but can wait for a while.
3 Those patients who are likely not going to make it with any amount of medical attention.

Care is then given in order to these three categories. 'Email triage' works in exactly the same way, except that the patients are the incoming email messages.

Let us suppose that you have been away from email for about twelve hours (horrors!) and return to your computer to find that exactly 100 email messages have arrived in your absence. You have about thirty minutes right now to respond to email. Obviously, it will be hard (impossible?) to read and respond to all 100 messages in that time. Begin your 'email triage' by quickly running through the messages paying attention to the subject field (yet another reason to make sure that the subject field of an email message you send is well crafted) and glancing at the text of the message itself. Divide the messages among the three categories below:

1 Email messages which require immediate attention. Go ahead and read and respond to these messages immediately – during the triage process. There should not be more than ten to fifteen of these out of any usual group of 100 messages. These could be situations where people are waiting on you before proceeding.
2 Email messages which will require your attention but can wait a while. Place each of these in a 'Pending' folder. Out of 100 messages there might be twenty to twenty-five of these. When you finish your triage (including responding to the immediate category messages), use as much of your remaining thirty minutes on the most important or time-bound messages in the Pending folder. Then, try to return to them as soon as possible. Any messages that stay in this folder for a long time without getting your attention probably should be moved to the folder discussed below.
3 Email messages which may require no attention. The remaining sixty to seventy messages should go during triage into your 'Later' folder. Address this folder only when all immediate messages are handled and the 'Pending' folder is empty. This folder will include messages that you just read and do not respond to, for example, messages in which you appear in the 'Cc' line. It can also include messages for which the time to respond is not important. Any messages that stay in this folder for a long time without getting your attention probably should just be deleted. In fact, the authors place a 250 message limit on this folder – deleting the oldest ones when we get more than 250 in it.

Multimedia email

The era of 'just text' email (words alone) is giving way to the possibility of creating, sending, and 'reading' email messages rich in content – including pictures, cartoons, sounds, background music and video. In fact, we are simply going to have to redefine what we mean by an email message. The definition is going to have to be wide enough to include sending from one person to another almost anything imaginable. Thus, we are already entering the era of 'multimedia' (meaning multiple types of media) email. This process has been given a kick-start by a set of Multipurpose Internet Mail Extensions (MIME) that are becoming the standard formats for creating, sending and viewing multimedia.

What is a 'Multipurpose Internet Mail Extension'? Quite simply, an extension is the suffix for a file. So, the filename 'beach.jpg' consists of the name 'beach' and the extension 'jpg'. The 'jpg' (sometimes 'jpeg') extension is the Joint Photographic Experts Group image format. The 'jpeg' is a technique for representing the pixel colours (see 'Multimedia' section in Chapter 4) that form a picture or image. A jpg file can be sent as an attachment to an email message and viewed by the receiver of the email message – in many cases embedded right in the email message itself. So, if you send an email 'postcard' to Aunt Harriet telling her how much fun you are having on the beach at Cozumel, you could actually let Aunt Harriet see a picture of you walking along the beach between the first and second paragraphs of your 'postcard'. The MIME are a set of such file types that are standard enough for most email tools to be able to both send and receive them.

But, the Internet's Simple Mail Transfer Protocol (SMTP) has a problem with image files and sound files and video files, and even many word-processing and database files. The problem is that such files use a binary representation that cannot be sent via standard email – which was created to handle simple text, i.e. letters and numbers. So, the problem is what to do about these non-text files. The solution is to 'encode' them. The encoding process takes an image, sound, video or word processing file and translates it into a series of letters, numbers and standard special characters like commas, periods and % signs. Thus, an encoded file contains all the information that was in the original file, but looks like random typing by an idiot. Most important, though, is that an encoded file can be sent via the standard email protocol. Here is an example of the first three lines of an encoded file:

M/$A434P^'CQ(14%$/@H\5$E43$4^365T86UA:6P@+2T@;75L=&EM961I82!E
M;&5C=')O;FEC(&UA:6P\+U1)5$Q%/@H*/']](14%$@Hl)D}$63X*/$@Q/DUE
M=&%%M86EL('TM(&UU;'1I;65D:6$$@96QE8W1R;VYI8R!M86EL/']](,3X*/$A2

When an encoded file arrives at an email tool (usually as an attachment to a text email message), the modern email tool 'decodes' it. The decoding process is a reverse translation going back from the letters, numbers and special characters to the original binary file. If the decoded file is an image in jpg format, it can be viewed by the email recipient. If the decoded file is a sound, it can be heard. If it is a word-processing document, it can be read and even further edited using the appropriate word-processing tool.

There is not just one single encoding and decoding procedure. In fact, there are several. These grew up from different computing platforms. But, most modern email tools understand them all, so that upon receipt of a file that was encoded in 'base64' (one of the competing encoding/decoding standards), it simply decodes it using its 'base64' decoder. The nice thing for most of us is that we really do not have to know how a file was decoded in order to receive and 'use' it.

4

The World Wide Web

The Internet and the World Wide Web

In spite of all the interest in the Internet and email, most of the latest excitement about the Internet has been because of the newest development – the World Wide Web. First, let us be clear about the difference between the Internet and the World Wide Web. The 'Internet' refers to the physical side of this global computer network plus the TCP/IP software and associated protocols for sending things around on the Internet. The 'World Wide Web' refers to a body of information – an abstract space of knowledge available on the Internet. The World Wide Web is a collection of information available from thousands of places in the world – all accessible as if it were coming from some common location or set of locations.

It has been said that if the Internet had not existed, it would have had to be invented to accommodate the World Wide Web. There had to be some way to transmit the enormous amount of information on the Web from one place to another quickly and easily. The Internet had already put in place the infrastructure for that purpose.

The origin of the World Wide Web

Unlike most of the major developments in the history of the Internet, the World Wide Web did not come from the USA. In fact, the origin of the Web is with a collection of European high-energy physics researchers located at CERN (Conseil European pour la Recherche Nucleaire). Members of CERN are located in a number of different countries. Although not computer scientists, they had become adept at using email and file transfer protocol (FTP; see below) for transmitting information among all the CERN participants. But, this was time-consuming and not particularly easy to do. They thought that there must be a better way to share scientific information (including charts, figures and illustrations) among the scientists. Furthermore, they really wanted a way – when looking at the information from one experiment – to be able quickly to access information about any of a number of related experiments.

In 1989 Tim Berners-Lee came from England to join CERN. He considered the CERN problem of information sharing. He proposed a hypertext system that became the forerunner of today's World Wide Web. Berners-Lee created the first Web software in October 1990. A system similar to what we now know as the World Wide Web was first made available outside CERN on the Internet in the summer of 1991. Berners-Lee's concept was that of a means of sharing research information and ideas effectively throughout an organization. (In 1994 Berners-Lee joined the Laboratory for Computer Science at the Massachusetts Institute of Technology [MIT] as Director of the World Wide Web Consortium which co-ordinates Web development worldwide.)

Hypertext

The underlying aspect of the Web that is most important is its use of *hypertext*. Hypertext has actually existed as a concept for a long time –

even before the Internet. In fact, the notion of what we now call hypertext was first discussed by Dr Vannevar Bush, Director of the US Office of Scientific Research and Development, in an article entitled 'As we may think' that first appeared in the July 1945 issue of *The Atlantic Monthly*. Ironically, this article appeared at about the time that early research was being conducted that would lead to today's modern electronic digital computers. Bush did not refer to his idea as 'hypertext'. Instead, he talked about a device, and coined the term 'memex' for it, that would allow an enormous quantity of information to be stored and accessed in an associative fashion in nearly exactly the way hypertext works on the World Wide Web. In one of those delicious ironies of science, it took over forty-five more years for the concept of computer and hypertext to get together in the World Wide Web.

A good way to envision hypertext is to imagine reading an encyclopaedia. You stumble upon an article in the 'W' volume about World War II. While reading that, you see a reference to US Army General George S. Patton. This momentarily catches your attention. You put down the 'W' volume in favour of the 'P' volume and begin reading about General Patton. While reading that article, you read about Patton's work as a tank commander and become interested in learning more about tanks. You put down the 'P' volume momentarily and begin reading an article in volume 'T' about tanks. What you have been doing is quite illustrative of hypertext. A reference in one article (World War II) has diverted your attention to another article (Patton) in which another reference (tanks) has sent you off to read yet another article. The terms 'Patton' and 'tank' are functioning exactly like hypertext works – allowing you to leave one body of information in favour of something temporarily more interesting. Of course, you can finish the tank article, return to read the remainder of the article on General Patton and, finally, return to complete your reading of the World War II article. This is the way that hypertext is often used.

The Web relies on hypertext as its means of interacting with users. Hypertext is basically the same as regular text. It can be stored, read, searched or edited. It does have an important exception – hypertext contains connections within the text to other documents.

Hypertext links can be followed with ease. After reading all or part of the information on any page, the Web user has the option to follow another hypertext link or return to the page from which the current one was accessed.

Hyperlinks

Hypertext links are called *hyperlinks*. The major organization of the Web is determined by the hyperlinks on each web page. Obviously, documents can themselves have links and connections to other documents. Continually selecting links takes you on a free-associative tour of information. Hyperlinks can create a complex virtual web of connections. In fact, if you are accessing web pages from several different geographic areas and drawing lines from one web page to another, the diagram you are drawing after a while will begin to look like a series of lines, not unlike the strands of a spider's web, connecting the various sites where web pages come from. Thus, the term 'World Wide Web' seems quite appropriate.

Client–server paradigm

How does all this 'clicking' and 'appearing' work? What is it about the Internet and the Web that allows a click on a hyperlink to cause a web page to appear? The principal characteristic of the Internet that allows this is the so-called *client–server paradigm*. The client–server paradigm has been a stalwart of the Internet from its inception. It predates the Web. The basic idea is that the Internet consists of millions of interconnected computers. Some have information that others want.

Let us think of a cafeteria line as an example. A person moving through the line is a 'client'. She desires certain types of food to be placed on her tray on request. For example, she asks for a plate of roast beef and creamed potatoes. She waits for the person behind the counter, the 'server', to retrieve the roast beef and creamed potatoes and to place it onto her tray.

This is exactly the way the Internet works. There are appropriate servers and clients for virtually every type of information transfer on the Internet – including email. But, let us investigate specifically how this process works for the World Wide Web.

A 'file' in computer terminology is a collection of related information. For example, suppose that a file is information about travel destinations in Spain. Each line of the file contains information about one location. All of the lines together constitute the whole file. Let us now see how this relates to sending information from server to client on the World Wide Web.

Any computer on the Internet with one or more web pages (files) must have some software running referred to as 'web server' software. Because of the demands for web pages from all over the world at any time of day, web server software really must run twenty-four hours per day and seven days per week. Otherwise, when a web page is requested, the requester will get no response and is unlikely to ask again for a web page from that location – and is likely to say bad things about the location to his or her friends.

Thus, web server software runs continually on an Internet computer and has no purpose 'in life' except to wait for a request for one of its web pages. Then, it springs into action – retrieving the web page and sending it over the Internet to the computer that requested it.

There is sometimes some confusion about whether the term 'server' refers to the software or a computer. The answer is, both! The web server software at the MPSNet Cancun website may certainly be referred to as MPSNet Cancun's web server. But, this software is running on the Internet node computer www.cancun.mpsnet.com.mx. (Thus, their website is accessible via **http://www.cancun.mpsnet.com.mx**). So, in a sense www.cancun. mpsnet.com.mx is the server computer. Therefore, it is perfectly acceptable to refer to the web server software being run on the web server computer – thus, referring to both software and computer as the 'server'. Context should make it clear which is intended in any instance.

Client software is any program (such as a web browser, which will be discussed in Chapter 5) that requests information from a server. Thus, the typical web browser (such as Netscape Navigator, Netscape Communicator, Microsoft Internet Explorer, etc.) is a client program. In response to a mouse click by the person using the browser, this client program sends a message (just like a small email message) to the appropriate server. It requests that a web page be sent and then waits for the arrival of the page.

Upon the arrival of the requested web page, the client software displays the page for the perusal of the person using the browser. Clients and servers communicate via TCP/IP over the Internet. Thus, the World Wide Web is intimately tied to the Internet. It is the communication path that clients use to request web pages from servers, and that servers use to send those web pages to clients.

As discussed above, there is sometimes some confusion about whether the term 'client' refers to software or a computer. The same situation applies as for the term 'server'. The web browser running on your computer may certainly be referred to as your client software. But this software is running on your Internet node computer, which is acting as a client computer. So, it is perfectly acceptable to refer to the web client software being run on the web client computer – thus referring to both software and computer as the 'client'. Again, context should make it clear which is intended in any instance.

Another useful feature of client–server interaction is what we call a *persistent connection*. Have you ever noticed that it may take a long time for the first web page to arrive from a server, but subsequent web pages from that same server seem to arrive somewhat faster? One reason for this is that clients and servers may establish a persistent connection so that the communication path between them is left open after the first page is sent. It should not be surprising that after looking at a web page from a server, there is a very high probability that the next web page requested might be from that same server.

Multimedia

The World Wide Web has come along at a very fortuitous time. There had been other attempts to collect a large quantity of information and make it available on the Internet, but these had not caught the attention of most people outside the scientific community. One of the major problems was that textual information (that is, letters and numbers) is a limited medium through which to communicate. Unfortunately, previous 'large quantity of information' attempts had been mostly limited to textual information. Typical email is a good example of this limitation. Until recently, most of us could only communicate words via email. It is only recently that the capability of email has evolved to allow us to communicate pictures and sounds.

At the time that the Web was becoming popular, another activity was happening simultaneously. Research into digitizing information was experiencing tremendous progress. Virtually all forms of media are now yielding to digitization efforts. For example, any of us who have listened to a compact disk (CD) version of a song were in fact listening to the result of translating the original music into a series of binary digits (bits) – ones and zeros. This digitization can be quite precise and can reproduce the sound later with almost breathtaking sameness. Digitized sound is not subject to 'wearing out'. Even more important from a computing standpoint, digitized sound can be stored in a computer file of ones and zeros and transmitted from one computer to another.

Simultaneously, research was proceeding into digitizing images. Suppose that an image appears to be a beautiful deserted island basking under the gentle glow of the setting sun. But, in reality the file that produces this image is nothing more than a table of row, column and colour numbers. Any image (photograph or drawing) can be placed in a scanner that moves across its surface from left to right and top to bottom breaking the image into a table of dot-like 'picture elements' (called *pixels*). The scanner decides the best colour to use for each pixel and builds a table of row numbers, column numbers and pixel colour numbers. For example, row 1 column 1 might be a dark brown pixel. Row 3 column 12 might be a light yellow pixel. Row 25 column 254 might be a pale green pixel, etc. How many colours may be used? That depends on how many bits can be used for each pixel colour. Using only one bit will work fine if the colours are all either black (0 bit) or white (1 bit) and will lead to a very small file. But, most images employ more colours than just black or white.

Three bits will allow eight colours, sort of like this:

000 black
001 red
010 green
011 blue
100 brown
101 yellow
110 orange
111 white

So, for example, if the pixel in row 25 column 254 is green, the digitized file would contain 010 for that pixel. Obviously, most pictures (particularly photographs) contain more than two, or eight, or 256, or 1024 colours. They contain millions of colours. By expanding the number of bits, it is possible to digitize an image so precisely that its rendering later is nearly indistinguishable from the original. The only price paid by using many bits to represent colours is that the file (even for a small picture) can be quite large. Why do we care about the size of a file that represents a digitized image? Because on the Web that file must travel from the computer where it is now (the server) to the computer where someone wants to see it (the client). With a slow telephone connection, a large image file might take several seconds to transmit from one place to another. And even though several seconds seems very quick, web pages often have five or six images (or more) – meaning it might take more than a minute for all the image files to arrive and be displayed.

Thus, images on the Web represent a continual push–pull between using large images with millions of colours versus using smaller images with just a few colours. The former leads to a very satisfying look, but can be frustrating in respect of the amount of time it takes for all the images to 'arrive'. The latter can generally be viewed very quickly, but may not have the professional look we have come to appreciate from magazines and television images.

Since it is now possible to digitize sounds and images, the next step is obvious. Combine the two to create digitized video. If the size of a single image can often be a performance issue, a video will contain thousands (or more) of such images along with sound. So, again, the speed consideration becomes important.

There are basically two ways to handle video on the Web. The first (and historically original) way is to send an entire video file from one computer (server) on the Internet to another. The receiving computer (client) waits for the entire video file to arrive before attempting to 'play' the video. This has been the tradition with most media on the Internet – wait to get the file before doing anything with it. This still works fine for small video files, but presents a problem for lengthy (or live) video. A lengthy video file can be enormously large – in fact, far too large to fit on the disk of most computers. The waiting time can also be annoying. The newer, more modern solution is what is called *streaming video*. In this situation, the video file is not delivered as one monolithic entity. Instead it is broken into smaller packets. Each packet is delivered from the server computer to the client computer. When enough packets have arrived at the client computer, it can begin playing the video. The beauty of this arrangement is that as each packet is used it can be discarded. There is no need to keep the entire file on a disk. This is the only sensible solution (and much like television works) for live video. By definition one cannot wait for all of a live video to arrive to begin viewing it. This same technique can be used for *streaming audio* as well.

Uniform resource locators

The World Wide Web consists of a tremendous amount of hyperlinked multimedia information located all over the world. The obvious question is how does one computer tell another that it wants a certain web page. This is accomplished by using something called a uniform resource locator. A URL is exactly like an address. It uniquely identifies some web page, resource or service. For example, the URL for the MPSNet Cancun website is **http://www.cancun.mpsnet.com.mx**.

Let us examine this URL. First, the term 'http' stands for HyperText Transfer Protocol (HTTP) – yet another of the many protocols that make the Internet work. Specifically, the HTTP is used to send World Wide Web information from one computer to another. The protocol is usually followed by a colon and two slashes. Next comes the name of the Internet node on which the web server is running. Thus, there is a computer (most likely located in Cancun, Mexico), named www.cancun.mpsnet.com.mx. Recall from the client–server section above that both this computer and the web software on it may be referred to as MPSNet Cancun's 'web server'.

The relationship between HTTP and TCP/IP is a situation similar to sending priority mail. Generally the item is first put into a plain envelope and then that envelope is put into another envelope as required by the priority mailing service (like Federal Express in the USA). When the outside envelope arrives at its destination, someone opens it and removes the inside envelope. It is generally marked in some way so that the recipient knows what to do with it. That is exactly what happens with the Internet with co-operating transmission protocols.

The web page is first put into the HTTP envelope. Then the HTTP envelope is put into the TCP/IP envelope. The TCP/IP envelope functions exactly like the priority mail envelope. It contains all the information and functionality to allow the file to travel from one computer to another on the Internet. It does not matter what is inside the TCP/IP envelope. It could be a web page, or an email message or a data file being sent from one branch of a business to another. Being inside the TCP/IP envelope allows it to travel in the appropriate manner along the Internet. Now, the TCP/IP envelope arrives at the computer that requested the web page. The computer opens the TCP/IP envelope and removes the inner envelope. It is an HTTP envelope. The receiving computer knows exactly what this is and hands the contents of that envelope over to the appropriate software (a web browser, see Chapter 5) so that the web page can be viewed.

So, that explains the 'http' at the beginning of most URLs. But, some URLs do not begin with 'http'. Some start with 'gopher' or 'ftp' or something else. The next two sections discuss Gopher and FTP.

Gopher

Gopher is an Internet-based information system that predates the World Wide Web. There is still a large amount of gopher information available on the Internet, but production of this material has almost come to a halt because of the popularity of the World Wide Web. The Gopher system features menus of items that can be selected by typing the appropriate letter or number or by clicking on the appropriate line with a mouse. But, Gopher was predominantly a text-based system. Nearly all Gopher information placed on the Internet consisted of just letters, numbers and punctuation – creating hardly the excitement engendered by today's visually appealing (and even occasionally aurally appealing) websites. Gopher was a useful system, but just did not generate much enthusiasm in the Internet community and certainly did not excite the non-Internet public.

But, all the existing Gopher information is still available using the Web. Any URL such as **gopher://soochak.ncst.ernet.in** requests information from the Gopher server (rather than the web server) at soochak.ncst.ernet.in (a Gopher site of travel information in India). Since gopher material is textual, this can easily be displayed by a web browser – even if it is usually not as visually exciting as web material.

File Transfer Protocol

File Transfer Protocol (FTP) is also a system which predates the Web. Suppose that you have written a report on travel in New Guinea and want to make it available to your friends. Before the emergence of the Web, there were two main ways to make such information available. First, of course, was the possibility of sending this report to friends via email. The obvious question is, which friends would be interested and do you really want to send out lots of (perhaps unwanted) email messages containing a long report. The other way was to use the File Transfer Protocol (FTP).

With FTP, you would copy the report to a special directory (or folder) on your computer. In fact, this would have to be a directory (or folder) accessible to an FTP server. Then, you would make your friends aware of the report via email or some other means. Then anyone interested in the report could use his or her FTP software (FTP client) to connect to your computer (and FTP server) in order to obtain his or her own copy of the report. File Transfer Protocol is a very simple system. In its typical use a file is simply copied from the remote computer to the local computer. That is, if one of your friends wants a copy of the New Guinea travel report, he or she uses the FTP client on his or her local computer to request that file from your FTP server on your remote computer.

All the FTP process does is to copy the file to the local computer. It is up to the person at the local computer to decide where to store that file and what to do with it upon receipt. For example, if your report is a Microsoft Word document, then the recipient might direct the guinea.doc file to be placed in the directory (folder) where he or she usually keeps Microsoft Word files. Then, he or she could start Microsoft Word and import the file to read it.

There are two basic ways in which the FTP process works – public FTP and private FTP:

1 In public FTP, any file that is available for FTPing on a computer may be accessed by anyone who knows the address of the file. No account number or password is required of the client to copy the file. You might want to do this with your New Guinea travel file if you really do not care who makes a copy of it.
2 In private FTP, the client must provide an account and password in addition to the address of the file. This allows file access only to those individuals to whom you have given the appropriate account and password, thus protecting the file from general access.

The most popular software for FTPing files these days is visual software that shows the files of the local computer on the left and the files of the remote computer on the right. File transfer can be done by clicking the mouse on the desired file and then either dragging it over to the local files or by clicking on a 'transfer' button.

By the way, FTP provides a lot more capabilities than have been discussed here. In some instances files can be transferred from the local computer to the remote computer (although this is rarely allowed in a public FTP situation). Also, it is possible to transfer groups of files by clicking on several of them at once and then dragging the whole group or clicking on the 'transfer' button.

A URL such as **ftp://wuarchive.wustl.edu/multimedia/images/jpeg/m/marvin.jpg** will work with a web browser. It simply requests the file from a public FTP site and brings it to the client computer. Some files can be viewed within the web browser (such as pictures, sounds and video). Others are handed over to *plug-ins* – software associated with the web browser to handle files that are not generally part of web pages. Finally, if all else fails, the web browser will simply ask where on the local computer a file should be stored. Then, the web browser can be exited and the file can be 'viewed' with some other appropriate software.

Websites, homepages and web rings

Generally, when creating information on the World Wide Web, this will consist of several web pages with links among them. This is called a *website*. The website beginning at **http://www.travelsites.com** consists of several web pages concerning such things as 'Where to go', 'How to get there', 'Where to stay', 'I need a vacation', 'Tickets now' and 'Travelsites membership'. The entire collection of interconnected web pages may be thought of as one considers a travel brochure or magazine – lots of related pages in one location or website.

In most cases when a URL appears in a book, magazine, newspaper, or even on another web page (such as **http://www.travelsites.com**) this URL addresses the web page that the creators of the website want you to visit first. This is very similar to the cover of a brochure or magazine – the page that typically has a link to each of the others and is the place to which you return to begin exploring other aspects of the website. This cover page is referred to as the website's *homepage*. Thus, a homepage is typically the web page by which you should enter a website.

Sometimes, a group of related websites (for example, fifteen to twenty travel sites in Spain) will contain links to each other. This creates what is called a *web ring* – a collection of related websites. Participating sites on a web ring are in effect jointly publicizing each other. Someone who visits one is just a click away from any other. This co-operation can be useful to avoid redundancy – so that a site on a web ring need not repeat information that is available at another. It also usually leads to more visits for each of the 'ringed' sites than if they were not part of the web ring.

The last word on URLs

The URL discussed above (**http://www.travelsites.com**) is not complete. In fact, few of the URLs used above are really complete URLs. That is because a URL should tell not only the protocol (http) and the location of the website (www.travelsites.com), but also the name of the file being requested.

A web page is represented by a file of text that tells what words are to appear on the page, what images are to appear on the page, what hyperlinks are to appear on the page and how all these items are to be displayed. In the vast majority of the cases these files are created using something called the HyperText Markup Language (HTML). HyperText Markup Language is a 'markup language' in the sense that a file created using HTML contains a number of tags such as TITLE (that tells the title to be used for the page) and BGCOLOR (that tells the background colour to use for the page).

Most files on the Web that tell how a web page is supposed to look are HTML files and end with the file extension .html. So, a complete URL would look something like **http://www.travelsites.com/wherestay.html**; that is, at the Travelsites website this requests the file wherestay.html – which is a file created using HTML and is presumably about where to stay when travelling. (At least that is what 'wherestay.html' would suggest to most people!) Thus, **http://www.travelsites.com/wherestay.html** is a complete URL.

You will usually see complete URLs that end in the file extension .html, but occasionally may see some that end in .htm. This is also an acceptable file extension for an HTML file. This is allowed because there are still some computers with files available to web servers that use an old file naming system known as the '8.3' system. In this system each file name could consist of a first word of no more than eight characters and an extension of no more than three characters. If the Travelsites website were on a machine that used the 8.3 system, then the URL **http://www.travelsites.com/ wherestay.html** would have to be something like **http://www. travelsites.com/wheresta.htm**.

Why does the URL **http://www.travelsites.com** 'work'? That is, why is the Travelsites web server able to send a file in response to this incomplete URL? Because, every web server has a default file that it delivers. In the case of the Travelsites website this file is one named index.html. So, the URL **http://www.travelsites.com** is equivalent to the URL **http://www.travelsites.com/index.html** and requests the web server at Travelsites to send the client the index.html web page. Nearly all World Wide Web servers have a default file like this. That is why so many URLs can be advertised or used with just a few words and without the .html file at the end. Any URL like **http://www.travelsites.com** is really a 'shorthand' way of saying **http://www.travelsites.com/ index.html** or **http://www.travelsites.com/homepage.html** or **http://www.travelsites.com/welcome.html**. The decision is made by the person in charge of the web server (called the *webmaster*) as to what file name will be sent if someone fails (as is often the case) to request a specific file name.

Sometimes a URL can be quite long, such as **ftp://wuarchive. wustl.edu/multimedia/images/jpeg/m/marvin.jpg** already mentioned above, or **http://www.travelsites.com/InternationalSites/ qantas.html**. What does a URL like this mean? Let us examine the latter in more detail. The 'http' for HyperText Transfer Protocol looks satisfactory. We can also tell that there must be web server software located on a computer named www.travelsites.com. Finally, the file this URL requests will be named qantas.html. But, what do we make of the word InternationalSites. This is a directory (or folder) name. Here is the way this works: When this URL is sent to the web server at www.travelsites.com, it proceeds to the standard directory (folder) where web pages are stored. But, instead of looking for the page qantas.html, it looks next for the sub-directory (sub-folder) named InternationalSites, goes to that directory (folder) and retrieves qantas.html there. By making several sub-directories website designers can keep related material in separate locations. But, this can sometimes lead to silly looking URLs like http://www.travel.com/international/spain/barcelona/downtown/hotels.html. Luckily, most such URLs are available by clicking on a hyperlink and do not require typing the whole thing into the web browser.

5

Web browsers

Typical web browser features

Web browsers are computer programs that make it very easy for you to look at web pages and other resources on the World Wide Web. The two most popular web browsers are Netscape's Navigator and Microsoft's Internet Explorer. At press time, each was about equally popular ... accounting for about 50 per cent of web activity on the Internet. The competition between these two has been fierce. One of the reasons for the US Justice Department law suit against Microsoft 'bundling' its Internet Explorer with Windows 95/98 is the perceived advantage (unfair or otherwise) that this gives Microsoft in its battle with Netscape for browser supremacy.

The competition between these two software giants has had some very positive effects – leading to excellent features being developed quickly for both web browsers. But, one of the negative effects has been that just about the time you get comfortable using one of these browsers, it is replaced by a newer version. At the time of publication both Netscape's Navigator and Microsoft's Internet Explorer are at version 4. The discussion in this chapter is mostly about Netscape's Navigator version 4, but Microsoft's Internet Explorer version 4 looks and works remarkably like Netscape's, so this discussion applies to the Internet Explorer as well. Buttons may just be in a slightly different place or be called something slightly different. The comments below also work for version 3 of either Navigator or Internet Explorer and, because most version changes have not been too dramatic, will likely work well for version 5 as well.

Web browsers are simply Internet client programs. Whenever the human user clicks on a URL, the browser sends the appropriate information out to the appropriate server on the Internet and displays the information sent in return.

Web browsers have the following typical features: They have a graphical interface with lots of buttons and icons and are mouse-driven – allowing the user to do almost anything by moving and clicking the mouse. Browsers display hypertext and hypermedia documents using a variety of type fonts, colours and type sizes. Browsers can display standard textual staples such as paragraphs, lists, titles, headings and horizontal lines.

Web browsers support multimedia information by being able to display many images (and even sounds) along with the rest of a web page. In some cases browsers spawn off separate programs in new windows for some multimedia image, sound and video files.

Most web browsers can support much more than just the viewing of web pages. They can be used to download files from public FTP sites (watch for URLs that begin ftp://) and to view information that was prepared for the old Gopher information system (watch for URLs that begin gopher://). Gopher is an Internet information browsing system that predates the Web. Developed at the University of Minnesota (where the athletic teams are nicknamed the 'Golden Gophers') gopher was simply a little ahead of its time. It was predominantly menu-driven and was not as convenient for accessing images and sounds. But, there is a lot of textual information available from universities, research organizations and the US federal government through URLs that begin gopher://. These look on the Web like a simple text file. By the way, another possible origin of the name gopher comes from the behaviour that the system could be used to 'go for' any information the user wanted.

Memory and disk cache

Web browsers keep a history of hyperlinks that you visit. Even more important, their standard configuration is to keep copies of web pages you have visited (and images on those pages) in a special place called *cache*. This makes it easy for you to revisit a web page. Let us investigate how cache works. A web browser sets aside a certain amount of computer memory for copies of web pages and images that it has displayed most recently. Suppose that you are looking at the Yugoslavian Travel Bureau's website. When you click on a link to the Czechoslovakian Travel Bureau's website, the last page (Yugoslavian Travel Bureau) and all its images go into memory cache. If you immediately (or some time soon) want to return to the Yugoslavian Travel Bureau, your web browser simply redisplays those pages from memory cache.

Have you ever noticed how quickly some pages reappear – even some pages that took a long time to appear initially from their web server? Most likely the reappearance was coming from memory cache. But, the memory cache is limited. What happens when the web browser needs to place the current page in cache (before loading a new one) and the cache is full? A very simple procedure is used – known to computer scientists as the least recently used (LRU) algorithm. Suppose that you have a drawer full of socks and your Aunt Harriet gives you a new pair of blue argyle socks. In order to fit these in the drawer you find that pair of socks already in the drawer that you wore least recently. (You do keep this kind of information on your socks, don't you?) Suppose you last wore that old pair of pink socks in November 1995. All other pairs in the drawer have been worn more recently. Toss out the pink socks and replace them with the new blue argyle socks.

A web browser uses the LRU algorithm to remove one or more web pages and images in order to accommodate any page and images that need to go into the memory cache. But, where does the web browser toss the 'pink socks' from the memory cache. It tosses them into *disk cache* – sort of like having another drawer below your main sock drawer. Disk cache is slower. If you want to return to a web page that is in disk cache, it will not reappear quite as fast as one in memory cache, but it will still appear quicker than returning to the server for the page and images.

Most web browsers are set up to get new copies of web pages the first time after starting up the browser, but to get those pages (and related images) from either memory or disk cache if at all possible during any one browser session. What if you want a new copy of a web page even if one is available from cache? Then you use the Reload button discussed below.

The components of a web browser

The major (and most important) feature of a web browser is the viewing window in which you see the current web page being displayed. If a web page does not completely fit on your screen, you will see a scroll bar (to move up and down through the web page) to the right of the viewing window and possibly even at the bottom of the viewing window (to move left and right). The up, down, left and right cursor keys may also be used for this purpose. Left-clicking on any hyperlinks on the current page, of course, leads to the display of other web pages.

Across the very top of the screen (above the viewing window) is a row of pull-down menus and a row of navigation buttons – both of which will be discussed in the next section. Just below the navigation buttons is a location field that displays the URL of the web page being viewed. Below the viewing window is an information field that shows the status of the retrieval of a web page, that is, it tells you the percentage of the web page text (and the same for each file on that page) that has arrived and the estimated time for it to be completely in place. This information field also shows the URL of a page that goes with a hyperlink over which you have placed the cursor. This tells you what page will be requested from its server if you click on the hyperlink.

Browser buttons

The Netscape Navigator web browser has the following set of buttons. By the way, these buttons can appear as icons only (for example, a little picture of a house for the 'Home' button) or as text only (the word 'Home' for the 'Home' button) or as a combination of text and icons. You can decide how you want your buttons to appear. Configuring buttons is discussed below.

Netscape's buttons

1 Back – return to the previous web page. While moving along through web pages, you will often want to go back to the previous page visited. This can

be done easily by clicking on the Back button. Repeated clicks of the Back button continue to take you back to previously viewed pages.

2 Forward – proceed to the next web page. This button can only be used if you have used the Back button to go backward. Then, the Forward button can be used to go in the other direction. Repeated clicks on the Back and Forward buttons allow you to go back and forth among previously viewed pages.

3 Reload – reload the current web page from its server. This process is actually a little more sophisticated and efficient than it sounds. Let us suppose that you are looking at Fiesta Travel Limited's upcoming cruises website at **http://www.fiesta-travel.co.uk/Royalcarib.htm**. If you want to make sure that you are looking at absolutely the latest cruise information (assuming that a new cruise might have been added to their repertoire in the last thirty minutes), click on the Reload button. What happens then is that your web browser sends a request to the server at www.fiesta-travel.co.uk for the Royalcarib.htm page. But, along with the request it lets the server know that the copy of this page you have is dated 10.31 a.m., 11 January 1999. If the server has a newer copy of this page, it sends it to your browser in response to the 'Reload'. Otherwise, your browser is notified that you have the most recent copy and valuable Internet resources are not taken up by sending you a copy of a web page that you already have. By the way, this button is called 'Refresh' on the Microsoft's Internet Explorer.

4 Home – proceed to the 'home page' for your web browser. Notice that the term 'home page' (also appears without the space as 'homepage') has two distinct meanings. When someone tells you to visit the 'homepage' of a website, this is the web page that the creators of the website want you to visit first (like a magazine cover, as discussed in Chapter 4). But, the 'home page' of a web browser is the page that appears when the web browser application begins running. This is generally the homepage of Netscape or Microsoft or (if you are using a web browser at work) the homepage of your company. You can decide what page you want to use as the 'home page' of your web browser. More about this later.

5 Search – bring on screen a page that can be used to search the Web for some information. From this page you will have access to one of the standard web search engines (see Chapter 6).

6 Print – print the web page that you are currently viewing. This sends to the printer a copy of the page. Be aware that only this one web page is printed, not the entire website. If you want to print several pages from the same website, you will have to visit each and click the Print button while there. Also, be aware that the Print button prints the entire web page you are

visiting – not just the portion shown on the screen. If you happen to be looking at a small portion of a rather lengthy web page, clicking the Print button will cause the whole page (which might be tens or even hundreds of pieces of paper) to be printed.

7 Stop – discontinue the attempt to load this web page. After clicking on a URL, you may grow tired of waiting for its web server to respond. It may be that the server is badly overloaded or, perhaps, not currently in operation. Eventually, your web browser will 'time out' the waiting process, but you can end it more quickly by clicking the Stop button. The Stop button can also be very useful for a lengthy web page with lots of images arriving slowly – if you decide at some point that you are really not interested in that page.

Pull-down menus

Across the top of the Netscape Navigator are six pull-down menus. Let us discuss the most interesting components of each.

File menu

1 New – the 'New' menu entry is actually the starter to a sub-menu that contains among other items 'Navigator Window'. You can bring on screen a second Netscape Navigator Window and then alternate viewing between them. This allows you to keep an important web page in one window while going off to view some other information in another window. By using the 'New' 'Navigator Window' option multiple times you can have three, four or more Navigator windows in use simultaneously. A word of caution – multiple Navigator windows all take system resources, so having several open simultaneously can slow down your computer.

2 Open Page – this selection brings up a little box on screen into which you can type the URL of a website you would like to visit. By the way, the same effect can be achieved by going to the location field (just above the viewing window) and typing in a URL. Normally the location field is simply the way the web browser has of telling you the URL of the web page you are viewing. But, you may also type into it to turn it into a way of opening another web page. Another thing that can be done with the 'Open Page' selection is to click on the 'Choose File' button. This allows you to view files stored on your own computer disk. This process can be used when creating web pages so that you may preview them to see how they are going to look before moving them to a location where they will be accessible to a web server.

3 <u>Print Preview</u> – before printing a web page, this selection allows you get an idea of how the information is going to print – specifically how many pieces of paper will be printed and what will be on each one.

4 <u>Print . . .</u> – this is exactly the same as the Print button. In fact every button has an equivalent on one of the pull-down menus, because you will soon see that you can remove the buttons from your web browser if you do not want them taking up valuable screen space.

5 <u>Close</u> – this entry closes the current Netscape Navigator window, but leaves open any others you may have opened. If you have only one Netscape window open, the effect of the Close entry is the same as the Exit entry below.

6 <u>Exit</u> – close all open Netscape Navigator windows and shut down the application. Using the Close or Exit entries in this pull-down menu is the best way to exit Netscape – causing all status information to be stored properly.

Edit menu

The first three entries in the Edit pull-down menu are standard Edit entries in most Windows 95/98 applications:

1 <u>Copy</u> – If you hold the left mouse button down and drag the cursor across some text, this text is highlighted by putting it into reverse video. Clicking the Copy entry puts this text into a text 'buffer' so that it may be used later.

2 <u>Paste</u> – equivalent to typing the text in the text 'buffer' into the application at the point where the cursor is currently located. This situation occurs occasionally in web browsing when you find a URL listed on a web page, but with no link to it. Copy it and then Paste it into the location field causing your web browser to request that web page.

3 <u>Cut</u> – this both copies and removes text from an application. Cut cannot be used with web pages, but makes sense when using a text editor in which you want to Cut some text, removing it from one place, and then Paste it into another.

4 <u>Find in Page . . .</u> – choosing this Edit pull-down menu entry brings up a little box labelled 'Find what:'. Type in the character(s), word or phrase that you want to find in the current web page. Most web pages are short enough that you can simply 'eyeball' them to find whatever word or phrase you are looking for. But, what if you are visiting a rather lengthy web page with lots of information about travel in The Netherlands and are specifically looking for information about shots you must take before entering Norway. Type in

'Norway' or 'inoculation' or some such and let 'Find in Page . . .' jump to each instance of that word. This can make your in-page perusal process go much faster. The little box allows you to search multiple times for the same phrase, to match case exactly (for example, normally searching for 'inoculation' would find 'Inoculation' as well), and to search both forward and backward in a document.

5 Preferences – clicking on this fairly innocent-looking entry brings up a window with a lot of choices that you can make to set up the web browser to work exactly the way you want. Some major Preferences include:

a) Appearance – on this page you can choose whether you want the buttons to be 'Pictures and Text', 'Pictures Only' or 'Text Only'.

b) Fonts – choose the style and size of font to be used for both Variable Width (normal) text and Fixed Width (special typewriter-like) text.

c) Colours – Choose the colours to be used for text (default is black), background (default is white), unvisited links (web pages you have not visited recently – default is blue) and visited links (web pages you have visited recently – default is purple).

d) Navigator – specify the 'home page' you want displayed whenever the Netscape Navigator is started or whenever you click the 'Home' button. Also, specify how many days must pass since you last visited a web page (turning its link purple) before it is to be considered unvisited, which really means not visited recently (turning its link back to blue).

e) Applications – specify the 'helper' application you want to run depending upon a file's suffix. Usually only advanced web browser users edit this information. Most of the major applications are already set up by default. For example, here you will find that files with the suffixes .gif, .jpg, and .jpeg are image files that are handled by 'Netscape (internal)' – that is, the web browser itself takes care of displaying these files. But, .ra, .rm, and .ram files are streaming audio and video files that are handled by Realplay software.

f) Mail & Groups – there are several screens of information that must be provided if you want to use Netscape to send and/or retrieve email for you. Major items involve specifying your name, return email address, and outgoing and incoming mail server information.

g) Advanced – here you can specify whether you want images loaded automatically (the default as opposed to asking for images to be loaded later when you find an interesting web page) and whether you want to accept or reject cookies (see below).

h) <u>Cache</u> – this is where you can decide the size of your memory and disk cache. (It is probably best not to change from the default sizes unless you really know what you are doing.) You can also decide how often you want to check with a server to see whether a newer version of a web page is available and should be sent by the server. 'Once per session' is the default and checks web pages the first time each is accessed after starting up the browser. 'Every time' is the conservative approach that asks the appropriate server to check the time and date of the current web page every time you access a page. 'Never' instructs your web browser always to used a cache copy if available and only to go to the appropriate server if a particular web page is no longer available in either memory or disk cache.

View menu

1 <u>Navigation Toolbar</u> – the 'Navigation Toolbar' is the set of buttons (Back, Forward, Reload, Home, . . .). You may hide them by choosing the entry 'Hide Navigation Toolbar'. You may get them back on screen by choosing the entry 'Show Navigation Toolbar'. Only one of these options will be available to you depending on the current state of hiding or showing the Navigation Toolbar. Now, the question 'Why would you want to hide these buttons?' They take space on screen away from the viewing window and every button has an equivalent on one of the pull-down menus. But they are very convenient, so most people leave them on screen (even if just as Text buttons).

2 <u>Location Toolbar</u> – the 'Location Toolbar' contains the location field and a button to get to your Bookmarks (see below). You may hide this toolbar by choosing the entry 'Hide Location Toolbar'. You can get it back on screen by choosing the entry 'Show Location Toolbar'. Again, only one of these options will be available to you depending on the current state of hiding or showing the Location Toolbar.

3 <u>Increase Font</u> – this is a way to increase both the Variable Width and Fixed Width font sizes to the next larger size – slightly faster than going through the Edit pull-down menu's Fonts screen.

4 <u>Decrease Font</u> – this is a way to decrease both the Variable Width and Fixed Width font sizes to the next smaller size – slightly faster than going through the Edit pull-down menu's Fonts screen.

5 <u>Reload</u> – This is exactly the same as the Reload button. Check with the appropriate server to see if you should get a newer copy of the current web page.

6 <u>Show Images</u> – if the Edit pull-down menu's Advanced screen has been set so that images are <u>not</u> loaded automatically, choosing this entry

requests all images for the current page from the appropriate server. Why would anyone <u>not</u> want to load images automatically? Usually, because someone has a very slow Internet connection. The text of web pages can be loaded much faster than images from those pages. When the user finds a page he or she really likes, he or she can then take the time to request the images for that page through this 'Show Images' entry.

7 <u>Refresh</u> – this is somewhat confusing because Netscape's Navigator and Microsoft's Internet Explorer mean different things by the word 'refresh'. The usual meaning (and that employed by Netscape) is to repaint the screen with the information for that page currently in memory. Thus, no request is made to a server to see if there is (and, perhaps, to retrieve) a newer version. Why would 'refresh' ever be necessary? Suppose that an error message has popped up on the screen, perhaps from a totally different application, that has messed up the screen's appearance. Refreshing the screen makes it appear like it did before the message messed it up. Unfortunately, Microsoft uses 'refresh' to mean 'reload' – having the side effect of refreshing the screen appearance along with getting a new copy from the server if one is available.

8 <u>Stop Page Loading</u> – this is exactly the same as the Stop button: discontinue the attempt to load this web page.

9 <u>Stop Animations</u> – some images are really collections of separate images that are repeated by the web browser to give the appearance of animation. Sometimes, particularly if there are several of these on one web page, they can become distracting, annoying and, even worse, can slow down your computer. This Stop Animations entry temporarily freezes all animated gif images on the current web page.

10 <u>Page Source</u> – this entry brings up a new window containing the HTML file that comprises this web page. This can be useful when creating web pages so that you may observe specifics of how other people display information.

11 <u>Page Information</u> – for the particularly curious, this brings up a new window containing information about the size of the web page, last modification date, location of the images it uses, etc.

Go menu

1 <u>Back</u> – this is exactly the same as the Back button: return to the previous web page.

2 <u>Forward</u> – this is exactly the same as the Forward button: proceed to the next web page.

3 <u>Home</u> – this is exactly the same as the Home button: proceed to the 'home page' for your web browser.

The remainder of the Go menu is a numbered list of the most recent pages (in order) that you have visited. The current web page is numbered '0', the one before that '1', the one before that '2', etc. By simply clicking on one of these pages you can leap back to a previously viewed web page much more quickly than by repeated clicks of the Back button. It is also easy then to return to the Go menu and click on page '0' to return to your original page much more quickly than by repeated clicks of the Forward button.

Communicator menu

This menu allows you to start the Netscape Navigator, Messenger (Netscape's email tool) and other Netscape-provided tools. At the bottom of this menu will be entries for each Netscape Navigator window that is open, thereby allowing easy movement back and forth among them.

Bookmarks

Often when visiting a website you may say to yourself (quietly if there are other people around); 'This is a really interesting website. I would like to be able to return to it again easily later.' What are your alternatives? If you got there via a hyperlink from some other website, you can always retrace that route again later. But that may not be very easy. If you have written down the URL, you may always retype it to the File pull-down menu Open Page entry or to the Location field of your browser. But, retyping a URL like **http://www.fiesta-travel.co.uk/Royalcarib.htm** is both time-consuming and error prone.

The best solution is to add such a web page to your Bookmarks. Every web browser has a file of websites selected by the user of the browser for fast and easy return later. When you are visiting **http://www.fiesta-travel.co.uk/Royalcarib.htm**, simply click on the Bookmarks icon on the Location Toolbar and select 'Add Bookmark'. Later, any time you click on the Bookmarks icon on the Location Toolbar, the Fiesta Travel Limited Cruise web page will be among those listed. Simply click on that entry and off you go to http://www.fiesta-travel.co.uk/Royalcarib.htm.

What we did above is really not the best way to establish a bookmark. It is usually best to add the home page of a website to your Bookmarks rather than just some page you find at the website. So, it is probably better to go to **http://www.fiesta-travel.co.uk**, the homepage of Fiesta Travel Limited's website and put that in your Bookmarks. From that page there are immediate links to airline travel, agency branches and cruises. So, you can still get to **http://www.fiesta-travel.co.uk/Royalcarib.htm** easily – just one click from Fiesta Travel Limited's homepage. Another reason why bookmarking the homepage of a website instead of a sub-page is a good idea is that websites are frequently reorganized, with web pages being moved and even renamed. A bookmark to a sub-page like Royalcarib.htm may not work after a while, but it is highly unlikely that a bookmark to **http://www.fiesta-travel.co.uk** will become defunct any time soon.

Occasionally you decide that a bookmark that was very useful for a while is no longer of much interest to you (like the one you created to the Afghanistan Hiking Society before your recent trip to Afghanistan). Click on the Bookmarks icon on the Location Toolbar and choose the entry 'Edit Bookmarks'. In the little window that appears, click on the Afghanistan Hiking Society and then select Delete from the Edit pull-down menu. The particular bookmark is now deleted from your list.

Cookies

At one point, there was quite a bit of interest in the World Wide Web containing a lot of 'pay-to-visit' information. Several information providers (like popular news magazines, newspapers and television networks) speculated that they would be able to charge people to visit websites. This could be done via a yearly subscription. For example, a news magazine that costs $100 per year for a printed subscription might offer unlimited access to its website with all the same information and images, and more, for only $25 per year.

The problem was how to do this efficiently. The proposed solution was an account and password combination. For example, suppose that Darrell Dawson wants a one-year subscription to *Travel World Magazine*'s website. He goes to the homepage of the website, clicks on a 'Subscribe' link, and provides identifying information including a credit card number. His credit card is charged the $25 yearly charge and Darrell is given the account 'dardaws' and password 'dws25qz4' to use. At any time for the next year Darrell may use his web browser to go to *Travel World Magazine*'s website, enter his account 'dardaws' and password 'dws25qz4' when prompted, and then have access to everything at the website.

The problem is that Darrell just might have a problem in remembering his account 'dardaws' and password 'dws25qz4'. So, he would have to write these down and keep track of them. What does he do if he loses them? Also, what about the tens (maybe hundreds) of other websites like this? Does Darrell really need to have tens (maybe hundreds) of accounts and passwords?

A solution for this problem is the use of a web 'cookie'. It works this way. When Darrell goes to the homepage of the website, clicks on a 'Subscribe' link, and provides identifying information, data called a 'cookie', is sent back to his web browser essentially containing the account 'dardaws' and password 'dws25qz4'. Think of this as a line that goes into a file – which is what it is. We may say that a 'cookie' has been placed in Darrell's web browser's cookie jar.

The next time Darrell goes to *Travel World Magazine*'s website, his web browser sends a copy of the cookie containing the account 'dardaws' and password 'dws25qz4' to the web server. The server verifies that Darrell is a valid subscriber to *Travel World Magazine*'s website and gives him access to the website. Darrell did not have to remember or even type in his account and password. This was handled automatically for him by the sending of a cookie from his browser to the Travel World server.

So, a 'cookie' is a little morsel of information sent initially from a web server to a web browser. After a browser receives a cookie from a server, whenever that browser requests a web page from that server it sends along that cookie.

Interestingly (and similar to what has happened a lot during the development of the Internet and the Web), using cookies in place of accounts and passwords at subscription websites has never really taken off. The problem is not with the cookie technology; instead subscription websites have in general been dismal failures. Since there is so much free information available on the Web, it is very difficult for someone to justify paying a yearly (or monthly or daily) fee for something that they can get for free at another website. Most websites that intended to be subscription websites instead are now replete with many advertisements (like commercial television or magazines). The advertisers in effect are paying for the service rather than subscribers.

But, cookies have flourished and are being used for a variety of other applications. For example, the first time Darrell visits *Travel World Magazine*'s website, he might be asked what types of things interest him – from a menu of items that includes airline tickets, hotel information, trip planning, rental car information, cruises, etc. Darrell's response to this will likely be embedded in a cookie. Suppose that he indicates an interest in airline tickets and rental car information. The next time he returns to *Travel

World Magazine's website, amazingly the homepage of the website will feature prominently information about airline tickets and rental car information.

Also, web commerce sites can keep track of Darrell's past purchases in order to highlight similar items on his future visits. A cookie can even serve as a 'shopping basket', keeping track of planned purchases from visit to visit until Darrell finally decides to take his basket to the 'checkout line' and actually purchase the items.

Some people who are concerned about privacy are very concerned about the implications of a cookie. This means that some organization (like *Travel World Magazine* or a commerce site) has available to it through a cookie some perhaps private and sensitive information. But remember, all information appearing in a cookie represents either information provided by the user or is based on the user's behaviour while visiting the website. So, if this concerns you, do not supply any information that you consider private (like home addresses, phone numbers, bank account numbers, etc.).

Some web users are incensed that cookies are kept in the web browser's cookie jar. 'Not only is *Travel World Magazine* intruding into my privacy, but they make me keep the information on my computer and send it to them!' This does not have the makings of a great social cause. Web servers could simply keep the same information at the website, never sending a cookie to your web browser. They are stored at the browser for speed purposes. Imagine walking into a clothing shop where you have been before. On a previous visit, the clerk filled out an index card about your preferences. He disappears for several minutes into the back of the store to find your index card from among the thousands stored in the shop. Can you see how much faster it would be if he had given the index card to you and you simply hand it to him as you walk in the front door? That is the idea behind keeping cookies at the browser rather than the server.

By the way, cookies can be expired, modified and even removed. Some cookies are good only for a month or so – assuming that your preferences might change with time. The associated cookie will have an expiration date. When your browser detects an expired cookie, it removes it from the cookie jar. On your next visit to that website, you will be asked for preferences again as if you were a first-time visitor. Some websites allow you to reverify your preferences (to keep the cookie from expiring) and to make modifications on any visit. Some websites even allow you to remove a cookie if you are not pleased with the process.

Mosaic, Netscape Navigator and Internet Explorer

Mosaic

The first major web browser that enjoyed tremendous success in its heyday was called 'Mosaic'. Mosaic was developed at the National Center for Supercomputing Applications (NCSA), at the University of Illinois. Mosaic was the first mouse-driven, icon-controlled, easy-to-use web browser that was available for general use. It set a standard – a look and feel – that was a precursor to Netscape's Navigator and Microsoft's Internet Explorer.

One of NCSA's missions was to aid the scientific research community by producing widely available, non-commercial software. Seeing great promise if only some user-friendly software were available to navigate the web, NCSA's Software Design Group produced a versatile, multi-platform interface to the World Wide Web and called it Mosaic. The name 'Mosaic' reflects the fact that web pages combine text and images to form a visually appealing entity.

Mosaic first appeared in 1993 and was the predominant web browser for about two years – until it was largely supplanted in 1995 by Netscape's first browser. The contribution of Mosaic to the popularity of the Web cannot be overestimated. In fact, to many people in 1994 the Web and Mosaic were one and the same. Some people even referred to the Web as 'Mosaic'.

The driving force behind Mosaic was a student at the University of Illinois, Marc Andreessen, who is to web browsers what Tim Berners-Lee is to the Web itself. Mosaic was created during a four-month period in late 1992 and early 1993 by Andreessen and several student colleagues. In early 1993 the first version of NCSA's Mosaic web browser was made available to the Internet community. It was an immediate smash hit due to its easy-to-use point-and-click hypermedia interface. Mosaic had set the standard for web interfaces.

Netscape Navigator

In late 1993 and early 1994 it became apparent that there were commercial opportunities with the Web. Among them was the possibility that companies might be able to market (or at least gain a significant market presence from) web browsers. Marc Andreessen was coaxed away from the University of

Illinois and named Vice President for Technology of a new company in California – Netscape Communications.

Andreessen was unable to bring along any of the software code from his Mosaic web browser, but he did not really want to do that anyway. He had learned valuable lessons from developing Mosaic – what was done well and what was done not so well. Netscape allowed him to start over with a clean slate and develop a brand new web browser. The first version of the Netscape web browser was made available in October 1994.

Netscape made even more of a splash than Mosaic had. First, it fell into the hands of a rapidly growing cadre of web users. Second, the few minor things that it did better than Mosaic caused a furor in the Internet community. For example, Mosaic displayed a blank screen until it had received the entire web page. But, Netscape used continuous document streaming – in which the user could view parts of a web page while it was still being received by the browser.

Netscape has also been responsible for advances in HTML as well. Netscape's creative team introduced new ideas – for example, web page tables – and supported them with their web browser even before they became web standards. In fact, by and large Netscape pushed the web standards to keep up with the new features they were adding to their browsers. Netscape also has done a good job of introducing new versions of their web browsers on a timely basis. It seems that Netscape users barely get comfortable with the current software when Netscape announces a newer, and better, version.

By the way, although the official name of Netscape's newest software is the 'Netscape Communicator', most people still refer to it as the 'Netscape Navigator' (which is what we do in this book). There are two reasons for this: first, 'Netscape Navigator' is a comfortable term for many people who have used this software for years; second, the web browser portion of Netscape's software is still known as the 'Navigator'.

Internet Explorer

At about the same time that Microsoft introduced its Windows 95 operating system (August 1995), it also introduced its own web browser – the Internet Explorer. Microsoft's Internet Explorer is very similar in terms of look and feel, as well as its capabilities, to Netscape's Navigator. This is not surprising, since both the Internet Explorer and the Navigator have their origins in the same software – NCSA's Mosaic.

At one point Microsoft and Netscape were negotiating to make Netscape the web browser that would be part of the Windows 95 operating system. But, when negotiations broke down, Microsoft purchased the rights to a very similar browser and began to mould it into the Internet Explorer.

The Internet Explorer has been developed specifically for use with Windows 95/98. In fact, Windows 98 uses the Explorer heavily for browsing, not only websites, but local files as well. However, the Netscape Navigator may still be used (and often is) by Windows 95/98 users.

6

Using the Web effectively

Finding useful information on the World Wide Web
Should you have a site on the World Wide Web?

Finding useful information on the World Wide Web

Special purpose search tools for the Web

The amount of information available on the World Wide Web is staggering and continues to double about every six months. Our best estimate is that the Web will consist of about 40 million websites (and remember that each of them might have several web pages) by January 2000.

The Web has been compared to a rather large and unruly library. First, information is being added to the library at an astounding rate (as suggested above). Second, virtually anyone can make a contribution to the library. (This has positive as well as negative effects – for example, some information added to the Web may not even be factually correct.) Third, there is no equivalent of the 'card catalogue' available for most libraries. In fact, the World Wide Web is a lot like a library with millions of books, all of them scattered about the library – on shelves, on tables, on the floor – in almost completely random order.

So, how can any kind of order be imposed on this unruly mess? We explore in this chapter several ways of finding information on the World Wide Web. Let us begin with some special purpose information websites. The following discussion is meant to give you just an idea of the ways that some websites have collected and organized links in order to make your access to information a little easier.

Actual libraries have been very quick to realize that they can play a significant role in helping people find information on the World Wide Web. One of the better examples is the Purdue University Library's The Online Resource (THOR) at **http://thorplus.lib.purdue.edu**. Note that this excellent website is being used as an example and this has nothing to do with the fact that both authors of this book are professors at Purdue University.

Among the links available on the home page of this website is one named 'Resources'. A click on this link leads to a wealth of 'Virtual Library Resources' including:

- The Virtual Reference Desk – here there are links to US census information, several English language dictionaries, international dictionaries (translating to and from English), thesauri, telephone books, maps, travel information, US State Department Travel Advisories, currency converters, world time zones, postal address information and zip codes.
- News, sports and weather – links to web-based newspapers from around the world including the *San Francisco Chronicle & Examiner*, *The News* and *Observer* from Raleigh, North Carolina, *USA Today*, the London *Daily Telegraph*, sports and weather information websites.

One of the links available from THOR – specifically the 'Virtual Reference Desk' is a website **http://www.mapquest.com** known as 'Mapquest'. This is a very special purpose web-based information site. Here you can get a map of many cities in the USA and throughout the world, zoom in and out in that map, and even get driving directions (complete with little maps) between any two cities in the USA.

Weather information is very popular on the World Wide Web. A good example of a weather source is WeatherNet at **http://cirrus.sprl. umich.edu/wxnet**. Here you may supply the name of a city anywhere in the world and receive the latest weather conditions and forecast for that city.

Address and zip code information for the USA is available from the National Address Server at **http://www.cedar.buffalo.edu/ adserv.html**. This little gem of a website allows you to enter a partial address, perhaps even one with some errors and to get back the correct version of that address. For example, entering the address:

212 West Broadwy
New York, New York

leads to the address:

212 East Broadway
New York NY 10002-5561

Note that the National Address Server determined the zip code 10002-5561, the fact that this is on 'East' (rather than 'West') Broadway, and even correctly guessed that we meant 'Broadway' in spite of misspelling it 'Broadwy'.

For most serious Web users, a quick turn to the dictionary to look up the meaning or spelling of a word is quickly being replaced by a visit to an online dictionary website. For example, *Webster's Dictionary* is available online from the University of California at San Diego at *http://work.ucsd.edu:5141/ cgi-bin/http_webster*. It can be used in 'Approximate' mode to look up a word when you are not really certain how to spell that word. For example, looking up the word 'innoculation' not only gives you the meaning ('taking a vaccine as a precaution against contracting a disease'), but also shows you that the word is really spelled 'inoculation'.

Many magazines have lately been turning to the World Wide Web. A Web version of a magazine can be provided as a convenience for subscribers, as a way for potential subscribers to sample the magazine, and even as a way to provide more detailed information than would fit in the pages of the printed version. For example, *TNT Magazine* ('for independent and free spirited travellers') is available on the Web at **http://www.tntmag.co.uk/**. Not only can you read the current issue of the magazine at this website, but many of the most popular articles from previous editions are available there as well.

A lot of government resources are available on the Web. Many of them provide an organized set of links to a wealth of government websites. For example, the US White House website at **http://www.whitehouse.gov** has links to the offices of the President and the Vice President of the USA, as well as commonly requested federal services such as Social Security,

Education services (for example student aid, fellowships and grants), Health services (such as Medicare and Medicaid), and Travel and Tourism services (like passports and travel warnings).

General purpose search tools for the Web

Even though the number of special purpose search tools (websites) is growing, the managers of such sites struggle to keep them up to date. New sites appear, sites change and old sites disappear (leading to 'link rot' – a link to a website that no longer exists). Also, there are many topics for which no special purpose website has been created. For example, to the best of our knowledge there is no special purpose website concerning soft drinks available in Chile.

So, in many situations we have to rely on general purpose search tools. Of course if you had unlimited time (not to mention unlimited patience), you could click around throughout the Web starting at some promising locations and hope that eventually you would locate all the websites relevant to a particular topic. For example, if you are interested in tennis tournaments in Indiana, you might start with the home page of as many tennis organizations as you can find in Indiana, as well as sports and community festivals in Indiana. But, finding those starting points is difficult as well. But, what if we had a general purpose search tool that would allow us to enter any phrase (like 'tennis tournament Indiana') and find a lot of websites with relevant information.

The Contributor-Indexing Process

The original idea was that we could convince Website builders to send information about a Website upon its completion to some organization that would keep this information and make it available. For example, suppose that you have just created a website for the Crawfordsville, Indiana, Strawberry Festival Tennis Tournament. You would send in the URL of the website along with several keywords that someone might use when looking for your website – like tennis, tournament, Indiana, Crawfordsville, Strawberry, Festival, singles, doubles, etc.

This information would be filed and made available through a *search engine*. What is a search engine? This is a website visited by someone who is looking for information on the Web. He or she supplies any number of search keywords. The website then starts up a program to look through its database of URLs and related keywords and returns to the visitor a page or more of relevant websites. The 'search' aspect of this is easy, but what does 'engine' mean. This is referring to the fact that the program involved acts like a little train engine running around through the database, loading into its cars only the information you really want.

The Contributor-Indexing Process seemed like a great idea. This would be a very simple way for website builders to communicate what they had built and for users to find websites relevant to any set of search terms. But, the Contributor-Indexing Process has turned out to be a failure. The problem is that no one seemed willing to send URLs and keywords to them. Why? The most common reason given is, 'No one would be interested in my little website.' The problem with this is that there are many people who might be interested in your website. Many websites that appear to be of limited general interest (like 'Water Sports in North Central Ohio') get hundreds of visits weekly. Another typical reason for not sending in a URL and keywords is, 'I haven't finished yet; I'll notify the search engine when the website is finished'. The problem with this is that no website is ever finished. They always seem to be in a state of modification. But, even a partially finished website may contain much information of interest.

Robots, crawlers, worms and spiders

Since the Contributor-Indexing Process never really took off, another means of implementing a search engine has become the standard. Think of it this way: If you had unlimited time, you could visit thousands of websites every day just by clicking on links from the website you are currently visiting. You could write down the URL as well as a few appropriate keywords for each website you visit before forging off on all the links from the present website. Over a period of several weeks and months, you could build up a fairly impressive (and searchable) database of websites.

But, to do what we suggest above would require someone with unlimited time. Since the Web is doubling in size every six months, websites are continually modified and some web pages are actually deleted from the Web, the process would be never-ending.

Well, of course, no human being would be interested in this job. But, computer programs can be written that can do this – much faster, more accurately and without fatigue. Such a program starts with a web page, records its URL, determines a few keywords and then one by one does the same with each hyperlink from that page. If the program starts with a fairly high-level set of good websites, it might be possible to go from them to most of the world's existing websites.

Such computer programs are called *robots*, *crawlers*, *worms* and *spiders*. 'Robot' recognizes that these programs are performing tasks as directed by their human masters. 'Crawlers' and 'worms' are computer programs that move from one Internet location to another. Sometimes such programs are related to nefarious situations – like illicit software vandalizing a site. But, in this case, all they do is to slow things down a little for a web server while they look methodically through all the web pages at a site. The word 'spider', of course, plays on the web aspect – something that crawls around on a web.

Of course the Web is now far too large for any human being to try running through all the web pages. (You cannot click on web pages as quickly as they are being added to the Web!) Not even one such spider can keep up with web growth and changes. Most search engines that employ robots, crawlers, worms and spiders have hundreds of such programs running simultaneously – continually changing the search engine's database.

Search engines

Each search engine discussed below has a database of many millions of web pages. Each receives in the region of five million visits per day from people looking for websites.

Lycos

One of the first such search engines was a result of the Lycos project begun by Dr Michael Mauldin at Carnegie-Mellon University in 1994. The name 'Lycos' comes from the arachnid family Lycosidae – large ground spiders, very speedy and active at night, catching their prey by pursuit rather than in a web.

Lycos is available at **http://www.lycos.com**. It has several categories (such as Business, Careers, Education, Entertainment, Games, Government, Health, News, Shopping, Sports, and Travel) that may be used along with general purpose searching by just supplying a search phrase. The website URLs are returned in decreasing order of how Lycos thinks this matches your search – from best to worst. Each link is accompanied by a synopsis of the web page as well as an indication of the website homepage to which this one is linked.

Yahoo

Perhaps the most popular search engine is Yahoo at **http://www.yahoo. com**. Yahoo was created by Stanford graduate students Jerry Yang and David Filo in 1994. The name 'Yahoo' either stands for 'Yet another hierarchical officious oracle' or is a corruption of 'YangFilo'. Yahoo's creators are delightfully vague on this point.

Yahoo also has several categories (such as Business & Economy, Entertainment, Government, Health, News & Media, Recreation & Sports, Society & Culture) that may be used along with general purpose searching by just supplying a search phrase. It also has links to the latest news, weather and sports. Yahoo has its own travel site at **http://travel. yahoo.com** and web guide for kids Yahooligans! at **http://www. yahooligans.com**. There are even foreign language versions of Yahoo – for example, Yahoo France at **http://www.yahoo.fr** and and Yahoo Japan at **http://www.yahoo.co.jp**.

Infoseek, Excite, WebCrawler, HotBot, AltaVista

Other popular search engines are Infoseek (**http://www.infoseek. com**), Excite (**http://www.excite.com**), WebCrawler (**http:// webcrawler.com**), HotBot (**http://www.hotbot.com**), and AltaVista (**http://www.altavista.digital.com**).

MetaCrawler

MetaCrawler is a clever search engine at **http://www.metacrawler.com** that has no robots or spiders of its own. When you ask MetaCrawler to find a search phrase for you, it calls several other search engines (principally the ones listed above), merges all their results and presents you with what you would have found had you gone to each of the other search engines separately. MetaCrawler ranks its results based upon the number of search engines that listed a particular website.

Savvy searching

One of the the most challenging things in using any search engine is trying to decide what keywords will be best to find just those web pages in which you are interested.

You would like to eliminate as much as possible the 'false positives' – web pages that end up on a list, but that you really do not want. For example, suppose that you search for 'music festivals Indiana'. What you do not want to get are 'false positive' web pages about music festivals in Ohio, art shows in Indiana or wrestling matches in Burma.

You would also like to eliminate as much as possible the 'false negatives' – web pages that you would like on the list, but that are not displayed by the search engine. For example, the 'Carmel Concert website' might not be displayed if the website does not make it clear that Carmel is in Indiana.

It is best to start with just a few keywords that are as descriptive as possible. For example, suppose that you are looking for information about orchestra concerts in the Indianapolis, Indiana area, you might start with 'music festivals Indiana'. If you seem to have a lot of false positives, add more keywords, such as 'orchestra', 'concert' and 'Indianapolis'. You might even have to eliminate a word – like 'festival' if it seems to be bringing in a lot of irrelevant websites. The trade-off is that the more search terms you use, the fewer false positives you will have. But, the more search terms you use, the more likely you are to have more false negatives – eliminating websites such as 'Carmel Concert website' even though Carmel is a suburb of Indianapolis. The best technique is to try several different sets of search terms until you settle upon a list of websites that seems to work the best.

Some search engines provide some additional options that help to eliminate both false positives and false negatives. For, example it is possible to specify whether 'all' the words in the search phrase must appear at the website or just 'some' of them. Choosing 'some' will generally lead to more websites found – although some may be false positives.

Also, some search engines allow partial word searches. For example, 'mus*' would match any word beginning with the letters 'mus', for example, music, musical, musician, museum, mustard, etc.

Problems with search engines

Search engines have been fairly successful, but they are certainly far from perfect. Let us examine some of the problems that need to be addressed by those in charge of the major search engines if they are to be as useful tools as most of us would like:

1 Their databases are usually out of date. Since the search engines are scanning their database for matches to your search phrase – rather than searching the entire web at that moment (which would be impossible) – they cannot include the most recent additions to the Web. In general most search engines reflect the content of the Web any time from several weeks to several months ago. It is frustrating to some website builders that it takes so long for search engines to rumble back through, find their website and include it in the database.

2 Some websites are improperly classified. The classification process that determines the keywords that can be used to find each website is a closely guarded secret by the managers of each search engine. It appears that their software looks at titles, headings, words that are repeated and words that appear early on the web page. But this can still lead to some bizarre classifications of web pages. For example, a search by one of the authors concerning the dangers and costs of drunk driving turned up a web page entitled 'How to get drunk' – not at all the kind of information desired.

3 Some sites are never classified. Search engines depend on reaching websites from other sites that they know. If a new website does not have the 'right' links to it, it will never be found by some search engines. Attempts to contact the manager of a search engine and to supply that information by telephone, email, fax or letter usually fail because the manager has no time manually to add or change information in the database.

Should you have a site on the World Wide Web?

Growing use of the Internet and the Web

One of the authors of this book recently received a phone call from the representative of a company in which she said that the company was exploring 'the possibility of perhaps sometime in the future maybe using the Internet and maybe even ultimately having a site on the World Wide Web'. Less than one month later, this same person called and said that her company needed a website 'by Friday'!

Such is the way that companies are moving to the Internet and the Web. Many companies begin haltingly – fearful that the use of the Internet will provide access to valuable company information to outsiders (like high school students in Kansas). Finding that the Internet provides an excellent means of communication among employees, most companies then jump in quickly and become significant email and web users. It does not take long for them to realize that their customers and potential customers are looking for products and services on the Web. They need a website in order to maintain a competitive advantage over their competitors.

Often the authors hear statements like: 'I was going to buy a new pair of water skis. I found this neat company on the Web that shows all of its skis including all of their features and variations. I could even order the skis using my credit card, so I did. They should arrive by the end of the week.' Obviously in this environment those companies who have attractive and useful websites have quite an advantage over their competitors. In fact, it may not be long until the absence of a website may be fatal to a company. Many companies are even finding a tremendous shift to communication with their suppliers, customers, and even potential customers via the Web away from the more standard means of communication such as phone calls, fax and office visits.

For a while there was only limited access to the Internet – principally among persons associated with schools, government and research organizations. But the Internet is now rapidly becoming available in businesses and homes as well. In fact, this is the most rapidly growing area of Internet access.

In addition, the Web and web browsers have made accessing textual and multimedia information so easy that most people can master it with almost no training. Anyone who can point and click a mouse has access to a 'World Wide Web' of information.

Web addresses, those URLs that are used to find a website, now are appearing in all sorts of media. On television, they are not just mentioned in advertisements. Even news, entertainment and sports programming display URLs for people to use to get additional information about the product, service or programme. Newspapers and magazines now have web addresses printed throughout the publication. One of the authors recently bought a soft drink that had the URL **www.snapple.com** printed on the label! In effect, the Web has become a pervasive part of our world. Sociologists tell us that no other development – not the printing press, not the airplane, not the radio or television – has moved so quickly from its introduction to general use than has the World Wide Web.

Benefits of having your own website

The obvious question is, 'Do you need a website?' The answer to the question depends to a certain extent upon who you are. If you are an individual, then the answer is based solely on whether you have some information you would like to share with the rest of the world. Do you have a complete collection of Frank Sinatra albums? Have you travelled extensively in the Pacific region and can give advice and information for future travellers? Would you like to be in contact with other people who share your professional interests or who perhaps enjoy the same leisure and travel activities?

If you are an organization or company, then the answer is almost certainly 'Yes, you need a website!' In fact, for all the reasons discussed in this chapter, if you do not have one, your organization might quickly lose its competitive edge.

A website is an easy way to communicate information using both text and graphics. If you have information in sound or video files, these can be made available via a website, as well. A website allows the capability of interaction – with visitors providing feedback on information you supply, and even ordering products or services.

A company website can also have hyperlinks to more details than some people would want, but they would be available to the occasional visitor who really wants to know them. For example, if your company 'Water Ski Webworld' sells water skis, most people really do not care about the research that went into developing the high-impact plastic from which they are made. But, those who are interested can click and read away to their hearts content on as many technical details as you care to provide and they care to consume. A website can even have hyperlinks to related companies. For example, Water Ski Webworld could have a hyperlink to a company that sells life preservers. You could provide this as a service to the website visitor, 'If you don't find everything for your water skiing adventure here, click on these links to other companies' (one of which would be the life preserver company). You could get the life preserver company to do the same thing, with a link to Water Ski Webworld. This creates a web ring (as discussed in Chapter 4) – a collection of websites that are in effect jointly publicizing each other. As we mentioned before, this usually leads to more visits for each of the 'ringed' sites than if they were not part of the web ring.

Catalogues, services and schedules

Printed catalogues are often out of date as soon as they are printed. You have to get pictures, specifications and prices of your water skis together and to the printer. This takes time, as does the printer (maybe even several weeks) to produce the catalogue. Then there is time involved in distributing the catalogue either by mail or fast delivery service. The point is that by the time the catalogue gets into the customers' hands, there will be several items of information, like specifications for some skis, prices of some and even availability of some, that will have changed.

That same information can be placed on a website as quickly as the pictures can be scanned and specifications and prices can be determined. The availability is immediate. A 'catalogue' placed on the Web at 9.00 this morning is available to the thousands of Water Ski Webworld's customers at 9.00. There is no printing cost involved. Anyone who wants a paper copy of any pictures or information can send that to their own printer – at their own expense. The most attractive thing about web-based catalogues, however, is that they can be kept completely up to date.

Suppose that the price of the Wave Crasher 4000 ski set is reduced from $750 to $650. That change can be made to the website immediately. Anyone who comes to the website, even one second later, sees the correct price along with any updated specifications, pictures or prices for every product you sell at Water Ski Webworld. The beauty of a web-based catalogue is that a change to a single file immediately updates that document for all employees, distributors, customers and potential customers.

Web-based catalogues also provide the capability for a great deal of information for the real ski enthusiast without incurring a terrible printing expense for those who are not interested. A photograph or schematic diagram of a product can be annotated to highlight special features or configurations. Each feature can be 'clickable' allowing the real ski enthusiast customer to proceed to very detailed information. For example, clicking on the foot bindings in the Wave Crasher 4000 diagram can bring up a page of information about the polyurethane material used in constructing them, the rated strength and flexibility of the bindings, data from actual research tests, and even information about alternative bindings that can be chosen to replace the standard ones if more strength or less flexibility is desired.

A website is also extremely useful for providing information about services and schedules. A business or organization that offers training and related services can use its website to display course descriptions. These can be kept completely current. Any time a training course changes even minutely, that can be reflected at the website. Schedules for when and where these courses will be offered can be kept up to date – even reflecting courses that were just added. A website is ideal for supplementing course descriptions and schedules with hyperlinks to related courses, prerequisites, registration forms, etc.

Frequently asked questions

Many organizations provide help desks, help personnel, and toll-free numbers to handle a fairly standard set of FAQs. For example, Water Ski Webworld might have a toll-free number and there might be a fairly consistent set of questions generally asked about the Wave Crasher 4000 ski set: 'How do I put them on?' 'How do I take them off?' 'Which end is the front?' 'Which one is the left (or right) ski?' 'What do I do if I lose one ski, but still have the other one?' 'How fast can the boat run before the skis disintegrate?'

These can certainly be answered (over and over again) via operators at the toll-free number. But, this can also be a job for Water Ski Webworld's website. A link to 'Wave Crasher 4000 FAQs' might contain these questions (and several more) answered by the most knowledgeable person in the organization. This can tremendously cut back on phone calls to a toll-free number and can even ensure that the answers to such questions are uniformly correct.

Other related information that can be available at the website includes troubleshooting guides. These can be detailed and step-by-step instructions for determining if the foot bindings are defective or just installed on the skis incorrectly.

In this sense a website can improve 'maintenance' after a sale. The customer has the sense that he or she has purchased not only a set of water skis, but also access to the expertise of your company's experts to help him or her use them most effectively. Often, this is seen by customers as a competitive advantage for your company over other companies that do not offer such a service and it can significantly increase customer satisfaction with the product and the company. It can also reduce service calls for products (like washing machines) where such calls might be part of the warranty.

Website contents

A website is a good means of communicating rapidly changing information and special offers. Such things as restaurant menus, listing of shows at a motion picture theatres, store specials, seminar topics and times, service bulletins, and information about upgrades and changes to products are ideal for a website.

Most visitors to a website expect it to be a source of company contact information as well. They expect to find phone numbers, fax numbers, email accounts, and maps and directions to company locations. A clickable map of the country or some region thereof is a handy way for potential customers to find the nearest company location.

Customer feedback, orders and surveys

Fill-in forms (with text boxes and clickable buttons) can be used to gather customer feedback, to take product or service orders and to collect survey information from website visitors. The form provides places to enter text (either a word or two or a paragraph). It can even allow the selection of various items from pre-configured lists: 'Choose below the type of ski boat that you are using.'

Information can be provided to the website visitor immediately for items easily accessible from the company's online database. Alternatively, requested information can be sent to the visitor via email, fax or letter after some human intervention.

Online ordering can be done using credit card numbers (with secure encrypting as discussed in Chapter 2). Potential and current customers may use the website to complete membership or service applications.

Special and internal information

The website is also a good place to provide the company history and background. This kind of information is not interesting to everyone (in fact, probably not to many people), so it should be offered only to those who click on a hyperlink for this type of information. Every visitor, however, should be notified of new products and services and given the opportunity to click on links to as many of these as interest them. A website can also be used for 'morale' purposes – providing special recognition for employees, suppliers and customers through a web-based electronic bulletin board.

Many organizations are finding that, in addition to websites meant for the external world, internal websites can be made available as part of the company intranet (see Chapter 2). Such a website would be constrained for viewing and use by company employees. It would not be available to the outside world. Such a website is ideal for such things as company policies, internal forms, handbooks and regulations. Company news, job openings (to be filled from within the organization) and internal databases can be made available internally via the intranet website. This, by the way, is probably the best location for the employees' 'morale' bulletin board mentioned above.

The intranet website can be made accessible to carefully-selected suppliers and customers. This can be done to more tightly connect these outsiders to the organization in situations where this benefits the company.

Designing (before building) a website

When a company decides that it wants (needs) a website, the most common mistake is to rush to get something prepared quickly without thinking about what kind of information should be on the website and how it should be organized. The typical statement is, 'Let's get something out there. We can always make it perfect later'. The sad truth is that the initial look and feel of a website often stands for years without change. So, if this is done badly at first, the website may suffer for some time.

First, think about what you want to present on the website. It is not likely that everything about the company will be available at the website. Choose that information and those services that seem best suited to web presentation. Plan for extension later as more items are added. But, make sure that the design of the website is well suited for what you are most certain will be its major use.

Diagram the website's topology (home page, sub-pages, and connections among them) before beginning implementation. What should be on the home page? Keep it visually appealing, but do not fill it up with lots of graphics that load slowly and run away the potential customer before he or she even sees the entire home page. A useful home page should grab the newcomer's attention immediately and invite his or her return.

What links should be directly below the home page? What things are typical visitors going to want to do the most? Make sure that all of those are just one click away from the home page. Other things should be just a click away from that set of pages. A good rule of thumb is that web pages that are more than three clicks from the website home page are unlikely to be visited very often.

Set up company website standards. Choose a set of images, logos and icons that will be used throughout the website – even if different people build different web pages. Determine common background images and/or colours that will be used for the website. Agree on a common style that will be followed throughout. For example, will each page consist of several paragraphs of information or will each have short lists that convey the same thing? Consistent images, logos, backgrounds and styles are important for the website to have a consistent look and feel. Websites that shift their look and feel from one page to another remind of us strange houses in which the room decorations seem to change dramatically from one portion of the house to another. This makes us uncomfortable.

There is some general agreement in the industry about what makes good websites. Here are a few main ideas:

1 Each web page should be fairly small and able to load quickly.
2 Each web page should have a hyperlink (an easily recognized button is nice) back to the website home page.
3 Each web page should have email and phone number for the person responsible for that page in case a visitor finds some incorrect information or there is some other problem with the web page.
4 Each web page should have a 'last changed' date indicating the day and time it was last modified.

5 Images should be used judiciously. Use clickable small images to get to larger images that load slowly, but only if the visitor wants to see them.

Determine who will author and review the content of each set of web pages. The author should be that person (or persons) who know the particular area best. These authors supply text and information. They can also build the web pages if they know how to do this. Otherwise, website builders can implement the pages under their direction. It is important that web page reviewers differ from web page authors. In general, web page reviewers should be those responsible for an area, perhaps the managers of the authors – those most likely to determine errors or missing information.

Keep in mind that the Web is a publication medium just like a press release, stockholder pamphlet or catalogue. The company website reflects the professionalism (or lack thereof) of an organization. A website should never look like it was created by a disinterested intern who knows very little about the organization. Be certain that spelling and grammar are correct.

Keep the information current on a website. Make sure that repeat visitors can tell that something is new – maybe a new product or service – since their last visit. Websites that seldom change rarely get visitors.

Most web pages have a line near the bottom saying something like 'This page last changed . . .' giving the date of last modification. The kiss of death for a website is if someone browsing a site in 1999 finds 'This page last changed 4 October 1994'. Make sure to keep time-related information up to date. No one should go to your website and find that the price list says '1995 Price List'.

The frequency with which a website needs to be updated depends on the type of information provided. Some information requires daily change to keep it current, while other information can stay on a website for a year or more without needing modification. (Perhaps the Wave Crasher 4000 skis will be available for two years before being replaced by the Wave Crasher 5000.) Frequent updates can be accomplished via automated tools. From time to time, manual review for out-of-date material is critical. In addition you should test frequently to make sure that all (local and remote) hyperlinks work – avoiding that dreaded 'link rot'!

Building your own versus 'outsourcing' a website

Should you outsource your website? Do you have the expertise and time available with existing employees for them to build and maintain your website, or should you contract with an outside company or individual to do this for you? In the early days of the Web few companies had any internal expertise for building websites. That is changing as employees learn these skills and tools become available to make website-building easier.

But still ask yourself, 'Do my employees have the time to do this well – including the maintenance and modifications that are necessary to keep a website vital?' Outside firms certainly have the expertise and will make the time, but of course this can be costly. Some companies prefer to keep their website building and maintenance internal so that they maintain complete control of exactly what is on each web page.

Should you have your own web server? Do you want your company web pages to be served from a computer within your company or by an ISP that provides this service? The benefit of having your own web server is the ease of access in changing information as soon as it becomes out of date. The disadvantage of having your own web server is the need perhaps to dedicate one computer to this task and this computer must be connected to the Internet twenty-four hours a day, seven days a week. There is also the security concern. Do you feel comfortable that you can create a sufficient firewall to keep website visitors from drifting over into other areas of your computer system – getting access to sensitive information.

If you run your own web server, you will have to designate someone as the 'webmaster'. This person (or persons) must keep the server running, respond to queries and comments internally and externally, while staying abreast of technology that is changing every fifteen minutes.

Whether your website is being served internally or by an ISP, you will likely want to establish your own Internet domain. This can be done by contacting InterNIC – the organization that registers domains for the Internet. You can do this yourself or ask for help from your ISP. Choose a domain name (like waterskiweb.com) and ask for that domain. Unfortunately, at this point many really desirable domains (like waterski.com, waterweb.com, ski-world.com and waterworld.com) are already taken. So, you may have to be creative to come up with a descriptive name that someone else does not already have.

If at all possible, choose a short, intuitive name (like cbs.com, sears.com and fedex.com). In our example above, waterskiweb.com really is not as short as we would like. But, it is the best we can do with all the short names already taken. Over 17 000 domains are registered with InterNIC every day.

Critical criteria for selecting an Internet service provider for your website

Suppose that you have decided, like many other companies, to have an ISP house and serve your website at http://www.waterskiweb.com. By the way, any ISP can serve web pages for any domain. This is simply part of the InterNIC registration process – telling where www.waterskiweb.com is located. Let us look at some selection criteria for choosing the best ISP for your website.

Consider network topology and speed. How many 'hops' must your web pages make from the ISP to the typical user? If the ISP is far removed from the Internet backbone, the number of hops can really slow down the receipt of your web pages. How is the ISP affected by outages? Do they have a single connection to the Internet backbone or do they have some backup system? How much capacity do they have available for peak demand periods? Will there be times that people will have a lot of trouble getting your web pages? Find out typical speeds and slowest speeds.

Consider technology and backup provisions. Does the ISP use leading edge computers and equipment, or out-of-date hardware? Does the ISP use the most up-to-date software – including state-of-the-art web server software? What delays will website visitors experience during peak times? What happens when the ISP's hardware or software fails? Can immediate backups be employed? For how long will your website visitors get the 'server not responding message'?

Consider Common Gateway Interface (CGI) capabilities and limitations. Common Gateway Interface programs are used for dynamic, interactive web pages. Responding to forms or presenting user-specific information usually depends on CGI programs. How easy is it to develop and maintain CGI programs with this ISP? What limitations does this place on CGI programs?

Consider security. Will this ISP allow some, but not all, 'sensitive' information to be made available to certain visitors, exactly according to your directions? How does the ISP protect this information from access by others? How does the ISP protect all information from vandalism? What about password protection?

Does this ISP provide 'Visitor Logs' – IP node names of website visitors? How are these summarized in reports?

Check on the experience of the ISP's technical staff in computer networking – not just in computing. Make sure that the ISP has adequate staffing to cover both usual and unusual situations. Find out about technical staff turnover. Is the network operations centre always staffed by at least one person? Is the network operations centre staffed by senior personnel during normal business hours?

May your contract with the ISP be terminated with reasonable notice and at reasonable expense? Avoid long-term contracts. The Web is a very dynamic entity.

Find out about the ISP's customer base. How many customers does the ISP already have? How many of those customers need services similar to those you require? How happy is that subset with the service they receive?

Find out about the ISP's business history. How long has the company been in the ISP business? What indications are there that they are likely to stay in business for a while? Are they likely to be purchased by a larger ISP? This is not necessarily a bad thing to happen. Is this ISP financially stable? Some have almost no previous business experience, are badly under-capitalized, and do not stay in business very long. Is this ISP actively upgrading hardware and equipment? Those that are not probably will not survive.

Do some comparison shopping. Do a cost–benefit analysis. Make sure you do an 'apples to apples' comparison – do not compare one ISP's no frills service with another's full service offering. Ask for customer references and talk to these customers.

7

Electronic library resources

Access to libraries around the world

As an Internet user, you can exchange information with other Internet users from Argentina to Zambia. By itself, that capability makes the Internet extremely useful. However, you can also use the Internet to access an incredible amount of information stored all over the world.

Over the last several years, most university libraries have switched from a manual card catalogue system to computerized library catalogues. The automated systems provide users with easily accessible and up-to-date information about the books available in these libraries. This has been further improved upon with the advent of LANs, dial-up modems and wide area networks (WANs). Through the Internet, you can access almost every college and university library catalogue in the country, as well as many catalogues throughout the world. In addition, many large public library catalogues are available over the Internet, and each month more and more such catalogues are becoming available. This is especially useful if you do not have access to a large library, since each of these catalogues can be accessed from a computer. Now you can check your local library's holdings or that of a library halfway around the world.

Many institutions of higher learning have made their library catalogues available for searching by anyone on the Internet. These include Boston University, the Colorado Alliance of Research Libraries (CARL), and London University King's College. To include a listing of some of the existing sites would not only be far too long for this book, it would also soon be out of date. However, several lists are being maintained and are available either by mail or via FTP. Those lists, as well as the Internet Resource Guide will be described later in this chapter.

Library catalogues

In some ways, library catalogues have similarities to the World Wide Web (WWW) and Gopher search engines. Library catalogues allow you to search an index of materials and retrieve a list of documents that match your search query, just as a web search engine allows you to query and retrieve web-based documents that match your query. Library catalogues usually provide both free-text and controlled vocabulary searching, similar to many web search engines. In addition, catalogues generally provide some type of Boolean searching.

Boolean logic is a system which allows for combining search terms when using a search engine. It hones web searches so that they produce a top-notch retrieval list, and cuts down the number of irrelevant documents received. Boolean operators are virtually connecting words, specifically, AND, OR and NOT. The system allows one to combine search terms in three different ways by using these three word queries. AND queries allow for restricted searches that return documents containing more than one search term. OR queries provide for expanded searches that return documents that contain any one of a number of search terms. NOT queries can exclude particular terms from being considered in a search.

- AND queries: Assume that you are writing a paper on the history of parks within the UK. Obviously, you wish to look for documents that contain both the word 'parks' and the word 'history'. If a document contained only one of these words, the search might not be relevant to your topic. Therefore, you would want to do a search for documents that have *parks AND history* in them.
- OR Queries: Remember that while AND queries are used to restrict a search, OR queries are used to expand a search. When you link two or more terms using the OR operator, in effect you tell the search engine, 'Show me the documents that contain any of the keywords I've typed.' OR queries return documents that have either the first term or the second term, or sometimes both terms. If you were searching for documents pertaining to the number of international visitor arrivals, you could use a number of search engines using the words, *tourism OR travel* . If you wanted to find everything on the Web pertaining to 'ecotourism', you might phrase every term that is relevant including *green, sustainable, appropriate*, etc.
- NOT Queries: The NOT operator provides a way to exclude unwanted documents from the retrieved list. Sometimes when performing a search, you may find that many of the returned items stem from another meaning of your search word. For example, when you search for the word 'travel', you may find a large number of pages devoted to travel agencies. To refine your search to exclude travel agencies, you can use the NOT operator such as *travel NOT agencies*. However, NOT queries are used a great deal less than AND and OR queries. In fact, many search engines only support the latter two types of queries, and do not support NOT queries.

Library catalogues and Internet search engines have some significant differences. Library catalogues provide an index to materials that are the property of a particular institution instead of being scattered throughout the Internet. When using a library catalogue, you can normally search for an author, title or subject of a work, but you cannot search the full text of the material itself. In addition, when you query a library catalogue, the results that you receive are bits of information about a physical object (for example, a book) held by the library, rather than the object itself.

In general, library catalogues do not provide indexes to journal articles themselves, but rather they provide only the titles of the journals. Although a few university library catalogues do provide indexes to journal articles, those catalogues are normally available only to faculty and students of that institution, not to the general public on the Internet. If you wish to look up specific journal articles, you will have to use an electronic or paper index that is not publicly available on the Internet but is still commonly found in libraries. However, increasingly, databases that index journal articles (abstracts and indexes) are available on the Web, but only by paid subscription.

Given both similarities and differences, the user searches a library catalogue for one of the following reasons:

1 To search for and locate a book, a journal, or other printed material with the intention of checking it out or looking at it.
2 To find bibliographic information about a particular item, i.e. an author, publisher or date of publication.
3 To see what books or journals are available on a particular subject or by a particular author.

A library catalogue is not searched if the user wishes to retrieve the material electronically, although it may provide specific references to how this may be accomplished.

Using library catalogues

One of the major problems with accessing library catalogues is that many different types of software are used in the catalogues, and each software package usually has its own command language. Compounding the problem is the fact that each institution often modifies its software in order to reflect the institution's needs, so that the same program appears different from site to site. In spite of these problems, library catalogues are designed to make searching simple in order to accommodate thousands of people who possess different levels of computer experience.

Although a number of library catalogues have been placed experimentally on the Web or Gopher, most catalogues are accessible only through a program called Telnet.

Telnet

Long before the World Wide Web arrived on the Internet scene, knowledgeable individuals were using a text-based tool called Telnet to tap into the wonders of the online world. Even today, many Internet users who have never even heard of Telnet are missing out on something very valuable. Telnet is the main internet protocol for creating a connection with a remote machine. It gives the user the opportunity to be on one computer system and do work on another, which may be across the street or thousands of miles away. Modems are limited both by their speed and the quality of phone lines, whereas Telnet provides a connection that is error-free, nearly always faster than the latest conventional modems, but may also be limited by the node connection itself. Since Telnet is text based, there is no pointing or clicking as all navigation is done via the keyboard.

Unlike the phone system, however, the Internet is not yet universal; not everybody can use all of its services. Almost all colleges and universities on the Internet provide Telnet access as do most for-fee public access systems. Some databases and file libraries can be queried by email, and most Telnet sites are fairly easy to use and have online help systems.

How to connect

Before you can connect to another remote computer with Telnet, you will need to know a few things. No matter what type of computer or connection you have, you must know the Internet address of that computer before you can connect to the other computer. Internet addresses come in two different forms: a series of letters or words connected by periods (such as **thorplus-.lib.purdue.edu**), or by a series of four numbers connected by periods (such as **128.79.22.11**) (see Chapter 2). When you are connected, you will need to enter a user ID (and sometimes a password) in order to log in and start using the service at that remote computer.

A number of Telnet sites do not require a user ID. For those sites that do require a user ID for entry, often you may log in and be connected by typing the word *guest* or *anonymous* as the password. Unless you are connecting to a fee-based service to which you have previously subscribed (like Compu-Serve or a BBS) you probably will never need a password when using Telnet.

Once you are logged in, you will need to pay careful attention to the instructions on the screen to determine how to navigate the Telnet site and log out when you are done. Do not take too much time between connecting and logging in since the computer may disconnect. When connected via Telnet you could end up on almost any type of computer – a UNIX computer at a university, a DOS-based BBS or an IBM mainframe – so the commands you use while logged in to the remote site will differ from site to site.

Using Telnet

As with FTP, the actual command for negotiating a Telnet connection varies from system to system. The most common is Telnet itself. It takes the following form: **telnet somewhere.domain** (IP node name).

To begin, use your local system as a working example. Hopefully, you know your site's domain name. If not, ask someone or try to figure it out. You will not get by without it. To open the connection, type: *telnet your. system. name*. If the system were hollis.harvard.edu, for example, the command would look like **telnet hollis.harvard.edu**. The system will respond with something similar to:

Trying 168.26.284.777. . .
Connected to hollis.harvard.edu.
Escape character is '~]

The escape character, in this example] (Control-]), is the character that will let you go back to the local system to close or suspend the connection. To close this connection, the user would type *]*, and respond to the telnet> prompt with the command close. Local documentation should be checked for information on specific commands, functions and escape characters that can be used.

Searching with Telnet

When login is completed, if you are in a library computer or similar system, you may see a list of library catalogues available for you to search. There are also a set of database labels or abbreviations for these catalogues. In order to search a particular catalogue, you simply type the name of the database label for the catalogue you wish to use. For example, at Purdue University, in order to search the general book catalogue, type *PCAT*, then press Enter. Most libraries allow searching by one or more of the following categories: author, title, keyword or subject.

Both author and title searches are performed the same way, following these steps:

1 To search the Purdue library catalogue for books by William Theobald, type *a=theobald william*, then press Enter. The a= means you are searching by author, last name first. If you do not know the author's first name, you could still search for a=theobald. However, you would get a list of all Theobalds in the catalogue.

2 To search for the book, *Global Tourism: The Next Decade*, type *t=global tourism the next decade*, then press Enter.

The most common types of searches are usually keyword searches. By using keywords as search terms, you could determine everything about the work: author, title, publisher, subject, etc. To perform a keyword search, first type *k=theobald*, then press Enter. The catalogue will retrieve works by any Theobald, as well as works about Theobald, and works with Theobald in the title. Some libraries support Boolean searching, but only for keyword searching. In order to find materials that contain both 'Theobald' and 'global', you would type *k=theobald and tourism*, then press Enter.

The final type of search is by subject. When you search library catalogues by subject, you perform a series of controlled vocabulary subject headings that the Library of Congress, British Library, etc. assign to each of the materials in the catalogue. For example, if you want to browse the literature on the topic of tourism, you would type *s=tourism*, then press Enter. The results will be quite different from those of keyword searches. What you would see are, for example below, the Library of Congress subject classifications:

Tourism
Tourism–Economic Aspects
Tourism–Europe
Tourism–Europe–History–20th Century–Congresses
Tourism–India–Kumaun Region–Planning
Tourism–Management
Tourism–Marketing
Tourism–Planning–Handbooks, Manuals, etc.
Etc.

Hytelnet

Several hundred libraries around the world, from the Carmel Public Library in the state of Indiana to the Library of Congress are now available to you through Telnet. You can use a tool that helps bring Internet-accessible international library catalogues into a single directory, a tool to find their names, Telnet addresses and use instructions. That tool is called Hytelnet and its universal resource locator (URL) is: **http://www.lights.com/ hytelnet**. Presumably, it provides the most comprehensive site for accessing library catalogues from around the world.

Telnet sites are indexed geographically and by sponsor. The Web catalogues are additionally indexed by library type. The hypertext navigation of such enormous files is awkward, but the results are dependable. Although many other Internet resources, such as bulletin boards and directories are included, Hytelnet's is primarily intended as a gateway to library catalogues.

Why would you want to browse a library you can't physically get to? Many libraries share books, so if yours does not have what you are looking for, you can tell the librarian where he or she can get it. Or if you live in an area where the libraries are not yet online, you can use Telnet to do some basic bibliographic research before you head down to the local branch. The Hytelnet information page is located on the World Wide Web at **http://www.lights. com/hytelnet**. The World Wide Web version of Hytelnet is located at **http://moondog.usask.ca/hytelnet**.

Searching with Hytelnet

There are several different database programs in use by online libraries. Ohio State University is one of the easiest to use. For example, in order to use Hytelnet to access a library catalogue, try obtaining a list of the books written by Richard G. Kraus that are available through the Ohio State University library. Kraus is both a prominent and a prolific author in the area of recreation and leisure studies.

In order to begin your search with your web browser go to the Hytelnet web version **http://moondog.usask.ca/hytelnet**. First, follow the link to *Library Catalogues arranged geographically*, then to *The Americas*. The sequence following is to select the *US (by state)*, followed by *Ohio*, then the *Ohio State University Library*. The resulting page provides you with four pieces of information:

- the Telnet address that you use to access the catalogue
- no user name or logon name is required
- the name of the library catalogue used is INNOPAC
- the command that must be used to exit when the search is completed.

Follow the *INNOPAC* link to the information page, which summarizes searches by type: title, author, subject, keyword and other search options. You want to search for all the works by Richard G. Kraus, so type *a* to search by author. Next, type the author's name, *Kraus, Richard G.*, then press Enter. The results of your query indicate that there are thirty-seven entries for Richard G. Kraus. The names and call numbers are listed, and you can type the number of the entry you are interested in for more information.

Finally, it should be understood that although many library catalogues are only accessible via Telnet, the number available on the World Wide Web is increasing rapidly, and should continue to do so. In addition, quite often Telnet applications may be accessed through a web page(s) in relatively seamless fashion.

Internet-accessible libraries

It is now possible to access remotely many of the world libraries through the World Wide Web. In the past, Telnet has been the program of choice in order to access global libraries. However, an ever-increasing number of libraries, especially those associated with institutions of higher education have placed their catalogues and collections on the World Wide Web.

File Transfer Protocol

Although this chapter does not attempt to address the many resources available via FTP, it is impossible to discuss any type of resource on the Internet without mentioning the supporting information available exclusively via FTP. Because so many of documents exist only as an online file, these brief instructions on using FTP are provided. Be sure to check with local system administrators, library staff, or other support groups for specific information.

File Transfer Protocol provides the capability to connect to a remote computer, execute a few simple commands (such as listing the directory) and copy files to or from the remote computer very quickly. To accomplish these tasks it is necessary to connect to the machine you wish to transfer files to or from. Normally you would be allowed only to transfer files to or from your own accounts, but some computer administrators have set aside areas on their machines which can be accessed anonymously (i.e., without an identification or password) for the purpose of distributing documents, software and other files.

To use anonymous FTP, log on to your computer as usual. Enter the command *ftp <machine name or numeric address>*. When you are prompted to log on, enter *anonymous*. When you are prompted for your password, enter *guest* or your email address. You should then be connected to the remote machine and can use FTP commands to look at directories and transfer files.

Most web browsers allow you to download files using FTP. You might arrive at an FTP site through a link from a web page, or you can specify an FTP site using the ftp:// prefix in the address. There are also available share ware applications such as one for Microsoft Windows called 'WS_FTP.' If you have a problem or any difficulty using FTP, type *help* or *?* for a list of FTP commands or consult documentation.

Internet guides

There is a list of Internet-accessible libraries and databases (often called the 'St George directory' because it is maintained by Art St George and Ron Larsen) available over the Internet via anonymous ftp. The directory is available locally at **sunsite.unc.edu in pub/docs**, and the file name is **library.guide**. The guide is available at **nic.cerf.net** in the directory, **cerfnet/ cerfnet_info/library_catalogue**. The file name for the listing is **Internet- catalogs** and has a date suffix. Users should FTP the most recent date.

Originally only library catalogues were included but the list has now expanded to include sections on campus-wide information systems (CWIS), and even bulletin board systems that are not on the Internet. The library catalogue sections are divided into those that are free, those that charge and international catalogues; they are arranged by state, province or country within each section. There is also a section giving dial-up information for some of the library catalogues. The information is updated periodically.

A second helpful directory complementing the St George guide is maintained at North Texas State University and provides not only an alphabetic list of libraries by organization name, but also the Internet address, login and logoff instructions, system vendor and information on how to use the database. There is also a news group that announces new libraries on the net and discusses other related topics. The group is called comp.Internet.library. You may access the directory via anonymous FTP from **sunsite.unc.edu**. The file is in the directory **pub/docs** and the file name is **LIBRARIES.TXT**.

A third directory, CARL, is a network of libraries whose resources are made available as a group. By selecting services, you move from one library site to another. Users should remember that usually *//exit* will return you *home*, to Denver, the site you began with.

In addition to posting card catalogues on the network, CARL also makes available a large number of databases. 'Facts on File' and 'Choice Book Reviews' are two interesting database resources they offer. To reach CARL, you can either find them on the Web at **http://www.csc.edu/_server/ site_index/site_index.html** or Telnet to **pac.carl.org**. If you wish further information on CARL, send an email message to **help@carl.org**.

Major libraries on the World Wide Web

A number of major world libraries including the Library of Congress (US) and the British Library among many others, can be accessed directly through the World Wide Web.

The Library of Congress

The Library of Congress is the US nation's library. Its services extend not only to members and committees of the Congress, but also to the executive and judicial branches of government, to libraries throughout the nation and the world, and to the scholars and researchers and artists and scientists who use its resources.

The Library of Congress, founded in 1800 and housed in a three-building complex across from the nation's capitol in Washington, DC, is a storehouse for knowledge and an active centre for research and creativity of all kinds – the world's largest and most open library. With collections numbering close to 100 million items, it includes materials in 460 languages: the basic manuscript collections of twenty-three Presidents of the USA and the papers of thousands of other figures who have shaped history; maps and atlases that have aided explorers and navigators in charting both the world and outer space; the earliest motion pictures and examples of recorded sound; as well as the latest databases and software packages.

The Library of Congress contains copies of all the books (and nearly all the magazines and newspapers) published in the USA. Although at present, only approximately 20 000 of the most useful books have been prepared for individuals to access through the Internet, but a number of library groups are currently working to have the entire collection ready for the Internet. University libraries across the country (Harvard, Yale, Illinois and Michigan are the largest) house all types of foreign research material not found in the Library of Congress. The Library of Congress also:

- aids other libraries throughout the nation and the world by cataloguing new publications in all languages
- works with research libraries worldwide in the exchange of information and scholarship

- applies new technology to preserve, restore, and transmit library resources
- documents ethnic heritage in its folk life archives
- advances scholarship through a Council of Scholars.

The Library of Congress website

The Library of Congress (LC) can be accessed in order to find information about the materials from its collections over the Internet. Their website's home page can be found at **http://www.loc.gov**.

The library's home page offers the following options: performing a search, finding out what is new on the website or access to, among others, the following categories of information:

- General information and publications – publications; searching LC's web and Gopher sites
- Library services – acquisition and cataloguing; research and reference
- Databases and resources – Library of Congress Information System (LOCIS); access to catalogues at other libraries
- Library of Congress online catalogue

The Library of Congress utilizes the World Wide Web to present information about and materials from its collections over the Internet. Any of the following categories of information may be accessed:

- General Information and Publications
  - Greetings
  - About the Library of Congress
  - News and Events
  - Publications
  - Search LC's Web and Gopher Sites
- Library Services
  - Acquisitions
  - Cataloguing
  - Research and Reference
  - Preservation
  - Special Programs and Services
- American Memory Historical Collections
  - List of Collections and Topics
  - The Learning Page

- More Databases and Resources
    LOCIS
    - Vietnam Era POW/MIA Database
    - LC MARVEL (Gopher)
    - Access to Catalogs at Other Libraries
    - Library of Congress Public FTP Site
- THOMAS: Legislative Information
- LC Online Catalog
- United States Copyright Office
- Exhibitions
- Global Legal Information Network
- Country Studies: Area Handbook Program
- Information for Publishers
- Standards
- Explore the Internet

The Library of Congress Classification System (LC System) is used to organize books in many academic and university libraries throughout the USA and the world. The LC System organizes material in libraries according to twenty-one branches of knowledge. Those twenty-one categories (labelled A–Z except I, O, W, X and Y) are further divided by adding one or two additional letters and a set of numbers:

A – General Works
B – Philosophy, Psychology, Religion
C – Auxiliary Sciences of History
D – History: General and Outside the Americas
E – History: United States
F – History: United States Local and America
G – Geography, Anthropology, Recreation
H – Social Sciences
J – Political Science
K – Law
L – Education
M – Music
N – Fine Arts
P – Language and Literature
Q – Science
R – Medicine
S – Agriculture
T – Technology

U – Military Science
V – Naval Science
Z – Library Science and Information Resources

Two of the most useful services provided on the Internet by the Library of Congress are described below.

Library of Congress Information System

The Library of Congress Information System is simply an extremely large library catalogue. It provides information about an enormous number of materials, including books and non-print materials catalogued by the Library of Congress, federal legislation, copyrighted materials registered with the Library of Congress, Braille and audio materials, bibliographies for individuals conducting basic research, and foreign law materials.

The Library of Congress does not provide the full text of the materials available through LOCIS since most of the materials contained there are copyrighted. However, the system is very useful for retrieving information about published works, particularly when you want to go to a library to locate the material. Although LOCIS can be accessed through Telnet, the most user-friendly way is over the Web, using a search system (or standard) known as *Z39.50*.

Z39.50 is a national standard defining a protocol for computer-to-computer information retrieval. Z39.50 makes it possible for a user in one system to search and retrieve information from other computer systems (that have also implemented Z39.50) without knowing the search syntax that is used by those other systems. Using a Z39.50 client, it is currently possible to search the Library of Congress bibliographic and authority files. Information that will be required to configure your Z39.50 client to directly search the Library of Congress server is provided in the library's *Z39.50 Server Configuration Guidelines*.

Searching other catalogue databases

It is now possible to search other national and world databases through the Z39.50 standard protocol through links provided by the Library of Congress. However, in order to take advantage of the information stored on library databases, you need a web browser or application that is conversant with the Z39.50 standard. The following college/university and national/regional libraries can be accesses with the Z39.50 protocol:

Acadia University – Nova Scotia, Canada
Albion College – Albion, MI
Amarillo College
Auburn University
Bibliothèque nationale du Québec
BIBSYS – Norway
Boston University
Brandeis University
British Columbia Electronic Library Network
Brock University – Ontario, Canada
Brown University
Brunel University – UK
Butler University
Carnegie Mellon University
Center for Research Libraries
Central College – Pella, IA
Central Missouri State University
Chinese University of Hong Kong
College of the Holy Cross – Worcester, MA
College of William and Mary (SIRSI)
Colorado Alliance of Research Libraries:
    Aims Community College
Arapaho Community College
Colorado School of Mines
Colorado State Publications
Lamar Community College
Luther College
Morgan Community College
Northeastern Colorado Junior College
Northeastern University
Northeastern University Law
Otero Junior College
Pikes Peak Community College
Pueblo Community College
Red Rocks Community College
Regis College
Teikyo Loretto University
Trinidad Junior College
University of Wyoming
Colorado College
Connecticut State University

Cornell University
Cornerstone College – Grand Rapids, Mich.
OPAC (CURL OPAC Project) Database – Manchester, England
COWLNET Consortium – Kansas
Des Moines Area Community College
Drake University
Dublin City University
Duke University
École Polytechnique de Montréal – Quebec, Canada
Edgewood College – Madison, WI
Emory University
Florida Center for Library Automation:
   Florida A&M University
Florida Atlantic University
Florida Gulf Coast University
Florida International University
Florida State University
University of Central Florida
University of Florida
University of North Florida
University of South Florida
University of West Florida
Four Colleges Database:
   Amherst College
Hampshire College
Mt Holyoke College
Smith College
Francis Marion College – Florence, SC
Government Information Locator Service Test Database – at Index
   Data in Denmark
Grambling State University
Hamilton College – New York, NY
Hong Kong Academy of Performing Arts Hong Kong Institute of
   Education
Hong Kong University of Science and Technology
Hull University – UK
Illinois State Curriculum Center
Indiana State University Consortium
Indiana University
Iowa State Library
Iowa State University

Italian National Library Service – SBN Servizio Bibliotecario
    Nazionale
Keene State College – Keene, NH
Kentucky Community Colleges
Lehigh University – Bethlehem, PA
Lewis & Clark College – Portland, OR
LIBIS-Net–Belgium
LIBRIS – Swedish Union Catalogue
Lingnan College – Hong Kong
Loras College – Dubuque, IA
Louisiana Online University Information System (LOUIS):
    Delgado Community College
Louisiana State University
Louisiana State University–Alexandria
Louisiana State University–Eunice
Louisiana State University Law Library
Louisiana State University–Shreveport
Louisiana State University–Other Libraries
Louisiana Tech University
McNeese State University
Nicholls State University
Northeast Louisiana University
Northwestern State University
Nunez Community College
Southeastern Louisiana University
Southern University–New Orleans
Southern University–Shreveport/Bossier
Southern University Law Center
University of New Orleans
Maharishi University of Management – Fairfield, IA
MARMOT Consortium – Western Colorado:
    Adams State College
Colorado Mountain College Library
Colorado NW Community College
Fort Lewis College
Mesa State College
Massachusetts Institute of Technology
MEDLINE Database – National Library of Medicine
Memorial University of Newfoundland
Middlebury College
Michigan State University

Minnesota State Colleges and Universities/Project for Automated
   Library Services
Mississippi State University
Missouri Southern State College
Missouri Western State College
Murdoch University – Western Australia
NEOS Consortium – University of Alberta
New York University
Newcastle University
North Carolina Central Database:
   North Carolina Agricultural and Technical State University
Winston-Salem State University
North Carolina School of the Arts
North Carolina Central University
Fayetteville State University
Pembroke State University
University of North Carolina at Wilmington
North Carolina Western Database:
   Appalachian State University
University of North Carolina at Asheville
Western Carolina University
North Carolina State University
Northwestern University
Ohio State University
Oklahoma State University
Pennsylvania State University
Portland State University
Purdue University
Purdue University Calumet
Queen's University
Radford University
Rogers University – Tulsa, OK
Royal Melbourne Institute of Technology–Multimedia Database
   Systems Group
Seton Hall University Law Library
Simon Fraser University – British Columbia, Canada
Simpson College – Indianola, IA
Sonoma State University
South Bank University – UK
Spring Arbor College – Spring Arbor, MI
Spring Hill College – Mobile, AL

State Library of Western Australia–LISWA
Stonehill College – North Easton, Massachusetts
Strathclyde University – Scotland
Texas A & M University–Corpus Christi
Texas A & M University Database:
   Texas A & M University
Texas A & M University at Galveston
Prairie View A & M University
Texas A & M International University
UNILINC–Sydney, Australia
United States Military Academy, West Point
United States Naval Academy, Annapolis
Université Laval
University College – Cork, Ireland
University College, Galway – Ireland
University College of North Wales – Bangor, Wales
University of Alabama, Birmingham
University of Alabama, Huntsville
University of Arizona
University of Arkansas, Little Rock
University of California – MELVYL System
University of California, San Francisco
University of Colorado, Boulder
University of Connecticut Health Center Library
University of Iowa
University of Illinois, Chicago
University of Illinois, Urbana
University of Kentucky
University of Manitoba
University of Massachusetts at Amherst
University of Michigan
University of Michigan School of Business Administration
University of Michigan, Dearborn
University of Michigan, Flint
University of Minnesota
University of Nebraska–Lincoln
University of Nebraska–Omaha
University of New Brunswick
University of North Carolina at Chapel Hill
University of North Carolina at Greensboro
University of Northern Iowa

University of Oklahoma
University of Pennsylvania
University of Pennsylvania Law Library
University of Queensland
University of Saskatchewan
University of Scranton
University of South Carolina
University of South Alabama
University of Sydney
University of Toronto
University of Western Ontario
University of Wisconsin, Eau Claire
University of Wisconsin, Green Bay
University of Wisconsin, Lacrosse
University of Wisconsin, Madison
University of Wisconsin, Oshkosh
University of Wisconsin, Parkside
University of Wisconsin, Riverfalls
University of Wisconsin, Stevens Point
University of Wisconsin, Stout
University of Wisconsin, Whitewater
University of Wollongong – New South Wales, Australia
Utah State University
Virginia Commonwealth University
Wayne State University
Wellesley College
Western Washington University
Wheeling Jesuit University – Wheeling, WV
Wright State University
Yale University

The British Library

The British Library's collections represent every age of written civilization, every written language and every aspect of human thought. The collections contain over 150 million items and were developed over 250 years. Individual collections have their own separate catalogues, often built up around specific subject areas. The collections include:

■ The national archive of monographs and serials received by legal deposit.

- Rich holdings of books and serials from overseas.
- The national archive of British and overseas newspapers.
- Western and oriental manuscripts from the beginning of writing to the present.
- The archives, library, prints, drawings, and photographs assembled by the former India Office.
- One of the world's finest collections of printed and manuscript music.
- One of the world's most important collections of printed and manuscript maps.
- Internationally important holdings of philatelic material.
- One of the world's largest archives of sound recordings and videograms.
- Business information in many forms.
- The world's largest collection of patent specifications.
- The world's largest collection of conference proceedings.
- Millions of UK and overseas reports and theses in microform.

Information about services provided by the British Library **http:/ /www.bl.uk** can be found from their *Portico* Service, and *OPAC*, their centralized online catalogue which offers access to a number of bibliographic databases covering Science, Social Science, Arts and Humanities, Engineering as well as a contents page. They provide:

- Reading Room and enquiry services for:
  - Humanities and social sciences – early and modern printed collections
  - Manuscripts
  - Music
  - Maps
  - Official publications
  - Philatelic material
  - Newspapers
  - Sound recordings
  - Oriental and India Office material
  - Library and information science
  - Science, technology and business
  - Patents
  - Material for loan held at Boston Spa
- A range of document supply services:
  - Document Supply Centre
  - Patent Express
  - British Library Reproductions

- Specialist information services:
  - Science and Technology Information Service
  - Business Information Service
  - Patents Information
  - Environmental Information Service
  - Medical Information Service
  - IRS-Dialtech (the UK national centre for the European Space Agency Information Retrieval System)
- Services for the library and information community:
  - Research sponsorship
  - Consultancy services
  - National Bibliographic Service
  - National Preservation Office
- Services for a wider public:
  - Exhibitions
  - Education Service
  - Events
  - Publications
  - The Friends of the British Library
  - The Centre for the Book
  - Eccles Centre for American Studies

OPAC 97

OPAC 97 is a relatively new service which provides free access via the World Wide Web clickable from **http://www.bl.uk** to the catalogues of the major British Library collections. It provides the opportunity to discover what material is held in the major Reference and Document Supply collections of the British Library. In many cases it is possible to request copies of documents from the library's Document Supply Centre. At present, individual collections have their own separate catalogues, often built up around specific subject areas. Many of the library's plans for its collections, and for meeting its users' needs, require the development of a single catalogue database which is being planned. An online OPAC 97 catalogue is available via the Internet.

At present, however, OPAC 97 can provide information about the contents of a number of the library's major collections. When researching a particular topic it is advisable to consult with the collection areas involved to ensure that all possible resources have been discovered since some may only appear in printed catalogues or indexes. Many areas have their pages on Portico or can be contacted by email, fax or telephone.

Reference collections represented on OPAC 97

1 Modern books and periodicals from Britain and overseas
2 Humanities and Social Sciences collection (1975–)
3 Science, Technology and Business collection (1975–)
4 Music collection (1980–)
5 Older books and periodicals from Britain and overseas
6 Older reference material collection (to 1975 only)

Document Supply collections represented on OPAC 97

1 Books, reports and theses collection (1980–)
2 Journals/Serials collection (1700–)
3 Conferences collection (1800–)

List of printed catalogues

1 British National Bibliography
2 British Library General Catalogue of Printed Books
3 Current Serials Received
4 Serials in the British Library
5 Index of Conference Proceedings
6 Eighteenth Century Short Title Catalogue
7 Incunable Short Titles Catalogue
8 Index of Manuscripts in the British Library
9 Catalogue of the Newspaper Library
10 British National Bibliography for Report Literature

For a wider range of databases and many additional facilities the British Library offers Blaise, a priced online bibliographic information service, and Inside, offering article title records from 20 000 journals and 16 000 conferences.

Blaise

Blaise is the British Library's Automated Information Service, an online information retrieval service **http:www.bl.uk** that includes access via a fee-based subscription that provides a user-friendly graphical interface on the World Wide Web. Blaise provides access to twenty-one databases containing over 18.5 million bibliographic records. It provides bibliographic records for material ranging from the very first printed books to the most up-to-date scientific report literature. Coverage extends to all subject areas and all countries in the form of books, periodicals, reports, conference proceedings, theses, official publications, printed sheet music and maps.

Many organizations in the UK and abroad subscribe to Blaise. However, Blaise is only one of a number of gateways to subscription (fee-based) databases available on the Web such as Dialog **http://www.dialog. com**. For information about local access to British Library online catalogues and databases, one should consult a university library or the nearest public library.

Inside

Inside **http://www.bl.uk** opens up the British Library's journal and conference collection to researchers, librarians and information professionals in education, business and government worldwide, providing users with instant access to one of the world's greatest sources of knowledge. Inside is currently available on the World Wide Web and on CD-ROM.

Gabriel

Gabriel is the World Wide Web server for Europe's national libraries represented in the Conference of European National Librarians (CENL). Gabriel aims to help bring national libraries in Europe closer together by providing a single point of access for the retrieval of information about their functions, services and collections. Gabriel may be accessed through the British Library's OPAC 97 service at **http://www.bl/uk**.

British university libraries

Catalogues of UK university libraries can be accessed via the National Information Services and Systems (NISS) Information Gateway located on the Web at **http://ihr.sas.ac.uk/ihr/niss.html**. Another gateway to NISS and the library catalogues is through **http://www.niss.ac.uk/ reference/index.html**. There is also a news group that announces new libraries on the Internet and discusses other related topics. The group is called comp.Internet.library. Finally, a good list of UK CWIS can be found at **http:/ /www.niss.ac.uk/education/hesites.cwis.html**.

Campus-wide information services

In addition to over 100 online library catalogues, the Internet also provides access to a growing number of campus-wide information systems. A current list of such systems is provided at the end of each release of 'Internet-Accessible Library Catalogues and Databases'. An electronic conference which discusses campus information systems is maintained on the list server at **CWIS-L@WUVMD.BITNET**.

The types of information and search capabilities provided by these systems vary widely. Common components include library hours; local campus news and information; activities and events calendars; directories of staff, services, organizations and computing facilities; course schedules and catalogues; employment and financial aid opportunities; descriptions of the campus and academic programmes and policies.

Specialized information databases

The offerings of the Internet extend far beyond library catalogues. One can also access various databases sponsored by other organizations, many with reference value. Many systems do not require a password, and for those that do, obtaining a password is often as simple as filling out an application.

It is difficult to categorize these databases since they are hybrids. They are often co-sponsored by government agencies and university departments, or funded by grants. Their content ranges from full text documents to statistics, and can include directories of researchers, bibliographies, schedules of research activities, or information on research in progress. They are also more difficult to identify than library catalogues since they are not tied together with a common administrative structure or service goal. The various network information centers are currently the best resources for finding out about these databases. Information may be posted to various list servers as they are discovered.

Companion databases to online catalogues

In addition to book and serials holdings, many online library catalogues provide access to locally mounted commercial databases or locally developed databases. Commercial databases range from major periodical and newspaper indexes such as the National Newspaper Index, to encyclopaedias and dictionaries, to current awareness and statistical sources. Due to contractual agreements, access to most of the commercial databases is restricted to the user community of the purchasing library. Occasionally, systems suppress the restricted databases from screens presented to Internet users; systems usually offer them as choices, but Internet users who are not eligible for passwords are denied access.

Examples of locally developed databases include indexes to local newspapers; library pathfinders; an index to television scripts; and regional statistics. These databases generally are open to outside users with no restrictions.

Selected sites accessible through links

Listed below are a selective list of sites that can be accessed through links provided by the Library of Congress. Unless otherwise noted, the sites listed in this directory are provided by organizations outside the Library of Congress and are offered as a convenience and for informational purposes.

General resources

- Finding Internet Resources in Library and Information Science (Lund University, Sweden)
- Library and Information Science (EINET Galaxy)
- Library and Information Science Resources (University of Denver)
- Library and Related Resources (University of Exeter)
- Libraries: Information Science (Yahoo)
- Libraries on the World Wide Web (Victoria Telecommunity Network)
- Library Resources on the Internet (Northwestern University)
- News Flashes/Libraries (H. W. Wilson Company)
- PICK: Quality Internet Resources in Library and Information Science (University of Wales)
- WWW Subject Tree: Library and Information Science (BUBL Information Service)

National libraries

USA

- The Library of Congress (USA)
- US National Library of Medicine
- US Department of Education Library
- The National Agricultural Library

Foreign

- Gabriel – Gateway to Europe's National Libraries
- National Library of Australia

- National Library of Austria
- National Library of Belgium
- The British Library
- National Library of Canada
- National Library of the Czech Republic
- Royal Library of Denmark
- National Library of France
- National Library of Germany
- National Library of Ireland
- National Library of Lithuania
- National Library of Malaysia
- National Library of The Netherlands
- National Library of New Zealand
- National Library of Norway
- National Library of Scotland
- National Library of the Slovak Republic
- National Library of Slovenia
- National Library of Spain
- Royal Library of Sweden
- National Library of Switzerland
- National Library of Turkey
- National Library of Wales

Library home pages

- The Canadian Library Index
- Libraries
- LIBWEB: Library Servers via WWW
- Medical/Health Sciences Libraries on the Web
- Nordic Libraries: Information Servers
- School Libraries on the Web: A Directory
- UK Higher Education and Research Libraries

Online catalogues

- Book and Library Catalogues
- INNOPAC Libraries on the Internet
- Library Catalogues
- Library Catalogues via Gopher
- Library Catalogues via Z39.50
- Online Library Catalogues

- Online Catalogues with 'Webbed' Interfaces
- webCATs: Library Catalogues on the World Wide Web

Research and reference

- Full Text and Ready-Reference Resources
- Internet Public Library Reference Center
- Ready Reference Using the Internet
- Virtual Reference Desk

Technical services

- ACQ Web
- Interactive Electronic Serials Catalogueing Aid
- Cataloguing Resources

Professional organizations (lists)

- Resources of Scholarly Societies – Library and Information Science
- American Library Association
- Association of College and Research Libraries
- Library and Information Technology Association
- American Society for Information Science
- Association of Research Libraries
- Coalition for Networked Information
- International Federation of Library Associations and Institutions
- Internet Library Association

There are now a large number of publishers making academic journals available on the World Wide Web, although they are often not the same as the printed versions. Often, they are made available by consolidators such as the Information Access Company **http://www.searchbank.com**. Library catalogues are increasingly continuing to develop cataloguing resources on the Web and are providing links to those resources as well as to academic journals.

8

University and college resources worldwide

Learning, the Internet and the World Wide Web

In its earliest form, distance education meant study by correspondence. Typical audiences for early distance education courses were adults who often sought advanced education or training at home, on the job, or in the military since their multiple responsibilities or physical circumstances prevented attendance at a traditional institution. As new technologies developed, distance instruction was delivered through such media as audio and videotape, radio and television broadcasting, and satellite transmission. Microcomputers, the Internet and the World Wide Web are shaping the current generation of distance learning. Now anyone is potentially a distance learner, a concept that has profound implications for the organization of educational institutions and for teaching.

Learning in cyberspace

Perhaps more than any other distance media, the Internet and the World Wide Web have helped overcome the barriers of time and space in teaching and learning. Educational uses of the Internet are burgeoning. The University of Wisconsin's Extension Distance Education Clearinghouse lists numerous institutions offering online instruction **http://www.uwex.edu. home.html.disted**. The magazine, *Internet World*'s October 1995 issue provides examples of 'The Internet in Education' including online degree programs offered by such traditional institutions as Penn State and Indiana Universities as well as non-traditional entities like University Online and the Global Network Academy.

Internet learning in higher education may take one of the following forms:

1 Email (delivery of course materials, returning assignments, giving or receiving feedback or using a course LISTSERV.
2 Bulletin boards/newsgroups for discussion of special topics.
3 Downloading of course materials or tutorials.
4 Interactive tutorials on the Web.
5 Real-time, interactive conferences using multi-user object-oriented systems or Internet relay chat.
6 The use of online databases, library catalogues, gopher and websites to acquire information and to pursue study-related research.

The advantages of delivering distance learning on the Internet include time and place flexibility, the potential of reaching global audiences, problem-free computer equipment and operating system compatibility, rapid development time, ease of updating and archiving content and, in most cases, low development and operating costs. Carefully designed Internet courses may enhance the interaction between instructors and learners, as well as among learners. A benefit of online learning is the relative anonymity of computer communication that has the potential to give voice to those students reluctant to speak in face-to-face situations. In addition it allows learner contributions to be judged on their own merit, unaffected by visual cultural markers. However, although the Internet has the potential to promote active learning, like television, it can also breed passivity.

Electronic tourism and leisure courses

Colleges and universities have had a presence on the Internet since its inception and are a rich source of information. This chapter provides information available from schools, departments and/or programmes in institutions of higher education, online educational institutions and online related courses, course materials, seminars and tutorials that deal with tourism and leisure subjects.

Whether people are professors, students, researchers or professionals, they will find the Internet invaluable. For example, if they wish to learn about marketing and their schedule or location prohibits attending classes, they can take an online course or even design their own self-study programme with online materials. Then, as they prepare a report, rather than reaching for an unabridged dictionary or thesaurus, they may log on to the Internet and look up the word in an up-to-date, perhaps even an interactive, dictionary.

If the user is a prospective master's degree student, a manager who wishes to research a topic in-depth, or a business owner who needs to consult with an academic expert, he or she may indeed find what he or she is looking for in this section. Almost every university worldwide has at least one address on the Internet. Those institutions with tourism and/or leisure departments or programmes may also often be found there. The chapter contains lists from which one may look up appropriate departments and programmes at colleges and universities worldwide. Also included are their home page addresses, where known.

CASO's Internet University

Cape software (CASO) is an indexing service [*sic*] Internet University website located at **http://www.caso.com**. Their website maintains an index of 2636 accredited courses, together with course descriptions that are available via the Internet. CASO does not teach any of the courses they list. Rather, they are taught by eighty-two colleges and universities located throughout the USA.

Examples of Internet courses currently available in the tourism, hospitality or leisure fields include the following undergraduate offerings:

1 Bed & Breakfast Management (HTM112) 3 cr. Email/WWW. Chemeketa Community College, Salem, Oregon
2 Cultural Heritage Tourism (HTM 111) 3 cr. WWW. Chemeketa Community College
3 Dynamics of Outdoor Recreation (R271) 3 cr. Indiana University, Bloomington
4 Food and Beverage Management (X407) 4 cr. UCLA (University of California at Los Angeles)
5 Hospitality Management (HFT1000) 3 cr. WWW. Brevard Community College, Hornbrook, California
6 Hospitality Marketing (HRMG205) 3 cr. SUNY (State University of New York, Albany, New York)
7 International Travel and Tourism (GY320) 3 cr. Auburn University, Auburn, Alabama
8 Introduction to the Hospitality Industry (HRMG100) 3 cr. SUNY, Albany
9 Introduction to the Hospitality Industry (HTM100) 3 cr. WWW. Chemeketa Community College
10 Leisure and Recreation Industry (HTM108) 3 cr. WWW. Chemeketa Community College
11 Marketing Hospitality Services (X491B) 4 cr. University of California at Los Angeles (UCLA)
12 Meeting and Convention Management (HTM126) 3 cr. WWW, Chemeketa Community College
13 Recreational Sports Programming (R324) 3 cr. Indiana University, Bloomington
14 Tourism Principles and Practice (BA160) 3 cr. University of Alaska, Fairbanks
15 US Destinations and Domestic Ticketing (TT131) 3 cr. SUNY, Albany
16 Worldwide Exposition Management (HRTM133) 3 cr. WWW. Golden Gate University, San Francisco, California
17 Worldwide Special Event Tourism (HRTM138) 3 cr. WWW. Golden Gate University

University of Wisconsin

The Instructional Communications Systems at the University of Wisconsin – Extension Service home page is **http://www.uwex.edu/disted/**. They offer the following courses in hospitality and tourism:

- Hospitality, Industry Law and Liability, 245-625(60)
- Hospitality, Industry Law and Liability, 245-626(60)
- Issues in Hospitality and Tourism
- Lodging Administration

Tourism and Hospitality Resource Centre

The Professional Development Institute of Tourism, a registered Hotel School located in British Columbia (Canada) is an academic partner with the Educational Institute of the American Hotel and Motel Association. The Institute's home page, **http://www.island.net/~htm/tourism3.html** provides links to:

- a selected number of organizations in the hospitality industry
- a selected number of colleges and universities offering tourism and/or hospitality degree programmes.

Hospitality organizations

American Hotel and Motel Association (AH&MA) Educational
  Institute
Pacific Rim Institute of Tourism (PRIT)
Hospitality Training & Management Consultants
Hotel and Catering International Management Association (HCIMA)
Internet Hospitality Index Hotel Chains
Culinary Resources on the World Wide Web

Colleges and university hospitality programmes

Algonquin College Hospitality Centre
Alpine Center for Hotel and Tourism Management Studies, Athens,
  Greece
Australian International Hotel School
Bethlehem University Institute Of Hotel Management and Tourism,
  Palestine
Boston University, School of Hospitality Administration
Brigham Young University, Hawaii Hospitality Programme
California State Polytechnic University, Pomona
Camosun College Victoria, British Columbia
Capilano College North Vancouver, British Columbia

Centre International de Glion

César Ritz Program at I.C.T.H.M., Sydney, Australia

Champlain College, Burlington, Vermont

Commercial Sciences University, Managua. Nicaragua

Conrad N. Hilton College of Hotel and Restaurant Management

Cornell University School of Hotel Administration

Ecole hôtelière de Lausanne

Euro CHRIE, Hotel Management School, Leeuwarden

Florida International University

Haaga Institute Polytechnic

Hawaii Pacific University, Travel Industry Management Program

Hospitality and Tourism Institute at Seattle Central Community
College/Washington State University

Hotel – Restaurant and Travel Administration, University of
Massachusetts

Hotel Institute Montreux, Switzerland

Hotel School Den Haag

Hotel School Glion, Montreux

Hotelschool Ter Duinen Koksijde Belgium

Hotelschool The Hague, Netherlands

Institut Hotelier 'César Ritz' Le Bouveret, Switzerland

International College of Hospitality Administration (ICHA) Brig,
Switzerland

International Institute of Tourism Studies, George Washington
University, Washington, DC

Kansas State University, Hotel, Restaurant, Institution Management
and Dietetics

Malaspina University College Nanaimo, British Columbia

Manchester Metropolitan University, Dept. of Hotel, Catering and
Tourism Management

Michigan State University

The New England Culinary Institute

New Hampshire College, Division of Hospitality Administration

North Island College Courtenay, British Columbia

Oklahoma State University School of Hotel and Restaurant
Administration

Oxford Brookes University

Pennsylvania State University, School of Hotel, Restaurant and
Recreation Management

Professional Development Institute of Tourism, Parksville, British
Columbia

Purdue University School of Restaurant, Hotel, Institutional and
   Tourism Management
Robert Gordon University, School of Food and Consumer Studies,
   Aberdeen, Scotland
Ryerson School of Hospitality and Tourism Management
School of Hotel and Catering, Galway, Ireland
School of Hotel and Restaurant Management
School of Hotel Management, Neuchâtel, Switzerland
Scottish Hotel School, University of Strathclyde, Glasgow
Shannon College of Hotel Management, Ireland
Southern Cross University, Australia
Swiss Hospitality Institute 'César Ritz' (SHI), USA
Temasek Polytechnic, Singapore
Thames Valley University, London
Tourism Training Institute
Trajal Hospitality and Tourism College, Tokyo, Japan
University College of the Cariboo, Kamloops, British Columbia
University of Brighton
University of Central Florida
University of Delaware, Hotel, Restaurant and Institutional
   Management Program
University of Guelph, School of Hotel and Food Administration
University of Missouri at Columbia
University of Queensland
University of San Francisco Hospitality Management
University of Surrey
University of Ulster
University of Utah Department of Recreation and Leisure
University of Wisconsin-Stout
Virginia Polytechnic Institute
Widener University, School of Hospitality Management

INFOTEC-TRAVEL

The purpose of INFOTEC-TRAVEL (**http://www.infotec-travel.com**)
is to provide subscribers with a moderated Internet emailing list dedicated to
the exchange of information about information technology in travel and
tourism worldwide. There are a number of selected links to online tourism
education sites including indices, schools and distance education.

Indices

Air Traveler's Handbook: Travel Careers
ASTA Travel School Members
Carl Braunlich's Tourism Hospitality Education Links
European Association for Tourism and Leisure Education Links
Education Tourism/Service Management
Excite Careers and Education: Hotel and Tourism
Hospitality Industry Links: Academic Institutions
Hyde's Travel Agent Resource: Education
Internet Hospitality Index: Hospitality Schools
Travel and Tourism sites: Educational
Rene Waksberg's Tourism Research Links: Schools
Harrah College of Hotel Administration: Educational Resources
UR Hospitality – Hotel School Links
USNews – edu: Travel/Hospitality – Hot Job Tracks
Yahoo! – Business_and_Economy: Companies: Travel: Schools

Schools

Alpine Center for Hotel and Tourism Management Studies
Echols International Travel Training
Education Systems Center for Travel Education
Griffith University Faculty of Business and Hotel Management
Heritage and Interpretive Tourism
Hosta Hotel and Tourism School
Institute of Certified Travel Agents
McConnell School, The
Michigan State University
Mundus World Institute for Travel and Tourism Studies
Purdue University Restaurant, Hotel, Institutional, and Tourism
Management
Southern Cross University School of Tourism and Hospitality
University of Westminster Department of Tourism

Distance education

AFTA Education and Training Australian Federation of Travel Agents
Education and Training's Internet-based IATA (International Air
Transport Association) Fares and Ticketing Refresher

Course preview
Cyber Travel Specialist
Tourism Education Network
Travel Education Center Distance Learning
Travel Navigator University

Other college and university resources

1 American universities on the World Wide Web **http://www.clas. ufl.edu/CLAS/american-universities.html**. In order to research US institutions of higher education offering undergraduate and graduate degrees, this website located at the University of Florida provides an alphabetically arranged, non-graphical list of websites.

2 College and university home pages worldwide **http://www. mit.edu:8001/people/cdemello/univ.html**. This website is considered by many to provide the most thorough and comprehensive links to colleges and universities worldwide. Non-graphical institutional information is provided alphabetically and also can be searched by letter. There is a link to the previous website (University of Florida) as well as links to mirror sites, one of which provides the same list, but arranged by geographic region.

3 Colleges, universities and other educational resources **http:/ /www.nosc.mil:80/planet_earth/uni.html**. At this website, the originator of the Planet Earth home page virtual library provides 'rooms' that contain a wide variety of resources. One such location, The Education Room, provides alphabetically arranged links to institutions of higher education. In addition, other education-related links include school rankings, telephone directories, faculty and staff home pages, and information about scholarships, careers and jobs.

4 Comprehensive list of academic servers **http://www.netgen.com/ cgi/comprehensive**. Located at Net Genesis, an index is provided listing every World Wide Web site at a college or university. If one wishes to obtain the list (quite long) of all edu servers contained in the index, select edu from the list box, then click on the Select button.

5 Universities arranged by country **http:www.yahoo.com/ Education/Universities/**. The search engine Yahoo provides a number of 'hot' links to colleges and universities by country of location, arranged alphabetically. For example, when selecting a country, in addition to viewing a complete listing of higher education institutions, there are often a number of indexes also provided.

Teaching materials, syllabi and course outlines

There are a wide and varied number of educational materials related to teaching and course work located on the World Wide Web. You may do a focused search for particular subjects using Boolean operators (connecting words that may be used to indicate the relationship among keywords in your search). For example, if you wished to locate courses in recreation or tourism subjects you might type *courses AND recreation OR tourism NOT golf*. Such a command would elicit those recreation and tourism courses found by a search engine, but would eliminate other unwanted subjects such as 'golf courses'. By using the infoseek search engine to execute the command above, infoseek found 1003 results including the following:

1 Teaching – **http://www.wau.nl/wrt/teach.html**
2 Department of Health and Leisure – **http://,www2.semo.edu/health/**
3 School of Environmental and Recreation Management – Courses – **http://www.unisa.edu.au/erm/Courses/home.htm**
4 Food Technopole – Partners – Sheffield Hallam University – **http://www.humber.ac.uk/technopole/partners/sheff.html**
5 Tourism management courses – **http://www.usiu.edu/courtour.htm**
6 Hotel, catering and tourism management: undergraduate courses – **http://www.doc.mmu.ac.uk/hol/ugcours1.html**
7 CCR Reef Research Centre online: Exploring Reef Science – **http://www.gbrmpa.gov.au/~crcreef/4news/Exploring/feat12.html**
8 UCDGSB Travel – **http://www.ucd.ie/gsb/courses/tourism.html**.

The following Web locations provide information on a number of courses that may be found online.

World Lecture Hall

http://wwwhost.cc.utexas.edu/world//instruction. This site located at the University of Texas is an alphabetical list of forty-six course categories from which one may see how faculty members at US colleges and universities are using the World Wide Web for distributing course information, schedules, lecture notes, assignments, examinations and online textbooks.

For example, World Lecture Hall provides, among others, course outlines and/or syllabi for such courses as:

1 Natural Resource Management (Management Category)
2 Research and the Internet (Business Category)
3 Marketing Strategies in Hospitality and Tourism (Marketing Category)
4 Recreation Geography Outline (Geography Category)

The Global Network Academy

http://uu-gna.mit.edu:8001/uu-gna/. The Global Network Academy is a consortium of educational institutions that provide online courses or serve institutions providing such courses. These online courses include a number of business and management courses that relate to leisure and tourism including marketing, development, information systems and strategic planning.

Online courses

The Internet provides you with the opportunity of studying course materials informally, or you may also take formal for-credit courses. For example, you may wish to find out how to market an organization or company on the Internet by reviewing the Research Program on Marketing in Computer-Mediated Marketing Environments. Although there are few subject-specific leisure and tourism available, nevertheless, there are two related courses of interest in management and business:

1 Economics of Businesses, Consumers and Markets – this online course **http://www.Vanderbilt.edu:80/Owen/froeb/mgt322/ mgt322.html** located at Vanderbilt University includes syllabus, lecture notes, problem sets and a reading list. Related to corporate strategies and international business, topics include among others, production and cost, demand and supply of foreign exchange, pricing and insurance, and managing service quality.
2 Research Program on Marketing in Computer-Mediated Marketing Environments and Interactive Marketing on the Internet – also located at Vanderbilt University, this site **http://www2000.ogsm.Vanderbilt. edu/links.cgi** deals with marketing on the Internet, and includes links to other marketing and advertising materials. Especially useful are lists of marketing: journals, research and resources.

Conferences and meetings

Whether you plan to attend a professional meeting or conference, this section provides information by listing conferences, expositions, meetings and trade shows by name, location and date.

Internet Conference Calendar

http://conference.calendar.com. This website provides up-to-date information on academic conferences and symposia, workshops, expositions, seminars and training courses. Three types of searches are available to users:

1 Simple search – by city, venue or event.
2 General search – by event, city, state, country, type of event or date.
3 Browse – by city, state or country.

EXPOguide

http://www.expoguide.com. The EXPOguide website provides a comprehensive listing of conferences, trade shows and expositions as well as providing specific information on conference services, associations and other related resources. You may search conferences alphabetically by name, location, date or keyword(s).

Conference Service Providers

Although this site suggests that it is under construction **http://www. netins.net/showcase/message/csp_home.html**, nevertheless, it provides ten extremely valuable links offering products and services that can assist in the conference process. These links include: Associations; Publications; Listings; Bureaus; Facilities; Internet; Logistics and Management; Miscellaneous Services; Producers; and Software.

Associations

American Society of Association Executives (ASAE)
Association of Conference and Events Directors – International ACED-I
International Association for Exposition Management (IAEM)
International Association Managers, Inc. (IAMI)

International Association of Conference Centers (IACC)
International Association of Fairs and Expositions (IAFE)
International Institute of Convention Management
Meeting Professionals International (MPI)

Conference industry publications

Exhibitor Magazine
Successful Meetings Magazine

Conference listing services

avinfo Trade Show Calendar
Computer Trade Show Calendar
Conference Listings
Internet Conference Calendar
Knowledge Web, Conference Listings
Medical Conferences and Meetings
Meetings and Events
Technical Conference Information Center
Trade Show Central

Convention and visitors bureaux

Alachua County, FL, USA
Anchorage, AK, USA
Atlanta, GA, USA
Birmingham, AL, USA
Champaign-Urbana, IL, USA
Charlotte, NC, USA
Colorado Springs, CO, USA
Cornwall, Ontario, Canada
Durham, NC, USA
Emerald Coast, FL, USA
Fairbanks, AK, USA
Fairfax County, VA, USA
Fort Smith, AR, USA
Fresno City, CA, USA
Greensboro, NC, USA
Hartford, CT, USA
Huntsville, AL, USA

Iceland Based in Reykjavik, Iceland
Kalamazoo, MI, USA
Kansas City, KS, USA
Lisboa, Portugal
Madison, WI, USA
Melbourne/Palm Bay, FL, USA
Miami, FL, USA
Montreal, Canada
Nagoya, Japan
Napa Valley, CA, USA
Nashville, TN, USA
Oneida County, Utica, NY, USA
Orlando/Orange County Florida, USA
Pennsylvania Dutch, PA, USA
Peoria, IL, USA
Philadelphia, PA, USA
Prince Edward Island, Canada
Sacramento, CA, USA
Salt Lake City, UT, USA
San Diego, CA, USA
Santa Fe, NM, USA
Santa Fe, NM, USA Sarasota, FL, USA
Scottsdale, AZ, USA

Facilities

Austin Convention Center, Austin, TX, USA
Chauncey Conference Center Princeton, NJ, USA
Ernest N. Morial Convention Center, New Orleans, LA, USA
Four Seasons Biltmore, Santa Barbara, CA, USA
George R. Brown Convention Center Houston, TX, USA
Georgia International Convention Center College Park, GA, USA
Grand Wailea Resort, Hotel & Spa, Maui, HI, USA
Hotel Roanoke and Conference Center, Roanoke, VA, USA
Hotel Sheraton Padova Corso, Argentina
Le Meridien New Orleans, New Orleans, LA, USA
Monterey Conference Center Monterey, CA, USA
Ramada Valley Ho Resort Scottsdale, AZ
Rancho Velencia Resort, San Diego, CA, USA
Salt Palace Convention Center, Salt Lake City, UT, USA
San Ysidro Ranch, Santa Barbara, CA, USA

Sun Valley Resort
Sydney Convention and Exhibition Centre, Darling Harbour, Australia
The Beaver Run Resort and Convention Center, Breckenridge, CO, USA
The Carter Center, Atlanta, Georgia, USA
The Coleman Center, New York, NY, USA
The Toll House Hotel, Los Gatos, CA, USA
Waterfront Plaza Hotel, Oakland, CA, USA

Internet resources

Association Network (information and resources for association executives, volunteers, meeting planners and consultants)
CyberEXPO
Event Planner (national Internet resource for event planning)
EventSource Community Uniting the Events Industry
Exhibitor Network from Exhibitor Magazine
Ferberts Internet Conference Registration Services [Image]
Florida's Internet Meeting Planners Site (IMPS) [Image]
Meeting Industry Mall
Meeting Resources an Index
Meeting Managers Association Meeting Planning Guide
The Meeting & Event Planning Center

Logistics and meeting management

Administrative Headquarters, Inc.
Ardenne International, Inc. Nova Scotia, Canada
Concepts Meeting Management CA, USA
Conference Planners, Inc. GA, USA
CONFERON, Inc. Meeting Planning Excellence
Coombs Productions, Inc.
Creative Expos and Conferences
Creative Management Services
Desa, Inc SC, USA
Destination St Louis, Inc., St Louis, MO, USA
Island Conferences and Events (along Georgia's colonial coast)
Jennie McNeill Enterprises, LLC New Orleans, LA, USA
JG&A Conference Producers in the UK
Meetings Management Group
Meeting Planning, Corporate Event and Destination Management Services

Perfectum Croatian Provider of Trade Show and Exhibitions
QTW – Conference, Meeting and Incentive Planning
Southern California Destination Management
Talley Management Group, Inc.
Tradeshow Network, Inc.
UK Sound and Vision Ltd, Worcestershire, England

Miscellaneous services

Banner Graphics (graphic banners, etc.)
Bright Life, Inc. Miami, FL, USA (decorative plants and foliage
   rental)
Causal Productions
Conference Publication on CD-ROM
Colorado Convention Connection
Conference Copy Inc. (conference recording services)
DISCscribe's Conference Documentation (documentation services)
Dynamic Magic Productions (entertainment services)
Edward Enterprises (quality printing for Hawaiian meetings)
Expertspace (experts, speakers, and conference talent)
Florida Speakers Association
Gerry Reid Speaking
HLC.net Show Services (Internet conference services)
IES Meeting Evaluation Services
Just You Naturally Image Services
Las Vegas Information Cybernet
Life Enhancement and Wellness Speakers List
M DOC Modular Custom Exhibits[Image]
Mike Powell Exhibitions European Exhibition Services[Image]
National Motorcoach Network (shuttle conference transportation)
Professional Balloon Decorating
Show Boat Agency
Speakers On-Line
Speakers, Consultants and Entertainment Directory
The Gifted Basket Gift Baskets
Westin Hotels, Meeting and Convention Services

Producer organizations (conference)

Advanstar Expositions Trade Shows and Exhibitions
American Show Management, Inc.

Blenheim
Graphic Arts Show Company, Inc.
Softbank Expos
21st Century Technology Events

Software providing specific conference-related functions

HOTELogic (search tool for over 35 000 hotels)
Quickspace (supplier of meeting computer technology information)
The Message Board System Conference Communications System
   (in-conference communications mechanism)

Tourism Conference Database

This database, listing the upcoming three months' tourism-related conferences and trade shows, is compiled by the Tourism Reference and Documentation Centre (TRDC) at the Canadian Tourism Commission in Ottawa, Ontario, Canada. Although not accessible through the World Wide Web, nevertheless, it is available by email to members of both the TRINET and MAILBASE 'tourism and hospitality' lists (see Chapter 10). For more information about the database or to add to it, you should contact the TRDC at *613-954-3943* (telephone), *613-954-3945* (fax), or by email at *trdc.ctc@ic.gc.ca*.

Other conference websites

Three additional conference postings include:

1 Therapeutic recreation conferences and workshops held throughout the world **http://www.pacificnet.net/computernet/trconf.htm** – in addition to lists of upcoming conferences and workshops, users may also submit conference or workshop information.
2 Travel-related conferences **http://www.cyberwonders.com/conf. html** – this site from CyberWonders primarily list conferences held in Europe and Asia. It also allows users to add conferences to the website.
3 Tourism and leisure-oriented conferences – this website, located at **http:// www.wu-wien.ac.at/inst/tourism/resinfo/tkonfere.html**[, provides a comprehensive listing of tourism, recreation and leisure meetings, conferences and congresses that are held throughout the world, with particular emphasis on those held in Western Europe.

Career information

The Internet provides a wealth of information for those seeking jobs and career guidance. Web-savvy companies, organizations and institutions post job openings on the Web and will accept resumes by email. With the entire web at your disposal, you can canvass many more potential employers than you could otherwise.

This section does <u>not</u> list all of the employment-related sites on the Web – there are simply too many to do so. However, the sites that follow are some of the best employment trailblazer sites including, where possible, the best searchable job indices. When using the Web as a job-search tool, begin with the trailblazer pages and the Yahoo index of job-listing sites located at **http://www.yahoo.com/Business_and_Economy/Employment/Jobs**/, then move on to the specific searchable indices.

You should also utilize InfoSeek, Lycos, or other web search tools to hunt for the home pages or organizations for which you would like to work. Many organizations list available jobs on their sites, and provide instructions for applying for those jobs. You might also wish to search for the names of cities in which you would like to work, since many metropolitan area sites have listings of jobs available locally.

AMI WWW Employment Opportunities and Résumé Postings

http://www.mountain.net/Pinnacle/amiwww/emppage.html.
At this single-page website, you can find links to many of the most popular job pages: CareerMosiac **http://www.careermosiac.com/cm/jobs.html**, Interactive Employment Network **http://www.espan.com/**, Employment Opportunities and Job Resources on the Internet **http://www.wpi.edu/mfriley/jobguide.html**, Job Hunting **http://.www.virginia.edu**, The Monster Board **http://www.monster.com/**, and Organizations with in-house job listings **http://www.ageninfotamu.edu/jobs.html**.

Employment trailblazer pages

These pages are excellent starting points to begin web job searches. Typically, they include hyperlinks to other pages with résumé writing suggestions, predictions about growing fields, and additional general information about the job market. Often, they include links to sites with job postings.

JobHunt

http://www.job-hunt.org/. If you are seeking employment, you might want to make JobHunt an extension of your homepage. This trailblazer page originally maintained by Dane Spearing has links to most of the resources listed in this section of the chapter, as well as links to human resource companies. JobHunt has links to professional employment consultants, who for a fee, will help you compose a résumé as well as links to home pages of companies with recruiting pages on their sites.

Employment Opportunities and Job Resources on the Internet (The Riley Guide)

http://www.dbm.com/jobguide/. Margaret Riley's guide to Internet employment is arguably the best job guide on the Internet. It is a database of useful Internet sites that provide resume information, international opportunities, minority opportunities, recruiter information, and job searches. Also included are reference sites, informative articles on the future of selected careers, and the benefits of additional education along with other topics.

Searchable databases

America's Job Bank

http://www.ajb.dni.us/. This Internet site is characterized by a highly intuitive interface based on a hierarchical search mechanism and database of jobs numbering in excess of 100 000 listings. America's Job Bank is a partnership between the US Department of Labor and the state-operated public Employment Service, gathering information from more than 1800 employment offices across the USA.

The Online Career Center

http://www.occ.com/. The Center claims to be the oldest and most frequently accessed Internet job search site. The Center offers a wide variety of job search resources, including an up-to-date database of job listings as well as useful information about the workplace and job search issues. The Center combines the best features of the Riley Guide with a database almost equivalent to that maintained by America's Job Bank.

CareerSite

http://www.careersite.com/. This Internet site is unique as it employs computer programs that are assigned to perform a specific job, i.e., to match your qualifications and interests to the needs of potential employers. It essentially performs the work of a human resources consultant, at no cost to you.

E-Span's Job Options

http://www.joboptions.com/esp/plsql/espan_enter.espan_ home. Although containing principally computer and technical jobs, E-Span is a very fast, up-to-date database which originates from submissions of employers who pay to have their advertisements posted at this site. There are six specific search categories available at the site: job search; search employers; post résumés; job alert; career tools; and human resource personnel and recruiters.

Career Mosaic J.O.B.S database

http://www.careermosaic.com/cm/jobs.html. As a part of the CareerMosaic Internet site, the J.O.B.S. database is a wonderful collection of web reference resources that allows users to specify search terms, then to seek specific employment opportunities in the CareerMosaic database. In addition to the J.O.B.S. database, the CareerMosaic site provides the opportunity to utilize their Usenet search tool in order to view selected company profiles.

CareerWeb

http://www.cweb.com. The CareerWeb Internet site provides a wealth of information on professional, technical and managerial jobs. For job seekers, you may search the jobs database, look for international jobs, file your résumé, and search jobs by employer. There are associated resources such as bookstore, career inventory and career doctor. The site is particularly useful for those individuals seeking careers in the allied health fields.

The Chronicle of Higher Education Job Openings in Academe

http://chronicle.com/jobs/. *The Chronicle*, a weekly newspaper dedicated to higher education has been recognized as the premier vehicle for academic job hunting. They were one of the first to provide job search tools on the Web. The Career Network site, a listing of academic jobs throughout the world is updated weekly. In order to access the current week's job listings, you must be a subscriber and a password is required. However, each previous week's listings may be viewed free. In addition to the current job announcements, there are links to other job resources on the Internet as well as a bookshelf with guides for the academic job seeker.

Graduate Horizons

http://www.gold.net/arcadia/horizons/. This large site contains both career and job information for recent graduates in the UK. It provides links under the categories: Graduate Employers; Careering Ahead; Dates for Your Diary; Careers Hotlist; and TalkBack.

InternNET

http://www.vicon.net/~internnet/. Although the Internet does not provide a list of jobs, it does provide postings of internships in leisure and tourism that might later lead to career positions. The listings are intended for students interested in commercial recreation and tourism, parks and outdoor recreation, environmental interpretation or education, therapeutic recreation, military recreation, municipal and non-profit recreation, sports, health and fitness. Students may access the list at no charge since costs are borne by those who post internship listings.

The Academic Position Network

gopher://wcni.cis.umn.edu:11111/. This national employment search service is aimed at those looking for a teaching position or other academic-related positions by US state or country and educational institution or company.

Association of Commonwealth Universities

http://www.niss.ac.uk/news/acu/ach.html. International higher education academic openings.

CareerPath

http://www.careerpath.com. CareerPath posts more than 250 000 new jobs on the Internet every month and is updated daily by newspapers across the USA, including the *New York Times*, *Los Angeles Times*, *Boston Globe*, *Chicago Tribune* and *Washington Post*.

Federal Jobs

gopher://caligari.dartmouth.edu:70/11/fedjobs. A career search to aid those interested in finding federal job openings as well as job lists downloaded from US government bulletin boards, state organizations and jobs available worldwide.

International Jobs List

http:/www.timeshighter. newsint.co.uk/THES/INTERVIEW/ CURRENT/ jobclass_menu.html. International academic positions.

Jobs Listing

http://www.yahoo.com/Business/Employment/Jobs/. This comprehensive list is composed of links to a wide variety of employment sites: commercial, organizations, government, etc. Also included are links to career advice and job indexes.

PeopleBank

http://www.peoplebank.co.uk/ten/candvac.htm. Jobs in Europe and the UK.

What Color Is Your Parachute: The Net Guide

Richard Nelson Bolles has adapted a chapter from the 1998 edition of his book, *What Color is Your Parachute?* into an online reference guide for job seekers and career changers **http://www.washingtonpost.com/ parachute** who want to use the Internet as part of their job search. The site is hosted by the *Washington Post* newspaper and is divided into five topics: job listings (where to find openings), résumés (creating and posting), career counselling (top advice sites), making contacts, and job-hunting research. Each of these areas provides a description of what is available on the Internet, how to use it, how effective it is and an annotated list of resources for each.

9

Electronic reference information, texts, journals and other Internet resources

Web-based reference works
Unified search interfaces
Finding texts
Tourism and leisure journals online
Dictionaries
Encyclopaedias
Other resources
Electronic newsletters and mailing lists
Other groups/lists

If you are unable to find what you are searching for by using search engines, subject trees, etc., it is possible that you need more specialized reference resources. There are a large number of searchable information databases covering almost every conceivable subject. It should be pointed out, however, that access to some of these resources requires a subscription.

Web-based reference works

What do we mean by the term 'reference works'? Enter any library, university or community and you will come across reference shelves filled with dictionaries, enclyclopaedias, directories and other general reference works. These heavily used works contain answers to commonly asked questions such as: 'Where is Guildford, Surrey, England?' 'What is the meaning of ecotourism' and 'How do you convert 40.47 hectares into US acres?'

Although the Internet cannot take the place of a good library, you can nevertheless find a number of excellent reference materials among its searchable offerings, such as:

- encyclopaedias
- dictionaries
- quotations
- telephone numbers
- frequently asked questions
- calendars
- thesauri

Unified search interfaces

Among the most popular web search services are two different types of unified search interfaces which provide access to several search engines all at the same time. Some unified search interfaces provide a list of search engines. They have text boxes that allow you to enter keywords in order to initiate a search. Other unified search interfaces provide only a single text box that sends keywords to several search engines at once.

If a high-quality, deep search is required, then you should go directly to a search engine. The reason for this is that the majority of unified search interfaces do not allow for using advanced search features. However, if a quick, approximate search is what is required, then a unified search interface may be used. Examples of unified search interfaces include:

1 Internet Sleuth. Perhaps the best place to start looking for searchable databases on the World Wide Web is the Internet Sleuth located at **http:// www.intbc.com/sleuth/**. The unique feature of Internet Sleuth is their directory of over 750 subject-oriented databases in an extremely large variety of fields. The databases are organized by topic, (such as

159

Government and Reference) and there are also links provided to popular search engines.

2 <u>E–Z Find</u>. A second unified search interface, E–Z Find can be found at the following location: **http://www.theriver.com/TheRiver/Explore/ ezfind.html**. E–Z Find allows you to type keywords just once, and you search just one service at a time. Advantages of this search engine include the ability to choose between default OR or AND searching, and you can turn case sensitivity on and off.

3 <u>Savvy Search</u>. This site, **http://www.savvysearch.com** allows the user to search many of the Web's search engines with a single query. You can type a keyword(s) in the search box, or select from some of the categories presented.

Finding texts

The Library of Congress Internet Resource Page contains a list of electronic texts and publishing resources, both public and private, that may be accessed from the following library web page links, **http://lcweb.loc.gov/global/ library**.

General resources

- Books in Chains
- Catalog of Projects in Electronic Text
- Directory of Electronic Text Centers
- Electronic Books on WWW
- Internet Book Information Center from the University of North Carolina, Chapel Hill
- Internet Resources Database on Electronic Publishing
- Library Electronic Text Resource Service
- Oxford Text Archives
- Usenet alt.etext Archives
- Whole Earth Lectric Link

Electronic text collections

- ACM (Association for Computing Machinery) Publications – Books
- Alex: A Catalogue of Electronic Texts on the Internet from Oxford University
- Book Links

- Canadian Children's Literature
- CCAT's Text Libraries at University of Pennsylvania
- Center for Electronic Texts in the Humanities
- Civil War Archival Collections
- Cyberstacks science and technology reference resources
- Electronic Classics Archive from the Wiretap Gopher
- Electronic Text Center from the University of Virginia
- Electronic Texts Archive from the Wiretap Gopher
- Electronic Texts from Sweden
- Entering the World Wide Web: A Guide to Cyberspace
- Eris Project from Virginia Tech
- From Webspace to Cyberspace
- Great Books of Western Civilization
- Hypertext Fiction on the WWW
- Labyrinth Medieval Studies server
- Libraries with Electronic Books
- Literature Links from Hong Kong
- Literature Links from New Zealand
- Medieval and Classic Literature from the University of Kansas
- Modern English Collection from the University of Virginia
- Mystery page url
- Online Book Repository via The Online Book Initiative
- Online Books FAQ
- Project Bartleby from Columbia University, includes the 1901 edition of Bartlett's Familiar Quotations
- Project Libellus from the University of Washington
- Russian Literature
- Skidmore Electronic Reading Room
- The Byrd Historical Electronic Archive
- The Dartmouth Dante Project
- The English Server from Carnegie Mellon University
- The Etext Archive
- The Gutenberg Project from the University of Illinois
- The Online Books Page from Carnegie Mellon University
- The Tech Classics Archive from the Massachusetts Institute of Technology
- The Tolstoy Library
- The Virginia Library and Information Network
- University of Chicago Philosophy Project
- University of Michigan Etext Archive
- Virtual Library of Virginia

Works by specific authors

- Arthur Conan Doyle: A Sherlockian Holmepage from the University of Waterloo
- Complete Works of Shakespeare
- Critique of Pure Reason by Kant
- Douglas Adams Related Sites
- Edmund Spenser Home Page
- House of Usher: Edgar Allan Poe Home Page
- James Joyce from Temple University
- Jane Austen from the University of Texas
- John Burroughs (1837–1921)
- Noam Chomsky Archive
- Stephen King Page
- Strunk, William. 1918. The Elements of Style.

Government and legal documents

- Consumer Information Center
- Government Documents in the News
- GPO Access
- Law Marks: Legal Resource Database
- Legal ResearchNet: Florida State University

Poetry sites

- Dickinson, Emily. 1896. Poems.
- Electronic Poetry Center
- Keats, John. 1884. Poetical Works.
- Shelley, Percy Bysshe. 1901. Complete Poetical Works.
- Whitman, Walt. 1900. Leaves of Grass.
- Wilde, Oscar. 1881. Poems.
- Wordsworth, William. 1888. Complete Poetical Works

Electronic-text newsletters

- Internet-on-a-Disk

Commercial electronic booksellers

- AAUP Online Catalog and Bookstore
- Amazon Books
- Bibliobytes

- BookDotOrg, Inc.
- Bookport
- Booksellers
- Elsevier Science books
- Enchanted E-Books
- Nomad Books
- The Antiquarian Booksellers Association
- The Student Market Locating College Textbooks

Electronic publishing and publishers

- Abiogenesis Software
- Ancestry Incorporated
- Bantam Doubleday Dell.
- Blackwell Publishers
- Book Arts and Book History
- Cambridge International Science Publishing
- Electronic Publishers Association
- Golden Gale Books (Australia)
- Hoover's Online
- Macmillan General Reference
- Macmillan Publishing
- Oxford University Press
- Que Publishing
- Random House WWW Site
- Sybex
- WWW Virtual Library: Publishers
- Yahoo: Business and Economics: Corporations: Publishing
- Ziff-Davis Net

Tourism and leisure journals online

There are a large number of tourism- and leisure-related professional journals, reviews and other periodicals that may be accessed online, most of which require a subscription to view the entire contents. The amount of information that may be secured varies according to the individual publication. Some journals publish selected articles in their entirety, some provide abstracts of important articles, and some provide a table of contents for each issue, while others simply provide subscription information. Those journals listed below are but a few that may be found on the Web.

Anatolia

http://members,tripod.com/~anatoliajournal/. Anatolia is a tourism and hospitality research journal which has been published solely in Turkish since 1990. The overall mission of Anatolia is to provide an outlet for innovative studies that will make a significant contribution to the understanding, practice and education of tourism and hospitality. Specifically, the objectives of Anatolia are to contribute to the dissemination of knowledge through publication of high-quality peer-reviewed research papers, reports and book reviews, while serving as a unique forum for case studies for instructional use. Through its updates on Mediterranean tourism, Anatolia also aims to heighten awareness of the Mediterranean region as a significant player in international tourism. Anatolia is dedicated to the provision of constructive, objective and timely reviews of research papers.

Annals of Leisure Research

http://www.gu.edu.au:81/uls/leis/services/anzals/. The Annals of Leisure Research, like its predecessor, the Research Series, publishes articles which promote the development of research and scholarship in leisure studies with a particular focus on Australia, New Zealand and other parts of the South-West Pacific region. In addition to articles, each issue of the journal features book reviews which, like articles, cover topics within the broad area of leisure studies, including recreation, tourism, the arts, outdoor recreation, entertainment, sport, culture and play, and may be of a theoretical or applied nature.

Annals of Tourism Research

http://www.elsevier.com:80/inca/publications/store/6/8/9/.
The Annals is a social science journal focusing on academic perspectives of tourism and is dedicated to the development of theoretical constructs. Its strategies are to invite and encourage articles from various related disciplines; to serve as a forum through which they may interact; and to extend the boundaries of knowledge, thereby contributing to the literature on tourism social science.

Articles in Hospitality and Tourism

http://www.lib.surrey.ac.uk/aht2/. Although not specifically a tourism journal, Articles in Hospitality and Tourism (AHT) is a current awareness service which is compiled by librarians at Oxford Brookes University and the University of Surrey in the UK. Articles provide hospitality and tourism references to, and brief abstracts of, articles in over 100 academic and trade journals. This fee-based database often has a direct link to the catalogue of the user's own library.

Asia Pacific Journal of Tourism Research

http://www.hotel-online.com/Neo/Trends/AsiaPacificJournal/ index.html. An official publication of the Asia Pacific Tourism Association, the journal is published semi-annually at the University of Houston, USA. The journal seeks to publish both empirically and theoretically based articles that advance and foster tourism education, research and professionalism in the Asia Pacific region. The journal welcomes submissions of full-length articles, research notes, critical reviews on major issues, and reviews of books and conferences with relevance to the Asia Pacific region.

Australian Leisure Management

http://www.spin.net.au/~leisure/. The first magazine covering all areas of Australian leisure, the magazine Australian Leisure Management is devoted to features, news, a diary of industry events and conferences, book reviews and advertising of recreation industry products and services. The magazine considers amusement and theme parks; aquatic centres and swimming pools; art galleries and museums; casinos and gaming; cinemas and entertainment; clubs; community recreation; environment and ecotourism; fitness; parks, botanical gardens and horticulture; outdoor recreation and education; sport; stadia and venues; theatres and performing arts; and wildlife parks, zoos and aquaria.

Cornell Hotel and Restaurant Administration Quarterly

http://www2.sha.cornell.edu/publications/hraq/. Like the hospitality industry itself, the editorial content of the Quarterly is broad, including topics in marketing, finance, human resources, international development, travel and tourism, and more general management. Each August the Quarterly publishes the 'Educators Forum,' a focus section of manuscripts dealing with the business of hospitality education.

Current Issues in Tourism

**http://divcom.otago.ac.nz:800/tourism/current-issues/
default.htm**. This quarterly journal seeks to encourage the full disciplinary
and interdisciplinary range of approaches that are available to the study of
tourism; bring together researchers from different subject backgrounds for
interdisciplinary debate; develop the theoretical base on which the study of
tourism is built; provide a basis for the development of critical approaches to
the study of tourism; disseminate new approaches, concepts, frameworks and
models which may be developed in the study of tourism; promote new
research; and assist in the creation of new networks of researchers.

Festival Management and Event Tourism

http://www.als.uiuc.edu/leist/fmet/aims.html. A quarterly journal,
Festival Management and Event Tourism, an international journal, is designed
to meet the needs of event managers, researchers, related businesses and other
individuals and groups dealing with the operation of festivals and tourism-
related special events. It chronicles related research progress, documenting
management and marketing developments, and fosters interdisciplinary work
relating to this phenomenon.

Hospitality Research Journal

http://www.access.digex.net:80/~alliance/pubresea.html.
Published three times each year, this Council on Hotel, Restaurant and
Institutional Education journal offers refereed articles which advance the
knowledge base of the hospitality field. Review Board approved articles on
empirical research findings and theoretical developments are presented.

Hospitality and Tourism Educator

http://www.access.digex.net80/~alliance/pubeduca.html. The
Hospitality and Tourism Educator is a refereed, interdisciplinary quarterly
magazine designed to serve the needs of all levels of hospitality and tourism
education through the presentation of issues and opinions pertinent to the
field. The main objective of this periodical is to facilitate scholarly
interchange among hospitality and tourism educators, industry practitioners
and educators from related disciplines. The magazine is published each
February, May, August and November.

International Journal of Contemporary Hospitality Management

http://www.mcb.co.uk/cgi-bin/journal/ijchm. The International Journal of Contemporary Hospitality Management aims to communicate the latest developments and thinking on the management of hospitality operations worldwide. A multidisciplinary journal, it publishes double-blind reviewed papers covering issues relevant to operations, marketing, finance and personnel, and encourages an interchange between hospitality managers, educators and researchers. The journal helps managers keep pace with research on consumer attitudes and innovations in technology and service.

International Journal of Hospitality and Tourism Administration

http://www.cofc.edu/~ijhta/. The International Journal of Hospitality and Tourism Administration is an applied, internationally oriented, hospitality and tourism management journal designed to help practitioners and researchers stay abreast of the latest developments and facilitate the exchange of ideas. The journal publishes refereed articles on best practices in hospitality and tourism management, applied research studies, and critical reviews on major issues affecting the hospitality and tourism sectors.

International Journal of Service Industry Management

http://www.mcb.co.uk/cgi-bin/journal1/ijsim. The journal concentrates on services management research and provides a communication medium for those working in the field regardless of their discipline, functional area or sector nationality. It focuses on customer satisfaction, flexibility and innovation, quality and productivity, quantitative applications and strategy, the service environment and technological applications and development.

International Journal of Tourism Research (formerly Progress in Tourism and Hospitality Research)

http://www.wiley.com/journals/pth/. The journal provides an international publishing platform for research practice in tourism and hospitality. It provides views and debates current in the field, focuses on methodological and best practice issues, and facilitates debate on issues of policy concern, related research issues and applications. In particular the journal encourages a fusion between tourism and hospitality approaches to research, aiming to make research practice across the fields available to both subject areas. The content of the journal is a mix of primary research, reviews consolidating previous work and papers providing future research agendas and issues of concern.

Journal of Applied Recreation Research

http://info.wlu.ca/~wwwpress/jrls/jarr.html. The Journal of Applied Recreation Research is prepared quarterly by the Ontario Research Council on Leisure and is devoted to applied research articles on a wide array of topics concerning recreation and leisure. Of interest to both academic researchers and practitioners, the journal emphasizes the practical implications of empirical and conceptual recreation and leisure research.

Journal of Convention and Exhibition Management

http://bubl.ac.uk/journals/bus/jcem/v01n0198.htm. The journal publishes topics including decision processes in determining convention destinations, consumer behaviour in destination marketing, antitrust issues in convention and exhibition management, dealing with general contractors and subcontractors, safety concerns, ethical concerns in marketing conventions, crisis management, customer satisfaction studies, forecasting demand, market planning, trends in market segmentation, technology and exhibition management, and marketing trade shows.

Journal of Gambling Studies

http://www.plenum.com/title.cgi?10505350. The Journal of Gambling Studies, co-sponsored by the National Council on Problem Gambling and the Institute for the Study of Gambling and Commercial Gaming, is an interdisciplinary forum for the dissemination of information on the many aspects of gambling behaviour, both controlled and pathological, as well as a variety of problems attendant to, or resultant from, gambling behaviour including alcoholism, suicide, crime, and a number of other mental health problems. Articles published in the journal are representative of a cross-section of disciplines including psychiatry, psychology, sociology, political science, criminology and social work, and are of interest to the professional and layperson alike.

Journal of Services Marketing

http://www.mcb.co.uk/cgi-bin/journal1/jsm. The journal concentrates on special characteristics of the field with emphasis on the practical applications of capturing and retaining customers in the service industry. It publishes contributions from both academics and practitioners, reporting the latest research, new developments and initiatives being applied today.

Journal of Hospitality and Leisure Marketing

http://web.spectra.net/cgi-bin/SoftCart.exe/cgi-bin/haworth/ jtitle_search?U+haworth+. The journal is devoted entirely to innovations in applied marketing for both academics and industry leaders in the hospitality and leisure fields. The journal publishes quarterly contributions from a variety of perspectives including those of the scholar, the practitioner, and the public policy-maker.

Journal of the International Academy of Hospitality Research

http://scholar.lib.vt.edu/ejournals/JIAHR/jiahr.html. The online Journal of the International Academy of Hospitality Research provides ten abstracts of current articles that may be accessed through their website.

Journal of International Hospitality, Leisure and Tourism Management

http://web.spectra.net/cgi-bin/SoftCart.exe/cgi-bin/haworth/ j-title_search?U+haworth+tojq3050+. This publication is a multinational and cross-cultural journal of applied research that highlights advances in hospitality, leisure and tourism administrative practices. This forum crosses two bridges at the same time: multinational, international and cross-cultural issues in applied hospitality research and practice, and cross-disciplinary applied research and practice in the interrelated fields of lodging, food service, travel, tourism and related fields.

Journal of Leisure Research

http://www.rpts.tamu.edu/jlr/. The Journal of Leisure Research is devoted to original investigations that contribute new knowledge and understanding to the field of leisure studies. Studies that do not clearly focus on leisure or recreation (i.e. do not use leisure or recreation as a central construct) are not suitable for the journal. Empirical reports and review papers as well as theoretical and methodological articles are accepted for review. Commentary, rejoinders and other critical papers are also accepted. Book reviews are typically invited but unsolicited book reviews are considered.

Journal of Park and Recreation Administration

http://www.rpts.tamu.edu/jpra/. The Journal of Park and Recreation Administration is the official publication of the American Academy for Park and Recreation Administration. The journal was established by the academy to bridge the gap between research and practice for administrators, educators, consultants and researchers. The journal provides a forum for the analysis of management and organization of the delivery of park, recreation and leisure services. The journal publishes original manuscripts that move theoretical management concepts forward in the field of park and recreation administration, and provide clear implications of theory and research for problem-solving and action in park and recreation organizations.

Journal of Service Industry Management

http://www.swets.nl/backsets/rtp0484.html. The International Journal of Service Industry Management focuses on services management research and provides a communication medium for those working in the service management field irrespective of discipline, functional area or nationality. The journal publishes papers from both academics and practitioners, concentrating primarily on 'for profit' concerns such as finance, transportation, tourism, hotel and catering, but is also relevant to public administration, health and welfare managers.

Journal of Sports Tourism

http://www.free-press.com/journals/jst/. The Journal of Sport Tourism, an electronic edition format quarterly publication, is the official publication of the Sports Tourism International Council. The journal serves as a communication link for groups and individuals associated with the sports tourism profession; as well, it provides an impetus for the investigation of key elements inherent within sports tourism. Research-oriented articles and experimental-based information provide the content foundation. Since its initiation in 1993, the journal has had one special issue, that being the History of Sports Tourism. These particular issues comprise a comprehensive historical overview of the role of sports tourism within the overall tourism industry.

Journal of Sustainable Tourism

http://www.catchword.co.uk/titles/09669582.htm. The Journal of Sustainable Tourism is published by Multilingual Matters and is available online using the reader, 'Real Page.' There are generally five issues published each year. Windows users may install the reader to access the journal online. Non-Windows users with Java-enabled browsers may use 'Java Real Page' to access the journal.

Journal of Tourism Studies

http://www.jcu.edu.au/dept/Tourism/JTS/jts.htm. Distributed in May and December, the Journal of Tourism Studies publishes articles on tourism from a range of disciplines including economics, commerce, social, biological and physical sciences and humanities. It is international in scope and inclusive in its coverage. Individuals involved in tourism and tourism-related activity at the executive level will find this journal especially relevant. It is also useful to those in planning, policy-making and consultancy positions, as well as academics teaching tourism and tourism-related courses. Publication material includes original research reviews, issue-oriented papers and descriptive, analytic discussions which have a relevance to those involved in the practice of tourism.

Journal of Travel Research

http://bus.colorado.edu/BRD/JTR.htm. The international quarterly publication of the Travel and Tourism Research Association (TTRA), the journal provides tourism educators and professionals with new and helpful information about travel research, new techniques, creative views, generalizations about travel research thought and practice, and a synthesis of travel research materials. Each issue of the journal contain articles on recent research efforts. The Travel Research Bookshelf section presents an annotated bibliography of recent studies published in the travel and tourism field. The section entitled Research Notes and Communications contains short articles and notes on pilot studies, innovative or exploratory research, announcements, and conference reports. Reviews are given of recently released books in the tourism field.

Journal of Travel & Tourism Marketing

http://www.hotel-online.com/Neo/Trends/JournalTravel TourismMarketing/index.html(alternate): **http://web. spectra.net/cgi-bin/SoftCart.exe/cgi-bin/haworth/jtitle_ search?U+haworth+**. The journal is a managerially oriented and applied journal. The aim of the journal is to serve as a medium through which researchers and managers in the field of travel and tourism can exchange ideas and keep abreast with the latest developments in the field. The journal publishes articles on travel and tourism as related to marketing management practices, applied research studies, critical reviews on major issues, and business and government policies affecting travel and tourism marketing.

KPMG

http://www.kpmg.ca/ht/. KPMG's Hospitality and Tourism Practice helps private-sector operators, industry associations, destination marketing organizations, financial institutions and governments meet their business challenges. They provide practical information, advice and judgement on the issues facing all sectors of the industry. In addition, they provide clients with current information and direct access to international trends and activities, international market information and competitive industry information.

Leisure Sciences

http://www.bmpub.com.JNLS/LSC.HTM. Leisure Sciences presents scientific inquiries into the study of leisure, recreation, parks, travel and tourism from a social science perspective. Articles cover the social and psychological aspects of leisure, planning for leisure environments, leisure gerontology, travel and tourism behaviour, leisure economics and urban leisure delivery systems. Also published are methodological notes and philosophical and policy treatises, calendars of research meetings and conferences, announcements and book reviews.

LARNet: The Cyber Journal of Applied Leisure and Recreation Research

http://www.nccu.edu/larnet/larnet.htm. LARNet; The Cyber Journal of Applied Leisure and Recreation Research is published free of charge to individuals, libraries, academic and commercial organizations. LARNet is part of a new publishing paradigm whereby scholars themselves retain control over all aspects of the scholarly communication process.

Loisir et Société/Society and Leisure

http://www.uqtr.uquebec.ca/loisir/Documentation/LetS/ls. html. Loisir et Société/Society and Leisure is an international refereed journal and intellectual resource for anyone interested in the leisure phenomenon in contemporary society. Its editorial policy allows researchers from around the world to publish their research findings on leisure and its relations to culture, politics, economy, education, health and work, etc.

TEOROS: Revue de recherche en tourisme

http://www.unites.uqam.ca/teoros/. This research review is published in French only at the University of Quebec at Montreal, Canada, and reports primarily on North American tourism research.

Terrain: A Journal of the Built and Natural Environments

http://www.bod.net/terrain/. Terrain: A Journal of the Built and Natural Environments is a quarterly online journal without definite boundaries that seeks to determine the integration among the built and natural environments. It is not only concerned with urban form, natural landscapes, human culture and ecology. Rather, it focuses on the symbiosis between the built and natural environments where it exists, and an examination and discourse where it does not.

Tourism Geographies

http://www.for.nau.edu/geography/tg/index.html. Tourism Geographies provides a forum for the presentation and discussion of geographic perspectives on tourism and tourism-related areas of recreation and leisure studies. It seeks the diversification of perspectives that fall under this subject matter, including both academic and applied research, and regional traditions from, among others, North America, Europe and Asia. In addition, the journal features disciplinary approaches from geographers and related professionals including social scientists, architects, planners, environmental scientists and managers.

Tourism Management

http://www.elsevier.com:80/inca/publications/store/3/0/. The primary concern of Tourism Management is centred on the planning and management of travel and tourism. The journal takes an interdisciplinary approach to planning and policy aspects of international, national and regional tourism as well as specific management studies. Its contents reflect an integrative approach, including primary research articles, discussions of current issues, case studies, reports, book reviews, a listing of recent publications and a schedule of forthcoming meetings.

Travel and Tourism Intelligence

http://www.t-ti.com/. Travel and Tourism Intelligence (TTI) publishes all of the travel and tourism titles formerly published by the Economic Intelligence Unit (EIU), as well as a series of new research reports. The TTI's publications on the international travel and tourism industry are available as either a series of single research reports available individually, or three subscription regular publications which include:

1 Travel and Tourism Analyst – a research publication designed and written for industry officials needing current information in order to monitor the key developments and trends within the industry.
2 TTI Country Reports – the leading source of analysis of the world tourism destination markets. A newly started series is called TTI City Reports.
3 Travel Industry Monitor – a monthly newsletter for industry decision-makers needing up-to-date objective industry information.

World Leisure and Recreation Association Journal

http://www.worldleisure.org/journal/index.html. A quarterly publication, the World Leisure and Recreation Association Journal provides an international and interdisciplinary perspective on a range of subjects related to leisure. Most of its issues are devoted to a specific theme with contributors from throughout the world.

Dictionaries

The World Wide Web has many natural applications including online dictionaries. Unlike paper dictionaries, web dictionaries take up no desk space, and for the most part there is no charge to the user. Also unlike paper dictionaries, users do not have to be familiar with alphabetical order. All they must do is to type in a word and see the results. In addition, web dictionaries free users from searching obscure foreign language dictionaries for projects that require such specific resources.

Four such online dictionaries that are available via the Web:

1 Hypertext Webster Gateway **http://c.gp.cs.cmu.edu:5103/prog/ webster**. This Carnegie-Mellon University website is based upon the popular UNIX program called Webster. It provides definitions of English words, and hyperlinks almost every word of the definitions to other

dictionary entries. Users type a word in the text box, then click on Perform Word Lookup to view the *Webster's Dictionary* definition of that word.

2 Free On-Line Dictionary of Computing **http://wombat.doc.ic.ac.uk/**. This dictionary, compiled at London's Imperial College by Denis Howe, contains over 8500 definitions totalling 3.3 megabytes. The dictionary is searchable by using keywords. To use the dictionary, you can browse its subject headings, or you can search directly. By default, searching is case-insensitive with automatic truncation. However, users can also perform an exact match case-sensitive search if they prefer. Definitions are brief but accurate.

3 Euralex: Resources **http://www.ims.uni-stuttgart.de/euralex/ info/Resources.html**. A web of online dictionaries, Euralex: Resources by Robert Beard at Bucknell University indexes online dictionaries, thesauri and suchlike containing words and phrases. The index of foreign language dictionaries contains over 150 languages from A, Afrikaans to X, Xhosa. Words are entered in the text box, starting and target languages are selected, then click the Search button to see the definition of the word and its equivalent in the target language.

4 One Look Dictionaries: The Faster Finder **http://www.onelook.com/**. This mega-dictionary indexes 428 individual dictionaries and contains over 2 million words. Users may choose from four separate categories: (a) special subjects, (b) general words, (c) spelling word lists or (d) all dictionaries. Users simply enter the word in the appropriate box, then press the LOOK IT UP button in order to see the result.

Encyclopaedias

At the present time, the World Wide Web contains a few encyclopaedias that are both free and comprehensive. The following resources may be used to access both specific as well as general information.

Free Internet Encyclopaedia

http://clever.net/cam/encyclopedia.html. This encyclopaedia is composed of information available on the Internet. Its two principal divisions are the MacroReference which contains references to large areas of knowledge, FAQ's, where available, and pointers to relevant areas of the MacroReference, and the MicroReference which contains short pieces of information and references to specific subjects, sometimes containing instructions on finding the specific subject inside a general reference.

Encyclopedia.com

http://www.encyclopedia.com/. This site conveniently places an enormous amount of information at the disposal of users. It contains more than 17 000 articles from the third edition of The Concise Columbia Electronic Encyclopedia which provides free, quick and useful information on almost any topic. There are extensive cross-references and convenient links to related websites and books.

Funk and Wagnalls.com

http://www.funkandwagnalls.com/. Similar to the Free Internet Encyclopedia, this site is also free and contains an an encyclopaedia composed of information available on the Internet. It consists of three divisions: a MicroReference, MacroIndex and MacroReference as well as a Search button. The MicroReference is an alphabetically arranged set of links to information, while the MacroReference is a themeatic arrangement with an index.

CIA World Factbook

http://www.odci.gov/cia/publications/factbook/info-frame. html. The World Factbook has been published annually by the Central Intelligence Agency (CIA) since 1962, but has only been available to the general public since 1975. Although not an encyclopaedia itself, the Factbook is one of the most informative and useful collections of published country-based knowledge that may be found anywhere in the world. Since it is in the public domain, it may be copied freely without permission. The full text of the Factbook is available online.

Other resources

There are a number of other college and university resources that may be of assistance to users in finding information on leisure and tourism subjects. These websites range from those providing specific information on books, periodicals, databases, abstracts, indexes, professional organizations and other links to World Wide Web sites internationally. It should be kept in mind that these sites provide information, not the resources (books and journals) themselves. For example, the following are but a brief listing and description of such sites.

Buckinghamshire University College, Library and Media Services, Leisure and Tourism Resources

http://www.buckscol.ac.uk/library/leisure.htm. The College's *High Wycombe Campus Library* (link) houses an extensive collection of leisure and tourism books and journals as well as information on CD-ROMs and computer databases. The *Wellesbourne Campus Library* (link) is devoted exclusively to this subject area, while the *Newland Park Campus Library* (link) covers management, company information and European information. Specific resources include shelf numbering system information which is listed on the computer system (OPAC), one of the most comprehensive listings of leisure and tourism journals, as well as subject matter abstracts and indexes.

Ithaca College, Library Subject Guides, Recreation and Leisure Studies including Therapeutic Recreation

http://www.Ithaca.edu/library/htmls/hshp.html   4RE and **http://www.ithaca.edu.library/biblio/recreation.html**. Resources located at the first website include: professional, scholarly, government and advocacy organizations; full-text and other journals; links to outdoor recreation sites, and fully annotated sites in leisure studies and tourism, recreation and outdoor education, and recreation therapy.

The second website includes: Library of Congress call numbers related to recreation and leisure studies; indexes and abstracts including computer databases and paper indexes; special collection microform publications; general reference sources; scholarly and trade journals and special interest magazines related to recreation and other web sources.

Nanyang Technological University, Library, Hospitality and Tourism Journals, Annual Reports, Yearbooks, Statistics available in the NTU Library

http://www.ntu.ac.sg/ ntu/lib/biblio/nyuhbib.txt. As the title above indicates, the library holds a number of titles, together with their call numbers of publications published by: the World Tourism Organization; James Cook University; Singapore Tourist Promotion Board; World Travel and Tourism Council; Hotel, Catering and Institutional Management Association; University of Surrey; American Society of Travel Agents; University of Colorado; ASEAN Tourism Association and others. Their files can be accessed and downloaded at these URLs:

> **http://www.ntu.ac.sg/ntu/lib/biblio/ntubib.doc** (Word 7.0)
> **http://www.ntu.ac.sg/ntu/lib/bivlio/ntubib.txt** (Text)

Tourism Research Links by René Waksberg and Tourism Montreal

http://www.tourism-montreal.org/tourism1.htm. This website is one of the most thorough and comprehensive compilations of tourism and tourism research to be found on the Web. It is intended for use by tourism researchers and industry practitioners, and may be accessed in English or French and may be viewed with frame menu or as a non-frames version. There are four categories of links provided:

RESEARCH
  Upcoming Tourism Conferences
  Government Tourism
  Tourism Journals Online
  Tourism News
  Tourism Associations and Organizations
  Tourism-Related Resources
  Resource Management and Planning
  Sustainable Development and Tourism
  Tourism Research
  Tourism Schools

INDUSTRY
  Upcoming Tourism Conferences
  Tourism Consultants
  Event and Exhibition Management
  Government Tourism
  Tourism News
  Tourism Associations and Organizations
  Tourism-Related Resources
  Transportation

NICHE MARKETING
  Cultural Tourism
  Gardening
  Gastronomy and Wine
  Gay and Lesbian
  Honeymooners
  Gambling

TECHNOLOGY
  Associations and Initiatives
  Global Distribution Systems
  Services

Tourism, Hospitality and Leisure Journals

http://omni.cc.purdue.edu/~alltson/journals.htm. This listing of refereed academic journals in tourism, leisure and recreation has been compiled by Allister Morrison, and provides links to over thirty-eight individual journal websites. In addition, there are links to North American hospitality and tourism trade journals, the *Lodging, Restaurant and Tourism Index*, and a list of publications published by the Culinary and Hospitality Industry Publications Service.

The Planning Exchange, Information Service, Tourism and Leisure

http://www.planex.co.uk/isla/leisure.htm. The Exchange's Information Service, a subscription enterprise is the most comprehensive such service available in the UK. They publish a weekly bulletin summarizing articles and documents for individuals working in the fields of economic, social or physical planning, whether in local government, public agencies, professional bodies or private consultants. In addition, their database, 'Planex', contains books, research reports, good practice briefings, case studies, journal articles, etc. which are collected, then sent to subscribers within specific subject areas.

Topics covered in the Tourism and Leisure category include sustainable tourism, ecotourism, tourist accommodation, heritage sites, visitor attractions, leisure complexes, community facilities, parks, playgrounds, open space, footpaths, sports stadia, marketing and promotion.

Electronic newsletters and mailing lists

Unlike LISTSERV mailing lists and Usenet newsgroups, newsletters and mailing lists may only receive information, news, etc., rather than participate in a discussion about that information or news.

INFOTEC-TRAVEL

INFOTEC-TRAVEL (travel and tourism commercial list) is a moderated Internet electronic mailing list owned by its moderator, Marcus L. Endicott, **mendicott@igc.apc.org**. The list's purpose is to exchange information about worldwide travel and tourism information technology. INFOTEC-TRAVEL's URL is located at: **http://www.infotec-travel.com**.

To subscribe to the list, send an email message without a subject line to **LISTSERV@PEACH.EASE.LSOFT.COM.** In the body of the message, type

SUBSCRIBE INFOTEC-TRAVEL.

To send a message to all the people currently subscribed to the list, just send mail to **INFOTEC-TRAVEL@PEACH.EASE.LSOFT.COM.** This is called 'sending mail to the list', because you send mail to a single address and LISTSERV makes copies for all the people who have subscribed. All commands must be sent to the 'LISTSERV address', **LISTSERV@PEACH.EASE.LSOFT.COM.**

Contributions sent to the list are automatically archived. You can get a list of the available archive files by sending an *INDEX INFOTEC-TRAVEL* command to **LISTSERV@PEACH.EASE.LSOFT.COM**. You can then order these files with a *GET INFOTEC-TRAVEL LOGxxxx* command, or using LISTSERV's database search facilities. Send an *INFO DATABASE* command for more information on the database search facilities.

You may unsubscribe yourself by sending a message to **listserv@peach. ease.lsoft.com** with only the words, *unsubscribe infotec-travel* in the body of the message. If unsuccessful, then a message must be send to the moderator at either, **mendicott@igc.apc.org** or **mendicott@ aol. com** indicating which list you wish to be removed from, and including all your former email addresses.

One word of caution, however, when considering subscribing to INFOTEC-TRAVEL. The sheer number of daily email messages emanating from this list can be daunting, and may discourage some list members from continuing their subscriptions.

Other groups/lists

There are a number of other discussion groups and/or LISTSERV groups in the areas of leisure and tourism available through the World Wide Web. A selected number of those groups with their topics include the following:

Green Travel

A moderated electronic mailing list, Green Travel is dedicated to sharing information regarding environmentally and culturally responsible (sustainable) travel and tourism worldwide, including ecotourism and adventure travel. The list's subscription address is **majordomo@igc.apc.org.**

TravelFlash

The purpose of the TravelFlash email newsletter, which is sent each Monday to senior executives within the travel industry as well as to corporate and leisure travellers, is to cover the weekly developments in the online travel news. The subscription address of the newsletter is **Majordomo@ListService.net.** The web address of TravelFlash is **http://www.travelgator.com**.

Hospitality and Tourism Global Forum

Developed by the MCB University Press, this forum publishes a monthly newsletter which provides three specific services:

- current awareness of trends, events and in-progress research
- conferencing on global key significant themes
- archival access to the online abstracts body of knowledge with full-text, global document delivery from the British Library.

The forum chairman is Richard Teare at the University of Surrey who is also editor of the International Journal of Contemporary Hospitality Management (IJCHM). One may register for the forum on-line by accessing their website located at **http://www.mcb.co.uk/htgf/**.

Intern-NET

This newsgroup provided free, current listings of available internships to students with interests in: commercial recreation and tourism; parks and outdoor recreation; environmental education/interpretation; therapeutic, military, municipal or non-profit recreation; sports; health and fitness. Intern-NET can be found at the URL, **http://www.vicon.net/~internnet/**.

Hospitality Net

A newsletter sent by email, Hospitality Net is sent weekly and provides news, job opportunities, spotlight articles, upcoming events and new topic forums to subscribers. Their site is located at **http://www.hospitalitynet.org/**, and those individuals who wish to register for the newsletter are directed to follow the link, **http://www.hospitalitynet.org/home.htm?/registration/contribute.htm**.

Tinet

The US Department of Commerce, International Trade Administration, Tourism Industries Bureau provides 'TInews,' an information service to subscribers. Tourism Industries provides monthly and quarterly data on US international arrivals, number of arrivals, country of residence and ports of entry. To subscribe to TInews, go to the website, **http://tinet.ita.doc.gov/ tinews/subscribe.html**. To unsubscribe, send an email message (without a subject) to **LISTSERV@tinet.ita.doc.gov** with 'SIGNOFF TIAN-NOUNCE' in the body of the message.

10

Electronic discussion groups

Usenet
Bitnet lists
LISTSERVs
Network etiquette
Leisurenet
TRINET
RTSNET-L
Mailbase Tourism
Tourism
Mailbase
Interact in Recreation Therapy
IGU Study Group on the Geography of
Sustainable Tourism
International Society of Travel and
Tourism Educators
Other lists

Usenet

Usenet is often confused with Internet. However, Usenet may be thought of as one component of the Internet. All Internet sites can carry Usenet, but so do many non-Internet sites, from sophisticated Unix machines to old XT clones and Apple IIs.

Technically, Usenet messages are shipped around the world, from host system to host system, using one of several specific Internet protocols. Host systems store all of their Usenet messages in one place, which everybody with an account on the system may access. That way, no matter how many people actually read a given message, each host system has to store only one copy of it. Many host systems 'talk' regularly with several others in case one or another of their links goes down for some reason. When two host systems connect, they basically compare notes on which Usenet messages they already have. Any that one is missing the other then transmits, and vice-versa. They run through millions of these comparisons each day. Every day, Usenet users pump upwards of 40 million characters into the system. Obviously, no one could possibly keep up with this immense flow of messages, so how does one find conferences and discussions of interest to them?

Usenet newsgroups

Usenet is an area of the Internet made up of thousands of topical discussion groups called *newsgroups*. The basic building block of Usenet is the newsgroup, which is a collection of messages with a related theme (on other networks, these would be called conferences, forums, bulletin boards or special interest groups). Each newsgroup is like an electronic bulletin board where participants post and read messages related to a particular topic.

Some public-access systems, typically the ones that work through menus, try to make it easier by dividing Usenet into several broad categories. If one of them is chosen, a given list of newsgroups in that category is provided. Then the user selects the newsgroup they are interested in and begins reading. Other systems allow compiling one's own 'reading list' so that they only see messages in conferences they want.

The range of subjects discussed in newsgroups is as wide as one can imagine. The name of a newsgroup generally indicates the topic in question. Newsgroup names start with one of a series of broad topic names. For example, newsgroups beginning with 'comp.' are about particular computer-related topics. These broad topics are followed by a series of more focused topics (so that 'comp.unix'groups are limited to discussion about Unix). Three examples might include the following:

1 *alt.business.hospitality*
2 *clari.biz.industry.tourism*
3 *rec.travel.europe.*

Table 10 1   Top-level news group hierarchies

Prefix	Represents
alt	Alternative information or unusual information
bit	Conferences originating as Bitnet mailing lists
biz	Business, marketing, advertising
clari	News primarily from wire services
comp	Computer and related topics
misc	Discussions that do not fit anywhere else
news	Discussion and news of the Usenet
rec	Recreational topics such as art and sports
sci	Scientific discussions
soc	Social issues and social groups
talk	Debate, discussion of controversial topics

As can be seen, newsgroup names have a hierarchical structure. Each segment of the name is separated by a period (although it is pronounced as 'dot,' e.g., alt dot business dot hospitality). The top-level hierarchy indicates a general category of newsgroup and is always shown first. Table 10.1 lists some of the most widely used top level hierarchies and what they mean.

With so much information to choose from, individuals will likely have their own unique Usenet reading list. However, there are a few newsgroups that are of particular interest to newcomers. Among them:

news.announce.newusers	This group consists of a series of articles that explain various facets of Usenet.
news.newusers.questions	This is where you can ask questions about how Usenet works.
news.announce.newsgroups	Look here for information about new or proposed newsgroups.
news.answers	Contains lists of FAQs and their answers from many different newsgroups. Learn how to fight jet lag in the FAQ from rec.travel air; look up answers to common questions about Microsoft Windows in an FAQ from comp.os.ms-windows; etc.
alt.Internet.services	Looking for something in particular on the Internet? Ask here.
alt.infosystems.announce	People adding new information services to the Internet will post details here.

There are more Usenet newsgroups, dedicated to the discussion of more different topics than one could even imagine. What are some of these newsgroups? For example, the following is a short list of leisure and tourism related newsgroups:

alt.business.hospitality	Hospitality-related businesses
bit.listserv.travel-l	Tourism discussions
clari.biz.industry.travel+leisure	Travel and leisure industries
fj.rec.travel.world	World travel
misc.business.marketing	Round table marketing topics
rec.arts.disney.parks	Parks, resorts, attractions, vacations, etc.
rec.travel.Europe	Travel in Europe

It should also be noted that all of the Usenet group names have periods (or, in Internet language, 'dots') in them. That is the preferred method of determining whether or not a group is a Usenet group or a mailing list (discussion) group which uses email for message distribution. The difference should be noted between the two examples of both Usenet groups and mailing list groups below:

GROUP	TYPE
gnu.emacs.sources	Usenet newsgroup
RHA-L	Mailing list
rec.birds	Usenet newsgroup
Navigate	Mailing list

How are postings in a Usenet newsgroup read? In order to access newsgroups, one must first have access to some software called a *news reader*. Many news readers are available and, in fact, many web browsers such as Netscape Navigator and Internet Explorer include a news reader. Local Internet providers will be able to suggest what Usenet reader you have access to, and will probably also be able to tell you some of your reader's commands. The news reader provides the ability to perform the following operations.

Subscribe and unsubscribe

Subscribing to a newsgroup simply means indicating to the host system the articles posted there that you want. The news reader keeps a list of groups to which you are subscribed and tracks the messages you read in each group. From the subscription list, you can choose which newsgroups to read. Unsubscribing means to remove a newsgroup from your subscription list.

Browse and read articles

The news reader displays a list of article topics in the current newsgroup. Select a topic to read the articles sharing that particular topic. Articles include a header that indicates the user who posted the article, the subject of the article and the message text.

Reply to articles

You can respond to an article in two ways: by posting a follow-up article or, emailing a personal reply. A follow-up article can, of course, be read by everyone in the newsgroup; a personal reply is read only by the person who posted the article (unless they choose to share it with others).

Post a new article

You can start a new topic of discussion within a newsgroup by creating a new article, assigning a subject to it, and posting it to the newsgroup.

Some of the more important Usenet reader commands that one needs to know in order to fully participate in a newsgroup are:

1 How to access a Usenet reader
2 How to access a particular newsgroup
3 How to subscribe/unsubscribe to a particular newsgroup
4 How to read a post
5 How to send a post
6 How to respond to a posting by email
7 How to save a post
8 How to move from one newsgroup to another
9 How to exit your Usenet reader

Newsgroup subscribers must be aware that articles do not remain in newsgroups indefinitely. Articles scroll off the board as they are replaced by new ones. In a busy newsgroup, i.e. one to which many articles are posted, articles may disappear in a few days. Typically, however, they remain accessible for a week or longer. It is always advisable to check a favourite newsgroup(s) regularly in order to stay current.

Bitnet lists

As if Usenet and mailing lists were not enough, there are Bitnet (Because It's Time NETwork) 'discussion groups' or 'lists'. Bitnet is an international network linking colleges and universities, but it uses a different set of technical protocols for distributing information than the Internet or Usenet. It offers hundreds of discussion groups, comparable in scope to Usenet newsgroups.

One of the major differences is the way messages are distributed. Bitnet messages are sent to a mailbox, just as with a mailing list. However, where mailing lists are often maintained by a person, all Bitnet discussion groups are automated, i.e. you subscribe to them through messages to a 'listserver' computer. This is a kind of robot moderator that controls distribution of messages on the list. In many cases, it also maintains indexes and archives of past postings in a given discussion group, which can be handy if you want to get up to speed with a discussion or just search for some information related to it.

If 100 people subscribe to the same Bitnet list, that means 100 copies of each message get sent on the Internet, whereas if 100 people read a Usenet message, that is still only one message that needs storage on the Internet. It can provide a major benefit if the discussion group generates large numbers of messages. Think of opening your electronic mailbox one day to find 200 messages in it – 199 of them from a discussion group and one of them a 'real' email message that is important to you.

When subscribing to a Bitnet group, there are two important differences from Usenet. First, when posting a message for others to read in the discussion group, you send a message to the group name at its Bitnet address. Using Econet (sustainable environment newsgroup) as an example, you would mail the message to: **econet@miamiu.bitnet**. Note that this is different from the LISTSERV address used to subscribe to the group to begin with. Use the LISTSERV address <u>only</u> to subscribe to or unsubscribe from a discussion group.

The second difference relates to sending an email message to the author of a particular posting. Some Usenet newsreaders let you do this with one key. However, if you hit the 'R' key to respond to a discussion-group message, your message will go to the listserver, and from there to everybody else on the list! This can prove to be a major embarrassment and be quite annoying to others. To be sure your message goes just to the person who wrote the posting, take down his email address from the posting and then compose a new message.

LISTSERVs

On Bitnet there is an automated system for maintaining discussion lists called a LISTSERV. Rather than have an already harried and overworked human take care of additions and removals from a list, a program performs these and other tasks by responding to a set of user-driven commands.

LISTSERV discussion lists are topic-oriented forums distributed by email, dealing with a wide variety of topics. Those LISTSERVs related to leisure and tourism notify to each of their subscribers news, current events, new publications and other items of interest. Several systems are used for email electronic discussion lists. The two most common are LISTSERV and Majordomo. Several other systems are also used for working with discussion groups, including COMSERV, LISTPROC, Mailbase and MAILSERV.

What is the difference between LISTSERV and Usenet? Essentially, the difference between a LISTSERV mailing list and a Usenet newsgroup is that a LISTSERV is a smaller, more homogeneous, intimate and focused place to discuss ideas and issues of mutual interest. Usenet, on the other hand, is a newsgroup that is significantly larger and much more open to 'everything and anything'.

Once you have subscribed to a LISTSERV discussion list, messages from other subscribers are automatically sent to your electronic mailbox. The LISTSERV service is like an electronic newspaper, except that every 'article' is sent to you separately. LISTSERV discussion groups contain news and articles concerning topics in which you are interested. They allow you to contribute messages that are then distributed to other subscribers.

Subscribing to a LISTSERV discussion group allows you and a computer program called a 'listserver' to communicate by email. You can find out what lists are available, then request a subscription or cancellation by sending email to a listserver. A listserver uses email to handle subscription information and to distribute messages to and from subscribers.

LISTSERV addresses

A discussion list and the LISTSERV program that manages the list will have different email addresses. To correspond with the LISTSERV program, the address is LISTSERV@address. To send a message to the discussion list itself the address is LISTNAME@address.

LISTSERVs may be on Bitnet or on the Internet. Many LISTSERVs are on both networks. However, the use of Bitnet is declining. To the average user most LISTSERV programs appear to work the same and have the same commands, so you do not need to worry about which LISTSERV program you are using.

Some LISTSERV lists are managed by a moderator. The moderator reviews all the messages submitted to the list and makes sure that they are relevant. With unmoderated lists, all messages sent to the lists are automatically sent to all list members. Depending on how much time you have to devote to reading your email, whether a list is moderated or not might be an important consideration.

LISTSERV commands

LISTSERVs are computer programs that can be customized with special commands. Many LISTSERVs also maintain an archive of past mail messages that can be searched. Here are some basic LISTSERV commands:

subscribe <listname> <your name> – subscribes you to a list
set <listname> nomail – suspends your mail while on vacation
set <listname> mail – restarts your mail when you come back from vacation
signoff <listname>. – cancels your subscription to the list
help – gives you a brief list of LISTSERV commands (like this list)
info – gives you a catalogue of available topics
info <topic> – get a particular file from a list of topics, for example info refcard gets a list of all LISTSERV commands
list global – the comprehensive list of lists
index <listname> – receive an index of archived files for a particular list
get <filename filetype> – receive a particular file from the index list
info database – receive info about the LISTDB program which can be used to search any list archives

Network etiquette

Regardless of which discussion group/list one subscribes to, there are a number of recommended guidelines for good manners when participating. When sending original messages or replying to posted messages, one should remember the following suggestions. They should help maintain a user-friendly atmosphere for everyone in the group (readers should also refer to the 'Netiquette'section in Chapter 3).

1 As with all email, you should provide a subject in the appropriate subject line for each posting.

2 Keep each line in your message seventy characters or less. Longer lines often create problems with some email systems.

3 When replying to someone else's message, do not quote it entirely. Selective quoting or paraphrasing is kinder to people's eyes and their mailboxes.

4 At the end of your message, include both your name and email address (your electronic 'signature'). Since it is often difficult to interpret email addresses, everyone should include their institutional affiliation.

5 Be extremely careful when replying to the author of a list message. The listserver will send your reply to everyone on the list if you simply use the reply command. If you really want to send to the entire list, please do so. However, if you wish only to reply to the sender, then use their name in the address line, 'To'.

6 Think before you post a message or reply to another. Do you really wish to say what you have written? It is always advisable to reread what you write, especially if you are posting to the entire list. Remember, once a message is sent, it cannot be retrieved.

7 Always be considerate of others. Through inexperience or limited software, a few members may inadvertently violate the above suggestions. A private message to the offender from an experienced friend or from the list owner is more appropriate than a public flame (an emotionally charged posting).

8 Lists have their own unique character, just like any 'real' grouping of people. Lists function best when people respect the character of the list. It is also good to respect the differences among list members and have a certain tolerance for individual member eccentricities.

9 DON'T SHOUT – unless you really mean it. The use of all uppercase letters is considered shouting, and therefore rude. Part of the problem with typing all caps is that they are harder to read than in mixed case. Also, since facial expression and tone of voice are missing from electronic communication, some way to express strong opinions (both positive and negative) is needed, so ALL CAPS has been designated.

10 Some common abbreviations found in email messages are as follows:

   (a) FWIW – For what it's worth
   (b) GOK – God only knows
   (c) HHOK – Ha, ha – only kidding
   (d) HHOS – Ha, ha – only serious
   (e) IMHO – In my humble opinion

(f) LOL – Laughing out loud

(g) OTOII – On the other hand.

11 You should save any important messages from LISTSERVs, especially those instructions you receive the first time you subscribe to an electronic mailing list. If you ever need to leave a list, you will be able to find the necessary instructions that you received. Also, by saving a copy of those messages (and of all future subscription notices from other mailing lists) in a special mailbox folder will give you instant access to all of the mailing lists that you have subscribed to. This may prove very useful the next time you go on vacation and need to leave the lists temporarily so as not to fill up your mailbox while you are away. You should also save the 'welcome messages' from the list owners that you will occasionally receive after subscribing to a new list.

On the following pages will be found a selected list of examples of some of the major LISTSERVs and newsgroups in the Leisure and Tourism fields.

Leisurenet

Leisurenet (Recreation and Leisure list at Griffith University) is an email discussion list for researchers, scholars and professionals with interest in the many areas in the field of leisure studies or recreation. The list was established by Anzals, the Australian and New Zealand Association for Leisure Studies. Leisurenet's URL is located at **http://www.gu.edu.au/guis/leis/services/lswp/lnetfrme.htm**.

Leisurenet provides information and contacts of value to individuals seeking to better understand leisure, leisure services and the leisure industry. Professional associations, service providers, e.g. journal editors and publishers as well as other leisure-related organizations, are encouraged to participate in this discussion group. The list is international in both scope and orientation and relies on contributions of subscribers for its content.

Subscription to Leisurenet is free, and the list is not moderated. The principal objectives of Leisurenet are to:

- distribute inquiries, information and papers to individual subscribers throughout the world who are interested in the serious study of issues and problems in the various sub-fields of leisure or recreation studies
- facilitate contact between scholars, researchers and professionals whose interests lie in particular leisure issues.

Leisurenet provides archived information on such topics as:

- leisure studies conferences
- leisure and recreation journals
- theses on leisure topics
- teaching and research positions in leisure studies and recreation
- leisure and recreation professional associations.

To subscribe to Leisurenet, send an email message to Leisurenet's list server, **listproc@gu.edu.au** with a blank subject line and stating in the body of the message: *subscribe leisurenet Givenname Surname*. For example, *subscribe leisurenet Catherine Thompson*.

To post a message to all Leisurenet subscribers, send an email message with a helpful subject entry to **leisurenet@gu.edu.au**. Subscribers should remember that when responding to a posting, they may either reply directly to the sender or reply to everyone through the LISTSERV.

A user may remain a subscriber to Leisurenet for as long as he or she wishes. However, if the user either chooses to discontinue his or her subscription or changes his or her computer logon to which Leisurenet communicates, then the user should unsubscribe (or signoff) from Leisurenet. The user may rejoin Leisurenet at any time from a different computer address.

To unsubscribe from Leisurenet, send an email message of just two words to Leisurenet's listserver, **listproc@gu.edu.au** with a blank subject line and stating in the body of the message: *unsubscribe leisurenet*.

TRINET

TRINET (Tourism list at University of Hawaii) is an electronic medium of communication among tourism researchers and scholars worldwide. Its purpose is to exchange research-oriented or scholarly information only. Information exchanges through TRINET are likely to include abstracts of current and proposed research, theses, published and unpublished references, upcoming conferences or their proceedings, ongoing research projects, information on grant proposals or funding, and discussion on tourism curricula in higher education. TRINET-L also allows researchers to request input on a subject or invite participation on a research project.

Before potential participants can subscribe to TRINET, they must first submit an email message to **TRINET@UHMTRAVEL.TIM.HAWAII.EDU** including a brief (less than 250 words) biographical sketch. Such sketches are necessary in order to ensure that all subscribers to TRINET are active researchers in tourism, and so that TRINET has this information on file for other subscribers of TRINET to access. Biographical sketches should include the following information:

> Name, position and affiliation.
> Mailing and email addresses, and telephone and fax numbers.
> Research interests (listed by topic area).
> Research publications and a brief summary of major work.

Biographical sketches should <u>not</u> be sent as attached files, but rather as part of the email message itself.

In order to send a message to the list (meaning that all subscribers to TRINET will receive your message), the address is **TRINET-L@ HAWAII.EDU**. However, if a subscriber wishes to send a message to the administrator's address should he or she have any problems with receiving mail from the list, unsubscribing or other queries or concerns, the following address is to be used: **TRINET@UHMTRAVEL.TIM.HAWAII.EDU**.

If a subscriber plans to be away on vacation and wishes to temporarily stop their subscription, send an email message to **listproc@hawaii.edu**, with the following information in the body of the message: *SET TRINET-L MAIL POSTPONE*. To resume, send a message to the same addressee with the following message: *SET TRINET-L MAIL ACK*.

To cancel a subscription to TRINET, send an email message to **listproc@hawaii.edu** and type the following in the body of the message: *UNSUBSCRIBE TRINET-L*.

Should a subscriber encounter any problems using the list, or wish to learn more about other commands that can be sent to the listserver, they should use the following address, **listproc@hawaii.edu**, with the word *HELP* typed in the body of the message.

RTSNET-L

RTSNET (Recreation and Tourism Geography list at the University of South Carolina) is a discussion group/LISTSERV of the Recreation, Tourism and Sport Specialty Group of the Association of American Geographers. It exists in order to facilitate the exchange of ideas and information among geographers and other scientists or practitioners who are interested in leisure research, especially that with a spatial (geographic) component. It is open to all interested parties, not just RTSers. The list is not moderated, therefore, messages are not screened. RTSNET's URL is located at **http://www.for.nau.edu/geography/rts/rtsnet-l.html**.

To subscribe, address an email message to **LISTSERV@ UNIVSCVM.CSD.SCAROLINA.EDU**. Leave the subject line blank and in the message area, type: *SUB RTSNET-L firstname lastname*. For example, *SUB RTSNET sharon kennedy*. Together with your subscription confirmation, you will receive instructions for using the RTSNET LISTSERV.

To send a message to all the people currently subscribed to the list, send mail to **RTSNET-L@VM.SC.EDU**. This is called 'sending mail to the list' because you send mail to a single address and LISTSERV makes copies for all list subscribers.

This address (**RTSNET-L@VM SC.EDU**) is also called the 'list address'. Therefore, any command sent to that address will be distributed to all of the people who have subscribed. All commands must be sent to the 'LISTSERV address', **LISTSERV@ VM.SC.EDU**. It is very important to understand the difference between the two addresses. The LISTSERV address is like a number that connects you to a fax machine, whereas the list address is like a normal voice line connecting you to a person. It works much the same way with mailing lists. The difference is that you are calling hundreds or thousands of people at the same time, and consequently you can expect a lot of people to get upset if you consistently send commands to the list address.

You may leave the list at any time by sending a *SIGNOFF RTSNET-L* command to **LISTSERV@VM.SC.EDU**. You can also tell LISTSERV how you want it to confirm the receipt of messages you send to the list. You may send a *SET RTSNET-L REPRO* command and LISTSERV will send you a copy of your own message. If you send a *SET RTSNET-L ACK NOREPRO* command, LISTSERV will mail you a short acknowledgement instead, which will look different in your mailbox directory. Finally, you can turn off acknowledgements completely with *SET RTSNET-L NOACK NOREPRO*.

Contributions sent to this list are automatically archived. You can get a list of the available archive files by sending an *INDEX RTSNET-L* command to **LISTSERV@ VM.SC.EDU**. You can then order these files with a *GET RTSNET-L LOGxxxx* command, or using LISTSERV's database search facilities. The list is available in digest form. If you wish to receive the digested version of the postings, just issue a *SET RTSNET-L DIGEST* command.

The *REVIEW* command, returns the names and email addresses of all list subscribers. If a subscriber does not want his or name to be visible, simply issue a *SET RTSNET-L CONCEAL* command.

Mailbase Tourism

Mailbase is a national service, providing electronic discussion lists and information-sharing facilities for the UK Higher Education and research community. Based at the University of Newcastle, the Mailbase Tourism discussion group is aimed at academics and researchers located primarily in the UK who are working in all areas of tourism. These include issues involved with the teaching of tourism at undergraduate and/or postgraduate levels, and research into tourism and its related areas. The home page of Mailbase can be found at the URL, **http://www.mailbase.ac.uk**. The Mailbase Tourism list has its own web page, **http://www.mailbase. ac.uk/lists/tourism/** where you can read archived messages, get information about the list, retrieve files and, owner permitting, look at membership details.

In order to join Mailbase Tourism, send an email message to **mailbase@ mailbase.ac.uk**. Leave the subject line blank and type the following command in the body of the text: *join tourism first name last name*. For example, *join tourism John Rogers*. You will then begin to receive messages from the list you joined.

The tourism web page may be used to retrieve old messages and files associated with the list. To retrieve archives and files by email, use 'index listname' to obtain the names of files and list archives associated with a specific list, e.g., *index mailbase-tourism*. The 'get' command retrieves files via email. Large files are automatically broken down into several messages, each 1000 lines long. For example, *get mailbase-news 1996-09* or *get mailbase-news introduction*. You may set your own file size, up to a maximum of 5000 lines, by using the 'line limit' command. If required, it should precede a send command. The minimum line limit value is 1000. For example, *line limit 2000* or *send mailbase-news 1996-09*.

To post a message to all list subscribers, send an email message to **mailbase-tourism@mailbase.ac.uk** with a subject specified on the Subject line, followed by your message in the text section. Below is an example of a message to the Mailbase Tourism (mailbase-tourism) list:

> To: mailbase-tourism@mailbase.ac.uk
> From: william theobald<theobald@purdue.edu>
> Subject: New Tourism Book
> (Body of message): *Colleagues. Today, Butterworth-Heinemann released a new book, titled, etc . . .*

Your message will then be sent to all members of the list.

One of the unique features of Mailbase is the opportunity use the 'suspend mail' command to temporarily stop mail. This is quite useful if one is away from their computer for any length of time, for any reason. To temporarily suspend mail from a Mailbase Tourism list, send an email message to **mailbase@mailbase.ac.uk** without a subject line. In the body of the text type: *suspend mail mailbase-tourism*. When you return to work, send another message (without a subject) with the words, *resume mail mailbase-tourism*.

To unsubscribe from Mailbase Tourism, send an email message to the same address as above (**mailbase@mailbase.ac.uk**) without a subject. In the text area below, type only the two words, *leave tourism*. The 'leave' command will remove your name from the list.

To receive further information relating to the list, contact the owner at **tourism-request@mailbase.ac.uk**. For queries relating to Mailbase, contact their help line at **mailbase-helpline@mailbase.ac.uk**.

Tourism

An electronic forum, Tourism is an information-sharing and issue-oriented discussion centred around extension and other service providers of tourism development assistance to communities in the USA and abroad. It promotes tourism and related economic development programmes and seeks to identify current and future tourism needs. The list's subscription address is **almanac@esusda.gov**. To subscribe, send an email message (without a subject line) to the address above with the words *subscribe tourism* in the body of the message. It is recommended that new subscribers also send to the group a brief, one paragraph, introduction of who they are and what their interests are in tourism development.

Mailbase

In an earlier section of this chapter, Mailbase Tourism was covered in depth. However, there are five additional Mailbase discussion lists that are strongly related to leisure or tourism.

Mailbase-Heritage

This Mailbase discussion list provides an unmoderated forum for academic and industry researchers to share experiences and information on all aspects of heritage, tourism, museum and cultural management. List members exchange information on such topics as conferences, seminars, journal articles, book reviews, general news and views. To join Mailbase-Heritage, an email message without subject line should be sent to **mailbase@mailbase. ac.uk** with the message, *join Heritage first name last name*, (e.g. *join Heritage Deena Burgess*).

Mailbase-lis-tourism-and-hospitality

This Mailbase discussion list is intended as a forum for librarians in the UK who have responsibility for the subject areas tourism and hospitality. To join Mailbase-lis-tourism-and-hospitality, send an email message (without subject line) to **mailbase@mailbase.ac.uk** with the message, *join lis-tourism-and-hospitality first name last name*. To get further information about the list or to access the archive of previous messages, their URL is **http://www. mailbase.ac.uk/lists/lis-tourism-and-hospitality**.

Mailbase-small-tourism-firms

This list focuses on issues and trends relating to management of small tourism and hospitality firms. Particular research and teaching emphasis is related to human resource management, finance, operations, general management and business development of small tourism firms. The list is owned by Martin Friel at the Centre for the Study of Small Tourism and Hospitality Firms, Leeds Metropolitan University. The list may be joined by sending an email message (without subject line) to **mailbase@mailbase.ac.uk**, with the following text: *join mailbase-small-tourism-firms last name first name*.

Mailbase-tourfor

Tourfor's objective is to stimulate and encourage discussion on sustainable co-development of tourism and forestry by identifying and promoting appropriate conceptual tools and sound practice within the European Union, particularly from the UK, Finland and Portugal. To join the list, send an email message without a subject line to **mailbase@mailbase.ac.uk** with the following text: *join mailbase-tourfor last name first name*. The list maintains a website **http://www.buckscol.ac.uk/leisure/tourfor/tourfor.shtml** where message archives and files may be accessed.

Mailbase-anthropology

The newest Mailbase discussion list is linked to the Tourism Commission of the International Union of Anthropological and Ethnological Sciences. The purpose of this list is to promote communication among individuals with an interest in tourism, with particular focus on both scholarly and applied research in the field of tourism and anthropology. To join the list, send an email message (without a subject line) to **mailbase @mailbase.ac.uk** with the following text: *join mailbase-anthropology first name last name.*

Interact in Recreation Therapy

This website provides the opportunity to communicate live with fellow recreation therapists in chat rooms, post and read messages in twenty-four therapeutic recreation (TR) related topic areas, take part in recreation therapy forums, and participate in one of several ongoing recreation therapy surveys. In addition to the TR Advocacy and Group Work forums, there are subject articles where readers may post feedback, as well as surveys and polls on issues of interest. Interact's URL is located at **http://www,pacificnet .net/computernet/board/index.htm**.

IGU Study Group on the Geography of Sustainable Tourism

This website **http://www.for.nau/geography/igust/** of the International Geographical Union (IGU) is available in English, French and Spanish, and may be accessed through Northern Arizona University. The objective of the study group is the development and application of an internationally comparable geographical research programme on the sustainability of tourism in various regions of the world. The group publishes a Tourist Info Newsletter, and members may access past newsletters and activities. There is also a membership directory, publications list, a forthcoming conference listing and a list of links of interest.

In addition to those activities listed above, the study group also maintains a discussion group list. The list is unmoderated. In order to subscribe, send an email message to **IGUST-L-request@lists.nau.edu** without a subject line. In the body of the message, type *SUBSCRIBE IGUST-L.* To unsubscribe from the list, simply reverse the process with the request, *UNSUBSCRIBE IGUST-L.*

Since the list is unmoderated, whatever is sent to the list is neither censored nor filtered prior to being sent to members of the list. In order to send messages to list members, the email address to be sent to is

IGUST@lists.nau.edu with the appropriate topic listed in the subject line, followed by the text of the message.

International Society of Travel and Tourism Educators

This website **http://members.aol.com/istte/travel/index.html**, which is available to AOL subscribers, is involved with training for individuals entering the travel and tourism industry. The list represents teachers and administrators in high schools, proprietary schools, community colleges, universities and graduate schools. In addition, textbook publishers and other vendors who provide products and services to educators and students are also affiliated.

Other lists

When searching the Internet for recreation LISTSERV's, L-Soft International, **http://www.lsoft.com/scripts/wl.exe?qL=recreation&F= L&F=T** produces the following leisure and/or recreation sites:

> **58-350F98@LISTSERV.UOGUELPH.CA** – Planning Recreation and Tourism:Engaging People in the Process.
> **58-350W98@LISTSERV.UOGUELPH.CA** – Planning Recreation and Tourism.
> **CALONTIR@CRCVMS.UNL.EDU** – Historical Recreation in the Kingdom of Calontir
> **CORE@HERMES.CIRC.GWU.EDU** – Campus Outdoor Recreation Enthusiasts
> **COREC-L@VM.CC.PURDUE.EDU** – COREC-L (Recreational Sports Student Staff)
> **CPS-SPORTANDLEISURE@NJCU.EDU** – College of Professional Studies Sport and Leisure Department
> **GLEIS-L@UGA.CC.UGA.EDU** – Graduate Students in Leisure Studies
> **KEEP@CRCVMS.UNL.EDU** – Historical Recreation at UNL by Scholar's Keep Student Organization
> **MN-LEISURE@LISTSERV.NE.JP** – MN-LEISURE
> **ORC-L@LISTSERV.TAMU.EDU** – A&M Outdoor Recreation Club
> **RCONSORT@LISTSERV.TAMU.EDU** – At-Risk Youth Recreation Consortium
> **REC-FACILITIES@MORGAN.USC.MUN.CA** – Recreation Facilities List

RECALUMN@ASUVM.INRE.ASU.EDU – Recreation Management and Tourism Alumni Forum

RECMAJOR@ASUVM.INRE.ASU.EDU Recreation Management and Tourism Students Forum

RTSTU-L@CRCVMS.UNL.EDU – Recreation and Tourism Student Communications Forum

SPRENET@UGA.CC.UGA.EDU – Society of Recreation and Park Educators

UNT-KHPR@UNT.EDU – Health Promotion and Recreation

VAHPERD@VENUS.VCU.EDU – Virginia Association of Health, Physical Education, Recreation and Dance

WISHPERD@SJSUVM1.BITNET Women in Sport, Health, Physical Education, Recreation and Dance

11

Searching the World Wide Web: software, computing, citation and troubleshooting

Researching the Web
Tips to search the Internet successfully
Shareware and freeware
Compressed files
Internet citation style
Troubleshooting

Researching the Web

The majority of World Wide Web users find information in two different ways: searching and browsing. *Searching* is what an individual does when he or she knows approximately what he or she wants. Searching often involves knowing the title, author or subject of the material sought. For example, suppose that you are looking for a resource that contains the text of a declaration recently passed by the World Tourism Organization. Since you know exactly what you want, you would most likely do a search involving the name of the declaration or the name of the organization that passed the declaration.

Browsing, on the other hand, tends to be less focused. Presume that you want to write a paper on leisure programme evaluation and need to know some of the key areas of research and methodology in the field. In this case, your need for information is not very focused. Certainly you know the subject area you are interested in, but not much more than that, and certainly not enough to look for specific authors, titles or articles. Most likely, you will probably browse the resources available on leisure programme evaluation, in the hope that something that shows up will catch your attention and lead to a more focused search for information. Chance or luck, the discovery of information not planned for is always the hope of a researcher browsing for information. For this reason, many search engines still provide the capacity to browse, although searching is a more efficient and effective means of finding information.

What is the best way to search the Internet? The following section of has been reprinted in its entirety, with permission, from an article by Bruce Maxwell published in the *USA Weekend*. (In addition, See 'Savvy Searching' in Chapter 6.)

Tips to search the Internet successfully

Trying to navigate the World Wide Web without help is like trying to do research in a library that has no librarians, a jumble of card catalogues listing just a fraction of the collection – and 320 million books. To flounder less and learn more in your maiden voyages on the Web, follow these tips.

1 If your subject is broad (cancer, archaeology, politics), start with a directory such as Yahoo! (http://www.yahoo.com) – that categorizes websites by subject. Just pick the most likely subject, then drill down through layers of subcategories until you find what you want.

2 If your subject is narrow (such as a particular bed-and-breakfast you want to try), choose a search engine: AltaVista (http://altavista. digital.com), HotBot (http:// www.hotbot.com), Excite (http://www. excite.com), Infoseek (http://www.infoseek.com) or Northern Light (http:// www.nlsearch.com).

3 For comprehensive research, use several search engines or try a meta-search engine such as MetaCrawler (http://www.metacrawler.com) that simultaneously queries numerous engines.

4 Before using a search engine, read any instructions it offers. Yes, these documents can be snoozers. But each engine has its quirks, and knowing them will help you craft a more accurate search.

5 When choosing keywords for a search engine, select six to eight words to help narrow your search. If you type just one or two words, you'll likely get thousands or even millions of documents. Use nouns whenever possible, and put the most important words first. Put a '+' before any word you want to include, and a '–' before any word you want to exclude (this works with most engines).

6 To increase your search's accuracy, use phrases instead of single words. Put quotation marks around the phrase.

7 Many search engines will let you refine the results of your initial query. Do it.

8 When you find a good website about your topic, check whether it provides links to similar sites.

9 You may be able to guess the address of specific sites. Many are 'www,' a period, the name or acronym of the site's operator, a period and three letters denoting the site's type. Thus: www.microsoft.com (commercial), www.fbi.gov (government) and www.harvard.edu (education).

10 Double-check your spelling. You'd be amazed at how many people misspell words in their queries.

11 Keep in mind that even if you type a precise query, many of the documents returned won't be applicable. Computers (and search engines) aren't perfect.

12 Remember: The Internet does not contain the sum of all knowledge. You may still need to hit the library.

(Maxwell, B. [1998] Tips to Search the Internet Successfully. *USA Weekend*, 6–8 November, 12.)

Shareware and freeware

Prior to the Internet becoming such a popular location for academic users, software developers used it primarily to receive and send software and programming modules, and to trade information on computer applications.

The Internet has a large number of sites containing shareware and freeware. Since universities were first among the main users of the Internet, a large number of those programs have accumulated on their computers. What is the difference then between shareware and freeware?

Shareware is software that may be tested or tried before purchasing it. Users of shareware are expected to pay for it, although most shareware is relatively inexpensive. *Freeware* is, as the term suggests, completely free. This is the case since developers are either altruistic, or they want to introduce you to a 'light' version of a program, hoping that eventually, you will purchase the complete version of the program.

This section of the chapter contains a few of the myriad shareware and freeware resources that are to be found on the Internet. The sites presented here provide applications for specific platforms, including Windows and Macintosh. These sites also suggest particular purposes including utilities, multimedia, business, travel, communications and, obviously, for using the Internet.

Users should keep in mind that whenever downloading shareware and freeware from any website or source, that they risk introducing a virus into their system. Therefore, it is always prudent not only to have a current virus checker available, but also to use it regularly.

Freeware and shareware sites, PC

1 Shareware and Freeware at 5 Star-Shareware:
http://www.5star-shareware.com/.
This website provides Windows 95/98/NT shareware for a large number of programs from anti-virus scanners to utilities.

2 Windows software, Shareware and Freeware from Oakley Data Services:
http://www.smartcode.com/.
Oakley, located in the UK, develops and publishes a range of popular software for the Microsoft Windows platform ranging from business to utilities programs.

3 DaveCentral Video Shareware, Freeware, Demos and Betas:
http://davecentral.com/video.html.
DaveCentral provides free downloads of the best Internet video shareware, plug-ins and players including MediaPlayer, MediaPlayer and Net Tool.

4 Download shareware and freeware programs at The PageCreator:
http://www.pagecreator.net/.
PageCreator provides a website where shareware and freeware authors can freely promote their web design-oriented programs by providing access to them by interested individuals.

5 PCWin Resource Center Home Page:
http://pcwin.com/index.html.
This site is an excellent Windows 95/98, CE and NT software and freeware resource located on the Web. It offers a very wide selection of software available for download.

6 32 bit.com: **http://www.32 bit.com/**.
   The 32bit.com software archive provides Windows 95, NT, CE and OS/2 software, shareware, freeware and demos. Included are business, Internet, utilities, programming and graphics programs as well as games.

7 Download.Net: **http://www.download.net/**.
   As the second part of their name suggests, Download.Net offers the best games and applications available for downloading on the Internet.

8 DownLinX Shareware: **http://www.downlinx.com/**.
   This shareware download site contains over 2500 shareware and freeware programs with descriptions, and they are sorted by category.

9 Shareware Shop: **http:///www.bsoftware.com/share.htm**.
   The Shareware Shop website provides not only shareware and freeware resources, but also games, reviews, want advertisements and a search engine.

Freeware and shareware sites, Macintosh

1 Dr Shareware's Download Site:
   http://www.rbi.com/~salegui/jim/download/.
   Often referred to as Dr Shareware or Dr Games, this website located at the University of Texas Archive contains some of the finest shareware programs on the Internet.

2 Macintosh Shareware:
   http://thyme.circa.ufl.edu/mac/ho_shareware.html.
   A Macintosh shareware archive accessed through the University of Florida, containing, among others, software that may be copied, tried and distributed free.

3 Karl Bunker Shareware and Programming:
   http://users.aol.com/Kark Bunker/.
   This website is devoted to the highly acclaimed and award winning shareware and freeware of Macintosh programmer, Karl Bunker.

4 Shareware/Freeware Sites:
   http://www.mir.com.my/mpug/software/shareware.htm.
   Programs and links to a large number of wide-ranging Mac shareware and freeware sites on the Internet.

5 CLUB MAC – SHAREWARE:
   http://www.auroranet.nt.ca/clubmac/s-ware.htm.
   An excellent source for obtaining shareware or updating software, this website is easy to navigate and provides excellent descriptions of a huge amount of shareware.

6 BeezleWare:
http://www.geocities.com/SiliconValley/Lakes/
2247/intro. . ..
Each week, BeezleWare provides those who access their website with the
hottest new Macintosh shareware and freeware.

Freeware and shareware sites, both PC and Macintosh

1 The Father of Shareware: **http://www.halcyon.com/knopf/jim**.
Jim Knopf, the 'father of shareware' provides a website containing links to
almost thirty other sites hosting shareware and freeware programs both for
the PC and the Mac.

2 InternetU software Library: **http://www.iu.net/software.html**.
The InternetU site allows users to search for Windows, Macintosh, MS-
DOS and UNIX software as well as other software archives from
Washington University and from Nova University.

3 Jumbo! The Official Web Shareware Site:
http://www.jumbo.com/Home_Page.html.
The Jumbo website contains almost 25 000 freeware and shareware
programs for Windows, DOS, Macintosh, OS/2 and UNIX. Software
categories include business, games, home and personal, programming,
utilities, and words and graphics.

4 Shareware.com: **http://www.shareware.com/**.
Shareware.com contains over 160 000 PC and Macintosh shareware
programs. Program links include demo, desktop, drivers, games, misc.,
sounds, personal information manager (pim), etc.

Other software resources

1 Free Database List: **http://cuiwww.unige.ch:80/~scg/FreeDB/**.
This website contains most of the free databases available on the Internet.
The majority of these databases are related to programming.

2 Global Network Navigator (GNN) Computer Page:
http://gnn.com/wic/wics/comput.new.html.
The GNN Computers Page furnishes a very long list of links where one
can find many of the top Internet computer resources as well as view the
most popular weekly sites. Links are arranged in such categories as:
Computer Dictionaries, Graphics, Languages and Programming, Hardware Manufacturers, Magazines, Miscellaneous Indexes, Publishing and
Multimedia, Software and Shareware, etc.

3 UCS Knowledge Base:
http://scwww.ucs.indiana.edu/ kb/index.html.
This Indiana University website helps users quickly find answers to general computer questions via an online database called *Knowledge Base*. The database contains over 3000 text files that address common computing questions.

4 Yahoo Computer Directory:
http://www.yahoo.com/Computers/.
This search engine (Yahoo) site originally hosted by Stanford University is a very popular online directory system. It provides hundreds of locations using a table of contents listing, and hosts more than 50 000 links to World Wide Web sites about computers.

5 Beyond.com: **http://www.beyond.com**.
Beyond.com allows visitors to their website to browse, evaluate, demo and purchase almost 8000 software titles for Windows, OS/2, DOS, Macintosh and UNIX. Purchases may also be made online.

6 Online Computer Manuals:
http://www.nova.edu/Inter-Links/misc/manuals.html.
This small non-graphical website from Nova University provides links to computer manuals for both languages and programs. For example, one may learn about Minitab, SPSS and SAS statistical packages. In addition, users may obtain information about Kermit and anonymous FTP.

7 Companies on the Web:
http://www.scescape.com/worldlibrary/business/ companies/.
Companies on the Web is a comprehensive site providing lists of companies, large and small, from advertising to travel agents. Companies are arranged by business type, with sub-categories from which you may select or click-on links for specific companies.

8 Computer Hardware and Software Vendor List:
http://sunsite.ust.hk/homepage/vendors.html.
This website provides a non-graphical page of hundreds of links to both hardware and software vendors worldwide. Company homepages may be accessed that provide product information, customer support, press releases and employment information.

9 World-wide Yellow Pages: **http://www.yellow.com/**.
The world-wide Yellow Pages administers a searchable database of worldwide businesses. Although most of the businesses in the index are relatively small, nevertheless, companies such as Apple, MCI, Microsoft and others are also listed.

10 Scientific Web Resources: **http://boris.qub.ac.uk/edward/**.
This website located at Queens University in Belfast has a large number
of links to scientific and other such resources on the Internet. Categories
of information include Campus-Wide Meta-Searches, Lists of the World's
Most Powerful Computing Sites, Company Meta-Pages (primarily
computer), Research Labs Meta-Pages, and University Meta-Pages, by
country.

Compressed files

The Internet provides thousands of files and software including shareware and
freeware (which will be discussed in the following section) that can be
downloaded directly into your computer. However, prior to filling your hard
drive with downloaded software and games, it is important to understand
about compressed files.

A compressed file is composed of one or many files that have been reduced
in size by a utility program, then saved as a single file. Compressed files are
useful for three principal reasons. First, they take up less disk space; second,
they both upload and download faster; and third, they are very handy for
packaging multiple files. Therefore, compressed files are extremely popular
on the Internet.

Many Internet servers contain multiple programs and files in the same
folder. Each of these compressed files contains a complete software program
composed of multiple files. If these programs were not compressed into a
single file, placing more than one would be impractical because it would be
next to impossible to distinguish which file belonged to which program.
However, since programs with multiple files are compressed into a single file,
downloading programs is simple.

Decompressing compressed files

When a file is compressed, your computer's operating system or the
application on which the file is meant to be run cannot read it. This occurs
because the file has been altered to reduce its size. Therefore, you must utilize
a decompression utility in order to expand the file to its full size.

Several different compression/decompression utilities are available. Unfortunately, the programs used for compression are quite different for UNIX,
Windows and the Macintosh operating systems. The following section
indicates how to uncompress a compressed file that has been downloaded
from the Internet using each operating system.

Uncompression with UNIX

Assume that you have received a UNIX file called *readme.tar.gx*. The tar.gz extension to the file name indicates that two different programs are needed in order to decompress this file. First, you need to use the gunzip program (to uncompress). Then you need to use the tar program (which unarchives). All UNIX systems have the tar program available, and almost all systems have gunzip.

To decompress a UNIX file, first type *gunzip readme.tar.gz*, then press Enter. The result is that the file *readme.tar* is left behind. Second, type *tar pfxv readme.tar.* then press Enter. This command unarchives the file into one or more component files.

Uncompression on the PC

Assume that you have received a file called MYFILE.ZIP on the PC. The ZIP extension indicates that this file should be uncompressed with the PKUNZIP uncompression program.

To decompress the file, first at the DOS prompt, go into the directory where MYFILE.ZIP is located. Then, type *pkunzip myfile.zip*. The file names of the expanded files will be displayed on-screen. You can then work with the resulting files as you would with any other file. Naturally, you must have the PKUNZIP program available on your computer in order to uncompress files.

Uncompression on the Macintosh

Unlike UNIX, the Macintosh uses several types of compression. Files compressed on the Macintosh end in extensions like .sit and .hqx, or even .sit.hqx. Fortunately, all these types of files can be managed by a single decompression program called StuffitExpander.

Providing your computer has StuffitExpander installed, you simply double-click the file icon ending in .sit.hqx, and the file will be decompressed automatically.

Internet citation styles

Unlike the Modern Language Association, the American Psychological Association or other manuals of style which provide specific methods for citing books and periodical articles, there is no accepted way to cite Internet resources, particularly those that are available through the World Wide Web and Gopher. This section provides one way of citing resources that are found on the Internet.

Citations are one of the fundamental aspects of scholarly writing, communication and research. In fact, in many publications and papers, the citations and bibliography are often as important as the text itself. Citations must accomplish two purposes: giving credit to the person or organization responsible for a certain idea, concept or phrase; and; allowing the reader to find, retrieve and read the source being cited.

Although there are no well-established standards for the citation of Internet resources, the following pieces of information must be included in any citation of an Internet resource:

1 The author of a particular work. The author may not necessarily be an individual, but may be an agency, organization or department. (When the latter is the case, the author is normally called a 'corporate author'.)

2 The date of publication of a particular work. Sometimes, the publication date may be difficult to determine. If a copyright date or date of publication can be found somewhere in the resource, use that date. If it is an email message or a newsgroup posting, use the posting date.

3 The title of the resource. In a Web-based document, the document's title may be the title of the home page. With email messages or newsgroup postings, the title may be the subject of the message or posting.

4 The location of the resource on the Internet. Although the URL has not been established as a standard, nevertheless, the resource's location should be provided. The URL provides the necessary information to retrieve the document from the Internet. If the resource is an email message, include an email address that readers may use in order to obtain the document.

Citing email messages

It is very important that when citing an email message, a copy be kept in the event it is needed to document the use of the message. The following form may be used for such a message: Message sender. (Year, Month Day). *Subject of the Message* (email to the name of the recipient). Available email: email address of the message recipient. For example:

Dann, Graham. (1998, December 20). *Is it Really Nostalgia?* (email to W. Theobald). Available email: graham.dann@luton.ac.uk.

Citing a newsgroup posting

The following form may be used for citing a newsgroup posting: Name of poster. (Year, Month Day). *Subject of the thread* (Usenet discussion). Available:news:name of newsgroup. Note the use of the URL in specifying the availability of the posting. For example:

> Endicott, Marcus. (1998, November 15). *New Tourism Organization* (Usnet discussion). Available: news:trinet.tourism.

Citing a Web document

The following form may be used for citing a Web document: Name of author. (Year, Month Day). *Title of the Document* (World Wide Web). Available: URL of resource. Examples include:

> Summer, Luke. (1997). *Recreation Facts* (World Wide Web). Available: http://www.thompson.ac.uk/web-elements-home.html.

> Purdue University Krannert School of Management (1995). *WWW Home Page* (World Wide Web). Available: http://www.krannert.purdue.edu/library.

> World Tourism Organization. (1999, February 12). *Economic Impact of Tourism* (World Wide Web). Available: http://www.world-tourism.org/.

Troubleshooting

For the majority of individuals searching the World Wide Web, they normally have one of three specific objectives:

1 Seeking specific information such as: What upcoming international conferences or meetings address the subject of sustainable tourism? Where is the text of a proposed Federal bill authorizing the purchase of land for a new national park?
2 Looking for general information in a subject area such as: What does the Web have to offer someone interested in hiking and backpacking? Spending a semester or a year abroad? Studying recreation therapy?
3 Finding everything on the Web in my subject area such as: all visual aids available that relate to tourism planning and development, or all books that

deal with the concept of life tenancy in the preservation of historic homes.

When utilizing a Web search engine in order to find information about one of the three previous topic areas, often however nothing shows up. This result may be due to a number of potential causes:

- It may be due to peak demand, the search engine may simply have too much traffic to allow you to connect to it. Try connecting again during off-peak hours.
- The search engine may simply be overloaded. First, start with a relatively specific list. Type the most important word first since some search engines afford greater weight to the first word in a query.
- Select search options if they are available. A number of search engines allow for searching different parts of Web documents, such as titles, document content, or hyperlink text.
- Check your spelling. You may have typed one or more words incorrectly. Make certain that you have typed the search term(s) correctly, then repeat the appropriate command.
- If your key words produce no results, try alternative keywords. For example, if you are searching for 'green tourism' and nothing shows up, try changing your keywords to 'ecotourism.' When searching without success for the keywords 'alternative tourism,' instead try 'sustainable tourism'.
- If the keywords you enter do not get results, try synonyms. If you cannot think of another word(s) for the same thing, use a free online thesaurus such as Roget's or Merriam-Webster.
- Try searching again with fewer search terms. A search for 'marketing a commercial recreation enterprise' may produce no results. Instead, first try 'marketing commercial recreation', then try simply 'marketing recreation'. Also, word inversion may be helpful.
- Failure might also be due to the fact that either the Web may not be an appropriate place to seek the kind of information sought, or if there is a fee involved, general search engines are not likely to find it.

The final part of this section dealing with the issue of troubleshooting is from a column written by Eric Taub (copyright © 1998 by *The New York Times*. Reprinted by permission):

Web Hears You Knocking But You Can't Come In
By Eric Taub

For anybody who wonders what the neighborhood would look like from the viewpoint of a low-flying aircraft, Microsoft's Terra Server – a database of aerial and satellite images – may provide an answer. But many who tried to visit the site after it went on line recently saw absolutely nothing (www.terraserver.microsoft.com).

Nothing, that is, except for an hourglass or a spinning ball, occasionally followed (with some browsers) by '403.9 Access Forbidden. Too many users are connected.'

Some futurists (and now, apparently, the cable giant TCI and the telephone giant AT&T, which intends to take over TCI) may believe that the World Wide Web and television will one day be indistinguishable, but it looks as though some work needs to be done first. While television programmes have always been available to all who tune in, Web pages too often are not.

The reasons why you may not be able to get to a website are numerous, and the 'explanatory' phrases that appear on the monitor are cryptic at best, useless at

**Behind that annoying hourglass or spinning ball
is often a Net traffic problem.**

worst. Like the Long Island Expressway, the Web often has trouble getting travellers to their destinations because of heavy traffic. And even when Web surfers manage to get to a page, many may find the door slammed in their faces because thousands of people are trying to squeeze simultaneously through the same narrow entranceway into the site's computer servers.

'When people can't access sites, it's usually not the PC's or the phone line's fault,' said Igor Shindel, vice president of technology for Time Inc. New Media, operators of Time Warner's Pathfinder site (www.pathfinder.com) and linked areas, which include Time, Fortune and People. 'The problem typically lies in the general load on the Web, or the load on the actual server farm.'

Requests for a site's material must go to a server, a computer (or a chain of them) that stores the information. The www.pathfinder.com site keeps its Web pages on eight Sun Microsystems multiprocessor computers running Solaris 2.6 and maintains five copies of the pages to protect the site from crashes.

The 300,000 pages of the Microsoft website (www.microsoft.com) are held on 58 Compaq computers, each with 4 processors. Each of these $25,000 behemoths contains a 30-gigabyte hard drive and 512 megabytes of RAM.

Duplicate (or 'mirrored') information is held in similar sites in Tokyo and London, said Tim Sinclair, Microsoft.com's editor in chief.

Like someone getting a busy signal when trying to make a phone call, a user who cannot get into a website should keep trying. Every person who ends a connection instantaneously makes room for another. Sites that offer software for downloading can get tied up for even longer periods. While viewing a Web page requires just a few seconds of connect time, downloading the latest version of Internet Explorer could require 20 minutes to 3 hours on line, limiting the number of people who can get to the servers.

Even the large capacities of the more popular websites do not mean easy access. A site may go down for many reasons, like a lost connection with an Internet service provider or a decision by the site's administrator to remove it from the Net temporarily to update its pages. If a smaller site goes down, the reason could be even more quirky – a child might have run behind his mother's desk and tripped over the server's electrical cord.

Sites may also appear to be unavailable when they are actually just loading at a snail's pace. Pages with lots of graphics will load slowly, causing some users to hit their browser's Stop button in the mistaken belief that nothing is happening. Sometimes your browser will tell you in a small window at the bottom of the screen just what it is trying to do – getting in contact with the host's server or downloading material, for instance.

Typing the wrong Web address (the URL, or uniform resource locator) – even if it is off by only one letter or digit – will also block access to the site. (Some website providers, especially those with pornographic sites, take advantage of misspellings by registering site names that are just one letter away from the spellings of popular ones, so unsuspecting users will go there by accident.)

Or you may click on a link from a home page or Internet search engine like Yahoo or Alta Vista but wind up going nowhere because the page is no longer there, even though there is still a record of it. According to a recent survey by the All Things website (www.pantas.org/atw), which explains how to set up websites, Internet pages are getting bigger, and the number of missing links, pointing to nonexistent pages, has ballooned in the past year. Today, the average page weighs in at 61 kilobytes, up from 44 a year ago, while the incidence of missing links has increased by almost 40 percent. Today, 23 percent of all pages have at least one dead link.

A consortium is trying to find ways to eliminate many of the problems with gaining access to websites. It is working on Internet 2, a next-generation service that will increase the size of the electronic road to websites (the bandwidth) making it 10 to 100 times as large, said a consortium member, Mario Geria, a professor of computer science at the University of California at Los Angeles.

The plan calls for an Internet that will sense when multitudes are trying to gain access to a particular site and will automatically copy that site's pages to another local server. Now if only someone can figure out how to keep that child from running into the computer power cord.

Here are the most common types of connection messages and what you can do to avoid some of them. The actual wording of the messages may vary, depending on the website.

The Server Does Not Have a DNS Entry

After you type a Web address, your Internet provider looks up its numeric Web Equivalent; this message indicates that it cannot find one.

Sometimes you have done nothing wrong, and trying again with the same address solves the problem. Sometimes the address was typed incorrectly. And sometimes there is a problem with the server.

Spinning Hourglass or Beach Ball

A connection is being made. If the hourglass or ball persists, 'an Internet router somewhere along the path to your site is down,' said Tim Brady, executive producer of the Yahoo search engine. Try again.

404-Not Found

You have arrived at the correct server, but the exact page you are looking for cannot be found. If you have not mistyped the address, the page probably no longer exists or has been moved.

Sometimes it helps to back up/remove every part of the address to the right of the first single slash. That way, you will see if the site is still active, and you can try to search within the site for the page you want. If the address ends in htm, try html, or vice versa.

503-Service Unavailable . . .

Too much network traffic, service
temporarily over-loaded, network
connection was refused by the server,
gateway timeout: these are variations on
the theme of site overload – too many
people are trying to get into a site at the
same time. The only solution is to keep trying.

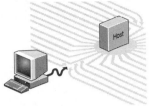

401-Unauthorized and 403-Forbidden

You have either failed to enter a
password or the one you entered is
wrong. Or the site may be available only
to users from a particular Internet
domain, like microsoft.com for Microsoft
employees.

(Eric Taub [1998] Web Hears You Knocking But You Can't Come In.
The New York Times, NE, 16 July, E13.

Appendix A:
Glossary of terms for
Internet resources

Anonymous FTP (File Transfer Protocol) – The procedure of connecting to a remote computer, as an anonymous or guest user, in order to transfer public files back to your local computer. (See also FTP and Protocol)

Bitnet – A co-operative computer network interconnecting over 2300 academic and research institutions in thity-two countries. Originally based on IBM's RSCS networking protocol, Bitnet supports mail, mailing lists, and file transfer. Now merging with CSNET and running the RSCS protocol over TCP/IP protocol (Bitnet II), the network will be called Computer Research and Education Network (CREN).

Client–server interface – A program that provides an interface to remote programs (called clients), most commonly across a network, in order to provide these clients with access to some service such as databases, printing, etc. In general, the clients act on behalf of a human end-user (perhaps indirectly).

Computer Research and Education Network (CREN) – The new name for the merged computer networks, Bitnet and Computer Science Network (CSNET). It supports electronic mail and file transfer.

Domain Name System (DNS) – The Internet naming scheme which consists of a hierarchical sequence of names, from the most specific to the most general (left to right), separated by dots, for example nic.ddn.mil. (See also IP address)

Downloading – The electronic transfer of information from one computer to another, generally from a larger computer to a smaller one, such as a microcomputer.

Electronic Bulletin Board – A shared file on to which users can enter information for other users to read or download. Many bulletin boards are set up according to general topics and are accessible through a network.

FTP – File Transfer Protocol allows a user to transfer files electronically from remote computers back to the user's computer. Part of the TCP/IP/ TELNET software suite.

Gateway – This term is used in different senses (e.g., Mail Gateway, IP Gateway), but most generally, it is a computer that forwards and routes data between two or more networks of any size.

Host computer – In the context of networks, this is a computer that directly provides service to a user, in contrast to a network server which provides services to a user through an intermediary host computer.

Internet – The series of interconnected networks that includes local area, regional and national backbone networks. Networks in the Internet use the same telecommunications protocol (TCP/IP) and provide email, remote logon and file transfer services.

IP – The Internet standard protocol that provides a common layer over dissimilar networks, used to move packets among host computers and through gateways if necessary.

IP address – The numeric address of a computer connected to the Internet; also called Internet address, for example: *128.10.9.154.*

Listserve lists (or listservers) – Electronic discussion of technical and non-technical issues conducted by email over bitnet using LISTSERV protocols. Similar lists, often using the UNIX readnews or rn facility, are available exclusively on the Internet. Internet users may subscribe to bitnet listservers. Participants subscribe via a central service, and lists often have a moderator who manages the information flow and content.

National Research and Education Network (NREN) – The NREN is a proposed national computer network to be built upon the foundation of the NSF backbone network, NSFnet. The NREN would provide high-speed interconnection between other national and regional networks. SB 1067 is the legislative bill proposing NREN.

Network information centre (NIC) – An NIC provides administrative support, user support and information services for a network.

Online Public Access Catalogue (OPAC) – OPAC is a term used to describe any type of computerized library catalogue.

Open Systems Interconnection (OSI) – This is the evolving international standard under development at the International Standards Organization (ISO) for the interconnection of co-operative computer systems. An open system is one that conforms to OSI standards in its communications with other systems.

Protocol – A mutually determined set of formats and procedures governing the exchange of information between systems.

Remote access – The ability to access a computer from outside a room or building in which it is located. Remote access requires communications hardware, software and actual physical links, although this can be as simple as common carrier (phone) lines or as complex as Telnet logon to another computer across the Internet.

Shareware – Microcomputer software distributed through public domain channels, for which the author usually expects to receive little or no compensation.

TCP/IP – is a combined set of protocols that performs the transfer of data between two computers. TCP monitors and ensures correct transfer of data. The IP receives the data from the TCP, breaks it up into packets, and ships it off to a network within the Internet. TCP/IP is also used as a name for a protocol suite that incorporates these functions and others.

TELNET – A portion of the TCP/IP suite of software protocols that handles terminals. Among other functions, it allows a user to log in to a remote computer from the user's local computer.

Terminal emulation – Most communications software packages will permit your personal computer or workstation to communicate with another computer or network as if it were a specific type of terminal directly connected to that computer or network.

Terminal server – A machine that connects terminals to a network by providing host TELNET service.

TN3270 – A version of TELNET providing IBM full-screen support.

Z39.50 Protocol – Name of the national standard developed by the National Information Standards Organization (NISO) that defines an applications level protocol by which one computer can query another computer and transfer result records, using a canonical format. This protocol provides the framework for OPAC users to search remote catalogues on the Internet using the commands of their own local systems. Projects are now in development to provide Z39.50 support for catalogues on the Internet. SR (Search and Retrieval), ISO Draft International Standard 10162/10163 is the international version of Z39.50.

Appendix B: Favoured leisure and tourism web sites

The thirty-six tourism and leisure web sites that follow are those that have been favoured by colleagues in an informal survey taken over the past few months. Obviously, this is but a very small number of such sites that are currently available on the World Wide Web. Depending upon the reader's perspective, there are a number of specific sites that they may feel should have been included in this appendix. However, it is simply not feasible to include all such sites.

Based on the nature of the web sites that have been included, it is quite possible, indeed it is even probable that sites which have been left out may be found through links provided by a number of related sites which follow.

Educational institutions

1 Academy of Leisure Sciences:
http://www.eas.ualberta.ca/elj/als/als1.html
The academy, an honorary organization undertakes various projects related to leisure and recreation studies including the publication of a series of 'White Papers,' and co-sponsors an annual Future Scholars Program.

2 Natural Resources Research Information Pages (NIRRPS):
http://sfbox.vt.edu:10021/Y/yfleung/nrrips.html
NIRRPS is an Internet resource guide for outdoor recreation researchers, practitioners and students interested in the field of natural resources. The guide provides several general catalogues and search engines as well as natural resources databases. In addition, a literature page provides links to other catalogues and guides, databases, publications and bibliographies on natural resource topics.

3 Study Group on the Geography of Sustainable Tourism:
http://www.for.nau.edu/geography/igust
The study group, part of the International Geographical Union has for its objective the development and application of an internationally comparable geographical research programme on the sustainability of tourism in various regions of the world.

4 Tourism, Hospitality and Recreation Research:
http://cac.psu.edu/~exs28/research/research.html
This website, maintained by Dr Eric Sirakaya, contains a comprehensive listing of useful links to tourism, recreation and hospitality sites that may be used by researchers. It provides links to Academic Journals, Associations, Data/Research, Programs, Conferences, Related Resources, Publishers, and Individual's Pages.

5 Tourism and Leisure Oriented Conferences:
http://www.wu-wien.ac.at/inst/tourism/resinfo/
tkonfere.html
As the name implies, this site located at the Institute for Tourism and Leisure Studies at the Vienna University of Economics and Business Administration provides a comprehensive listing of meetings and conferences held throughout the world, including dates and, where available, conference web homepages and names of contact persons or organizers.

6 Leisure Studies Web Page:
http://www.gu.edu.au/school/1st/services/lswp

This website provides information on leisure research and scholarship found on the Web including: Sport, Tourism, Community Arts, Culture, Festivals, Conservation And Recreation Parks, Outdoor Education, Play and Therapeutic Recreation. The aim of the site is to increase understanding of the aspects of leisure including the planning, provision and management of leisure services, and analysing leisure issues and concerns.

Government agencies

7 Association of National Tourist Offices (ANTOR) UK:
http://www.tourist-offices.org.uk

ANTOR UK has a membership of over ninety national and regional tourist offices, whose tourism officials represent nations worldwide. The Association is a voluntary non-political organization whose aim is to facilitate travel outbound from the UK. The website contains information from the tourist offices of countries in Africa, America, Asia, Australasia and Europe.

8 Countryside Commission:
http://www.countryside.gov.uk

The Commission, a public agency funded primarily by government is the statutory adviser on countryside matters throughout Britain. Their main aim is to be sure that the English countryside is protected. Their website offers visitors the opportunity to download or order free publications including their Annual Report. In addition, they provide research notes, press releases and new initiatives, as well as links to a directory of related websites such as The Great Outdoors, Greenways and Quiet Roads.

9 International Trade Administration (ITA) Tourism Industries:
http://tinet.ita.doc.gov

As described more fully in Chapter 10, the ITA's Tourism Industries Office provides statistical information relating to US visitor arrivals and departures, tourism export news and assistance, market analysis, tourism policy, an online catalogue of current and archived information, as well as a number of links to other tourism websites.

10 Leisure Information Network (LIN):
http://www.lin.ca

The LIN is supported by the Ontario (Canada) government. Their goal is to provide a focus and infrastructure for the collection, dissemination and exchange of information among leisure service professionals. Various technologies are used to promote and facilitate the availability and use of that information to its members.

11 Tourism Research Links by René Waksberg and Tourism Montréal:
http://www.tourism-montreal.org/tourism.htm

This site contains one of the most comprehensive and thorough links to tourism web pages found anywhere on the World Wide Web. The site is intended for use by tourism researchers and industry practitioners in order to bridge the gap between the two. It contains links to organizations that manage, consult or research tourism, as well as tourism schools. There are three broad categories of links: research, niche marketing, and technology.

Organizations

12 Canadian Parks and Recreation Association (CPRA):
http://www.activeliving.ca/activeliving/cpra.html

The CPRA is dedicated to the enhancement of quality community leisure services, lifestyles and environment for Canadians through advocacy, education, information sharing, policy development and national initiatives. Some of those initiatives that may be accessed on-line include Playground Safety, Benefits of Parks and Recreation, Youth-at-Risk, and Making All Recreation Safe – Harassment and Abuse Initiative.

13 European Association for Tourism and Leisure Education (ATLAS):
http://www.atlas-euro.org

Based at Tilburg University in The Netherlands, ATLAS promotes the teaching of tourism, leisure and related subjects throughout Europe. This is accomplished by the provision of a forum to promote the encouragement of student and staff exchanges, discussions of educational issues and curriculum development, the promotion of curriculum research, and the facilitation of tourism and leisure professional development initiatives.

14 International Association of Convention and Visitor Bureaus (IACVB):
http://www.iacvb.org

The association's website contains information that allows users to identify and contact convention and visitors bureaux throughout the world.

In addition, they also provide information on services for meeting professionals.

15 National Recreation and Park Association (NRPA):
http://www.nrpa.org
The homepage of the NRPA website affords visitors with the opportunity of looking for information related to Public Policy News, Parks and Recreation Magazine, Branches, Sections and Regional Offices, NRPA State Affiliates, Press Releases, Conventions and Meetings, Playground Safety, and a number of other related areas. In addition, the site allows users to look up parks and recreation products and services, and to post a position announcement on their National Job Bulletin.

16 Organization of American States (OAS) Inter-Sectoral Unit for Tourism:
http://www.oas.org/EN/PROG/TOURISM/home.htm
In 1996, the OAS created the unit that is responsible for matters directly related to tourism and its development in the hemisphere. Among other objectives, they support the formulation of tourism policy and sustainable development, conduct research and analyses of tourism issues, and promote co-operation with international, regional and sub-regional tourism organizations.

17 World Leisure and Recreation Association (WLRA):
http://www.worldleisure.org
This international organization is dedicated to discovering and fostering those conditions that best permit leisure to serve as a force for human growth, development and well-being. Members of the WLRA represent interests in tourism, recreation and parks services, the arts and culture, sport and exercise, children's play, theme parks and entertainment centres. Their services include research, advocacy and education.

18 World Tourism Organization (WTO):
http://www.world-tourism.org
The WTO website URL leads directly to their Information Centre. The centre contains information on their Publications, Statistics Service, Upcoming Meetings, Members and Other Services. In addition, there is current tourism news, frequently asked questions, and users may call up previously released WTO newsletters and press releases.

19 World Travel and Tourism Council (WTTC):
http://www.wttc.org
This URL is the homepage of the WTTC, the global business leaders' forum for travel and tourism. Its members include chief executive officers

from all sectors of the industry. The goal of the council is to work, in conjunction with governments, to realize the full economic impact of the world's leading industry – travel and tourism.

International bodies

20 Hospitality and Tourism Global Forum:
http://www.mcb.co.uk/htgf
The forum has two principal components: Current Awareness which provides access to a list of constantly updated areas providing the latest thinking and discussion within the tourism and hospitality field; and Resources and Archives, a body of professional and academic knowledge linking seven supporting journals.

21 International Conference on Information and Communications Technologies in Tourism (ENTER):
http://www.tis.co.at/enter
ENTER provides the opportunity to discuss the development of information and communication technologies in the international tourism industry, and its implications for global marketing. The website contains information on previous conferences held at Innsbruck, Istanbul and Edinburgh, which contain both scientific and applied research tracks.

22 International Federation for Information Technology and Tourism (IFITT):
http://www.ifitt.org/ifitt
The aim of IFITT is to promote international discussion about information technologies in the field of tourism. Federation members are either individuals working in tourism, or institutions such as companies and research institutes.

23 International Scientific Committee on Cultural Tourism (ICOMOS):
http://www.icomos.org/tourism
The ICOMOS is one of sixteen international scientific committees of the International Council on Monuments and Sites, and its aim is to maintain and protect historic properties.

24 International Tourism Research Links:
http://webhome.idirect.com/~tourism
This tourism web ring site contains a directory of links for consultants, academics and researchers specializing in the tourism and hospitality field. In addition, the site contains information on international work/study opportunities.

25 Worldwide Hospitality and Tourism Trends Forum (WHATT):
http://www.mcb.co.uk/htgf/whatt
The WHATT is an online database for hospitality and tourism academics, practitioners, researchers and students. It provides monthly interactive discussion columns on topical issues (Current Awareness Bulletin), global perspectives on both the academic and professional journal literature (World Trends), and details of current research (International Hospitality and Tourism Research Register).

Research and statistics

26 Big Volcano Ecotourism Research Centre:
http://www.bigvolcano.com.au/ercentre/ercpage.htm
The centre contains comprehensive information on ecotourism practice, tourism management, ecologically sustainable development (ESD), environment, outdoor recreation, adventure travel, and general tourism best practice management sites, worldwide.

27 CheckIn: The Internet Tourism Database:
http://www.checkin.com
CheckIn provides a sub-menu of tourism databases including Agency Chains and Consortia, Airlines, Airports, Country Tourism Boards, Cruise Lines and Ferries, Hospitality, Trade and Consumer Press, Rail and Bus, Rental Car, Technology, State Tourism Boards and Tourism Offices.

28 Consumer Culture Research Site:
http://www.gold.ac.uk/~soa01ds/consumer.htm
This site provides a resource for scholars and others interested in the study of consumer culture and related topics such as leisure and critical investigations of everyday life. It provides multidisciplinary coverage of resources and communications links for scholars and the website is a research node providing a consumer culture bibliography, course outlines, researchers and contacts, and resources and links including: the mailing list, Consumer-studies Mailbase; and an Asian region research network, ConsumAsiaN.

29 Hospitality and Tourism Indexes, Abstracts, Bibliographies, and Tables of Contents Services:
http://info.lib.uh.edu/indexes/hosp.htm
This website is located at the University of Houston (Texas) Libraries, and essentially provides links to those reference materials which are contained in the title above.

30 Reference List for Research on the Impacts of Tourism:
http://www.geocities.com/Paris/9842/impref1.html
This commercial website provides an extensive listing of books, academic journals and both government and other organizations' reports dealing with the economic, social, cultural and environmental impacts of tourism development.

31 Tourism Bibliography, Research Resources, References, Publications, Textbooks and Monographs:
http://omni.cc.purdue.edu/~alltson/bookss.htm
This site is maintained by Alastair Morrison at Purdue University and is a supplement to the following entry. As the title indicates, this website provides bibliographic information on over 300 tourism books and similar materials published throughout the world.

Related resources

32 EnviroLink Network:
http://www.envirolink.org
This network is a grassroots online community dedicated to providing the most comprehensive and up-to-date environmental resources to organizations and individuals in more than 150 countries throughout the world. In addition to being a clearinghouse for environmental resources, the network also provides no-profit organizations with website hosting, automated mailing lists, interactive bulletin boards and chat rooms, and other services, the majority of which are provided without charge.

33 OuR-TOWN:
http://ourtown.com
OuR-TOWN is a combination of Internet-based tourism information services and community-based tourism development information resources. Their goal is to improve the competitiveness of tourism-related businesses and communities by providing community leaders and business owners through education, technical assistance and market-oriented planning.

34 Partners in Responsible Tourism (PIRT):
http://www2.pirt.org/pirt/about.html
Partners is a network of individuals and representatives of tourism companies concerned with the impact of tourism development on local environments, especially as they affect indigenous culture. PIRT holds

educational seminars on tourism, the environment and opportunities for alternative forms of travel.

35 Recreation and Leisure Studies: Resources on the World Wide Web:
http://www.geog.ualberta.ca/als/risres.html
Although this site has not been updated since 1998, nevertheless, it provides a great deal of information and links to among others, Academic Departments and Programs in Recreation and Leisure Studies, Resources for Research on Leisure, Recreation and Tourism, Recreation and Leisure Studies: Organizations and Mailing Lists, Related Resources Pages, and Other Recreation and Leisure Sites on the Web.

36 Tourism and Hospitality Bibliography:
http://omni.cc.purdue.edu/~alltson/books.htm
The bibliography, a guide first published by the Association of Tourism Teachers and Trainers (ATTT) contains what they considered to be the best 100 tourism and hospitality books in print. Presently, this reference information has been compiled and supplied by Marylebone Books in the UK. They have agreed to stock most of the books listed on the bibliography, and where available, they may be mail-ordered directly from them.

Index